Don't Blame Me

DON'T BLAME ME

NOBODY BELIEVED HE WAS A SHALLOW, SELFISH DEVIL WITH THE SCRUPLES OF A SHARK

Diana K Robinson

A CIP catalogue record for this title is available from the British Library.

ISBNs
Paperback: 978-1-80541-292-2
eBook: 978-1-80541-291-5

About the Author

DIANA ROBINSON was born on a farm in what was then Rhodesia, now Zimbabwe, in 1958. In 1980 she moved to South Africa at the end of the country's civil war. Diana has travelled extensively and now lives with her husband in England. She has two sons, the eldest lives with his family in Canada and the youngest is a passionate conservationist and reptile expert and lives in South Africa. Diana has two grandsons who live in Canada.

Dedication

This fiction tale is based upon the true story of one woman's extraordinary life. This is not just a story, but a lesson.

My grateful thanks go to my patient husband, without whose support this book would have taken me ten times longer.

Acknowledgements

To my special friend, aka Elizabeth, who shared her dramatic life story with me and suggested I should write her tragic tale. You inspire me with your amazing inner strength and fortitude. Thank you for giving me the opportunity to tell the world your story.

A Message from "Elizabeth"

My grateful thanks go to my children. Thank you for standing beside me through all our dramas. I could not have survived it without your support.

Special thanks also go to the author who knows me better than I thought!

The biblical quote "Lead us not into temptation" is very apt in my story and it is my hope that it conveys a useful message to anyone else who may decide to do what I did. Don't do it!

Chapter One

1971

Standing in the foyer of the nurses' residence in Bloemfontein, seventeen years old, painfully shy, rurally raised and frighteningly naive, I felt an uncomfortable mixture of excitement and anxiety whirling around in my tummy, tugging and teasing every part of it. I was lost. I had lugged my bags up and down long passages and I couldn't find room 26. An irrational panic threatened common sense. I searched for signs for room 26. Left Wing maybe. That was to be my room for the year ahead.

A maze of passages branched off of the long corridor and I felt quite bewildered. I sat on top of my suitcase and thought about the mouse trails in the cornfields at home. The thought made me smile; they never confused me as I skipped along them! Those thoughts comforted me.

I took a deep breath and considered how the mice knew where to go in the fields. They always found the entrance to their little burrow after running across vast expanses of land, hiding from predators flying overhead. I envied them their skills in that moment. They didn't have signs.

I stood up, tears hovering along the rims of my eyes as I dragged my heavy luggage further down the corridor telling myself to grow up, calm down and think. I stopped near the entrance to another passageway. Glancing down at my watch,

I noticed it was midday. While everyone was enjoying their scrumptious Sunday lunch on this lazy afternoon in January 1971, I stood alone on the brink of my nursing career, feeling insecure, overwhelmed and homesick. Suddenly, I wanted to be a mouse.

I pulled the introduction letter from my bag. I'd not misread the directions. As I stuffed them back in my bag, a friendly voice came from behind me.

"Hi, are you lost?" asked the voice and I swung around, being instantly drawn to a pair of warm smiling green eyes that were looking up at me.

"Yes, I think so," I answered.

Relief tipped those tears over the edge and my bottom lip quivered, though I managed a rather pathetic smile.

"I'm looking for room 26 in the left wing," I stammered and was about to show her my introduction letter when she squealed with excitement.

"Hey, what a coincidence, I'm also in room 26. Howzit? I'm Amelia van Tonder." She beamed and thrust her hand out for me to shake. I felt instantly envious of her self-confidence.

"Elizabeth Pieterse, it's nice to meet you," I said with relief, taking her warm hand in mine.

At last, I wasn't alone in this maze of unmarked passages. I had to look away from her, and as I did, I noticed the room number signs high up on the wall ahead of me. They were facing away from the direction in which both Amelia and I had accessed the building.

"That's dumb," I said, pointing out the room signs. "Why don't they make them visible from both directions?" Shaking my head and wiping my cheek with the back of my hand, I added, "I thought it was just me being stupid. So, judging by the sequence of numbers on that sign, our room must be down the next passage."

"Aagh, no!" Amelia groaned. "These cases are so darned heavy." She rounded her shoulders and screwed up her face, not happy that she had to haul them along again.

I'd been struggling with the weight of mine, and I was at least five inches taller than her, plus she had more luggage than I did. Though I wanted to help her, all I could do was smile when she looked up at me. Off we went, dragging our suitcases down to the next passage where we turned into the entrance and finally located our room.

"Do you have any preference on which side you want to sleep?" Amelia asked, hauling her luggage through the door.

I'd always liked to sleep next to a window and wake to the call of birdsong, but as both our beds faced the only windows, a French door with windows on either side of it, I guessed it was irrelevant.

"No, I don't mind which bed I take."

We were both being very polite, yet it felt to me like I'd known Amelia for years.

"Perfect," she said and threw her handbag onto the bed she was closest to.

Taking a deep breath, I glanced around our room. "Not bad!"

"Much better than I expected. What a nice surprise."

Installed between two cupboards was a vanity table and mirror which served as a dressing table. The bathrooms were down the passage, but there was a wash basin in our room; apparently a luxury. Not all the rooms had a wash basin in them. We were in the newer wing. We could fill up our kettle, wash our hands and face, and clean our teeth without standing in a queue. Sharing a bathroom with anyone other than my family wasn't a comfortable thought.

Pretty floral curtains hung on either side of the French doors that opened onto communal gardens filled with wise old trees, standing tall above manicured lawns; it was a perfect place to study.

"I think we can manage living here." Amelia beamed as she unzipped one of her suitcases, then suddenly burst out laughing. "Gee, how tall are you?"

I was very self-conscious of my height, but for the first time, I found myself laughing too, responding with unusually good humour on such a sensitive subject.

"Well, the long and the short of it is…" And we both roared with laughter. "Seriously, I'm half an inch off six-foot. Much too tall for a girl. I hate being so tall."

Amelia chuckled. "Let me tell you, it's far worse as a real shorty like me."

"We're never happy with what we have, are we? I'm tall and want to be shorter. You're short and want to be taller. You have gorgeous auburn curls, my favourite hair colour. Don't tell me you wish you were blonde!"

"Yes, of course I do. Blondes have more fun. It's a known fact."

"I don't know about that," I responded, blushing furiously. I was way too shy to comment.

"Jokes aside…" She paused, looking a little sad. "I was teased unmercifully at school. Short arse, shorty, copper nut and rooi kop were just some of the horrid names they called me. Kids can be so cruel to each other, can't they?"

I could see how deeply the teasing had affected her.

"I was also bullied at school. I was mocked constantly for being shy until I finally learnt to stand up for myself."

I looked at Amelia's lovely doll-like face and found it hard to believe she had been so ragged. She was angelically beautiful. I couldn't imagine how anyone would want to tease or insult her.

"We're like Laurel and Hardy. Completely different. I like that, don't you?" I chuckled to lighten the mood.

"Ja, me too," Amelia agreed and pulled the next heavy bag close to the wardrobe and unpacked it.

Banter between us was easy. I felt incredibly fortunate to have Amelia as my roommate for the year. It had worried me that I would have to share a room with someone I didn't like.

"I feel like we've known each other for years, don't you?" Amelia stood up with an armful of clothes, echoing how I felt.

"I've just been thinking the same."

We went on nattering about what we had in common. It took us ages to unpack. Framed photographs of family members, best friends and special pets were the final decorative bits we added to make the room feel more like home.

Finally, Amelia plonked her childhood teddy on her pillow and looked at me.

"Don't laugh. He goes everywhere with me." She stroked its face affectionately. "I've had Harold since I was three and we're inseparable. Plus, he always brings me luck."

I felt a little tug of sadness as I thought back to my beautiful teddy whose arms and legs moved, and whom I'd adored. I would wrap Teddy's arms around my neck when I couldn't sleep after Papa died. It was the comfort I craved as a six-year-old. Mom had never been one to show much affection. She had found it hard to comfort me, for she too was grieving. Several months after Papa passed, she bought me a puppy: a fluffy crossbreed whom I fell in love with until he ripped Teddy apart. I never did get another. Mom couldn't afford it, but I eventually forgave my ever-faithful canine companion.

"What made you want to do nursing?" Amelia asked, her eyebrows raised, and a line creased between them. She had noticed my mood was pensive and she was too polite to ask what was wrong. I told her anyway.

"My father passed away when I was little. Mom bravely took over the farm, and too many of the years since, she has struggled. She couldn't afford to keep me in school this year. You know we've had drought conditions for a long time. After Papa passed, blistering hot sun and even more severe droughts persisted, lasting four long difficult years, burning the lifeblood out of my beloved papa.

"Mom once mentioned that the stress of losing my eldest brother during the on-going drought became too much for Papa. A heart attack sent him to an early grave. Tough years continued for us after Papa died, but Mom managed to keep the farm running and provide for us, but now, once more, another bloody drought, which has almost bankrupted her."

There was an awkward sombre silence between us for a moment, then I continued my story.

"I've always wanted to be a nurse, though I did want to finish my schooling first, but it wasn't to be. I know Mom feels very guilty, but there is nothing she can do. Some tough Voortrekker roots are embedded in her DNA which keeps her pressing on year after year. Even though she has my brother's help, she is amazing. It's difficult to break through her tough exterior though, and for years, I've craved her affection."

"I'm so sorry." Amelia reached out and hugged me. "Shame, Elizabeth, that's such a sad story. Thanks for sharing something so difficult. So, where's your farm?"

"Near Brandfort."

"I know Brandfort. Hey, remember how we all learnt that crazy town's history at school?"

"Yeah, and anyone born in Brandfort is always labelled a racist." I laughed.

"So, are you one?" Amelia prompted playfully.

"No. I don't think so, nor is my mother. We understand and respect our differences. None of my family was partial to the ways of that asshole Verwoed, and I do remember wishing he'd never been born in Brandfort."

"Gee, you've had a tough time. I know how hard farming is. My dad has only survived the droughts because we irrigate and the dams are good. Otherwise, I'm sure we'd have been in the same position." Amelia's voice was filled with genuine empathy, and for the first time in my life, I felt comfortable chatting about my childhood.

Bloemfontein was, and still is, the university town of the Free State province in South Africa. For student nurses in the seventies, it was a great city to be in as young teenagers. We fluffed out our youthful feathers, and there was no shortage of lively teenagers either, many of whom were from the surrounding farming districts like Amelia and me. We were mostly wide-eyed innocents ready to take on the world enthusiastically.

It was an era of fabulous music. The fashion was colourful and outrageous. Life was fun and we revelled in it, especially those of us raised in very conservative households, like I was. It was like being released from the coop. Mega conservative parents were horrified by the way the world was going: young "men" with long hair and facial hair growing in outrageous abandon down the side of their cheeks. The old folk couldn't tolerate the rebellion, but for me, coming to live in a city was an exciting and welcome change.

Living in residence was an education on its own. There were an assortment of interesting characters, but the behaviour from some girls in our wing shocked us both rigid. The city teenagers were far more advanced in the ways of the world than those of us raised on farms. Amelia and I had heard that a few of the girls had snuck a man or two into their rooms during the second week in res; we were shocked. However, we secretly enjoyed the gossip when we got sick of studying.

One afternoon, I had got back to our room earlier than Amelia and was lying on my bed reading my new notes when she burst through the door excitedly.

"Hey, ready for a party?" she screeched happily. "We've been invited to join the rest of our wing at a party tonight."

We'd been together in res just over a month by then.

"Oh, okay, great. Where?"

"I don't know. Some dude's house in town. Probably one of the guys who has been snuck in here on a few occasions. We're all to meet in the foyer at 7 p.m." She winked at me. "So, shall we go?"

She cocked her head to one side while one hand rested on her hip. The other hand she flicked out to the front with a theatrical questioning gesture. I couldn't help my laughter.

"For sure." I chuckled at her theatrics. I was game for a party. "Time to prove we are not the 'prudes' everyone thinks we are."

Amelia screwed up her face and raised her shoulders. She knew neither of us was the type of girl who wanted to be known as slutty or cheap, so prudish was fine for now.

Off we went, and we were not disappointed by Mr Rich Kid's selection of sixties and seventies music either. Popular songs of the day thumped out through the sound system in the garden. We did rock around the clock, drinking, laughing and eating off the barbecue until after eleven, then the music livened up and everyone gathered around the swimming pool. It was a perfect summer's evening; the air was still and warm, and by midnight, the party got interestingly raunchy. Daring couples (or drunk couples) stripped off, dived into the pool and shagged each other openly. Most of the girls participating were from our wing. Apart from being stunned, I was acutely embarrassed too. I'd never seen such urgent grappling, nor had I such wicked laughter in an open display of raw sexual lust. Amelia and I didn't know where to look. We both felt awkward, but, like insects drawn to bright light, we couldn't help staring.

Soon it got too raunchy to go on gawping; it was time to head back to res. That was our first taste of the wilder side of life in the city and from then on, we couldn't resist hooking up with the city-born teenagers. They behaved like racing pigeons and we flew from one party to the next. After our first, rather raw, introduction, Amelia and I joined in. Not for the sexual whirl, but the social rush.

Studying, working and partying became too much. It was a juggling act, but somehow we got through the first year with excellent results. I went home for the Christmas break and Mom dropped the bombshell. She announced she couldn't afford to pay the residence fee for the following year; government subsidies were only available to student nurses who'd completed their high school examinations and passed.

My world and my dreams were shattered. I was devastated. With a heavy heart, I searched for employment. I finally found a job in a pharmacy as a shop assistant, and a tiny bed-sit flat quite a long walk from the nurses' residence. I wanted to be close to the res for Amelia was still there. In the new year I began a seemingly directionless life and felt the loneliness of it like an abandoned child.

Chapter Two

The Corner Pharmacy, situated on the corner! It was how it got its name. It was situated on the other side of the city from my little flat. This meant, for the first time in my life, I'd have to learn to commute to work on the 6.30 a.m. bus. I panicked, thinking that, for a white farm girl to travel on a bus, would be an unusual occurrence. Would I be safe? My naivety and lack of self-confidence was painful, but real.

Having a sheltered, rural background had some prickly disadvantages. I understood the way nature ticked, but didn't have the vaguest idea how life outside of the farm, college or nurses' residence operated. I had assumed it was only black people who travelled on buses.

Standing alone at the bus stop, shivering as a gentle breeze passed over me seducing my heightened tension, I tried to think of my stupid fears as funny. Lots of people travelled by bus. While I was trying to convince myself I was safe, it arrived. I took the steps into the interior and handed my money to the driver: he was white! I felt less nervous then, and noticed I was the first passenger.

"Ah, a pretty new face to greet me in the mornings," the bus driver chirped as he took my fare and introduced himself.

I could not have wished for a more cheerful face to settle my nerves.

"Oom Paul," he said and popped the fare I'd given him into a blue leather pouch that was strapped around his rotund belly. (Oom is Afrikaans for uncle).

"Elizabeth," I said and returned a shy smile.

I sat down close to the door. The journey across town, with endless stops along the way, lasted just under forty minutes. I didn't give my nerves a thought on the journey as I watched more white people get on and off the bus.

The following morning, Oom Paul kindly informed me that regular commuters bought a monthly ticket and by doing this, I'd save a fortune. On my small salary, I was touched by his thoughtfulness. He was a dear old man, and in a matter of days, I'd learnt everything there was to know about the city, commuting by bus, his three beautiful daughters, his wife, how long he'd been a bus driver, where he'd attended school, when he learnt to drive and what his likes and dislikes were. He even described his favourite meals and, judging by the size of his tummy, food was high on his agenda. He loved teasing and joking with the commuters, so it was always a cheerful welcome start to the day. He reminded me of a joyful Father Christmas.

As we got to know one another over the months, he assumed the role of my fatherly protector. To begin with, I wasn't sure how to receive his light-hearted banter, paternal affections and concerns, but in time, I found it all very comforting, even though it evoked a longing to have known my father.

"Going home this weekend?" he asked as I climbed into the bus one Friday morning.

"Not home, but out to Amelia's parents' farm. I'm looking forward to it. I haven't seen Amelia for ages. We're having lunch together today and heading out after that."

"Have a wonderful time, my girl." Oom Paul knew all about my friendship with Amelia and our farming backgrounds.

"I will. You have a good weekend too, Oom Paul. See you Monday." I jumped off the bus, but on Monday, I felt anything but cheerful; I was getting sick.

An hour at work was all I could endure. I headed home, catching a different bus. Three days later, I went back to work.

"How are you feeling today?" Oom Paul asked, his usual beaming smile spread across his face.

"Better, thank you. How did you know I was sick?"

"Ah, because you haven't been on the bus since Monday." He smiled. There was a hint of mischief on his face and a twinkle in his eye that I'd not seen before. It looked like he was about to ask me a question, but he didn't.

When I stood up to leave, he winked at me and pulled gently at my arm, saying in a naughty whisper, "I have someone special for you to meet."

My body temperature soared, my face turned crimson and I didn't know what to do with myself.

"I don't do blind dates, Oom Paul," I answered quickly, but he took no notice and chuckled. "Why are you laughing? Blind dates scare the shit out of me. I'll see you tomorrow."

I hopped off of the bus before he could press for an answer. He was like a fox terrier who wouldn't let go. He asked again in the morning.

"So, what's the verdict?"

"Okay," I said, smiling at him. How could I resist his charms? "When?"

"Well, my girl…" He paused, interrupted by another commuter wanting to pay their fare as we talked across them. "He's, um… he's looking for a partner to take… to the New Year's Eve party at the Methodist Church Hall."

He was interrupted again while scratching to find the right change in his navy blue leather pouch.

"He's a good chap, Elizabeth. I think you'll like him."

I wondered whether I should trust that wicked grin. He read my mind.

"Go on, be a devil," he teased, raising one bushy eyebrow. The twinkle of enquiry lay within his glistening eyes.

"I'll think about it and let you know after the weekend."

I'd heard some gory endings to blind dates while in res. I wasn't sure I'd be doing the right thing agreeing. Though I trusted Oom Paul, I needed to bounce the idea off of Amelia first. I felt sure Oom Paul wouldn't set me up with a serial killer or a drug pedlar. Not that they were a dime a dozen in Bloemfontein in those days, but I still wanted to talk it over with Amelia. I wanted to know what she would do.

"Hey, you look happy," Amelia commented as she flung the car door open and bounced into the driver's seat. As soon as we were on our way, I blurted.

"How do you feel about blind dates?"

"It depends, but it looks like you're excited. Tell me more."

I explained that Oom Paul knew of a friendly chap who was looking for a date for the New Year's Eve party at the church hall.

"Oh, come on, Elizabeth, now who's being the prude? If the old man knows him, you'll be fine," she said, laughing mockingly. "You can't stay a virgin forever."

"This is an invitation to a dance, Amelia, not an invitation to a night of bonking. I don't even know the bloke."

Amelia caught the rising laugh in her throat and nearly choked.

"Hey, you'd… better… let me know… what he's like," Amelia stammered then swallowed hard. Composed again, she drove on while we merrily chatted about boys for the rest of the journey.

On Monday morning, I gave Oom Paul my answer he roared with delight.

But agreeing to go to the dance created a new problem. On my pathetic salary, buying a ready-made, off the peg, boutique evening dress was out of the question. I was good at sewing, so I decided to make a dress. That would occupy the lonely evenings during the week.

Amelia and I went shopping.

"You would blow his mind in that," Amelia teased when I moved the Butterick pattern book next to her and pointed to the dress I wanted to make.

"It's gorgeous, isn't it?"

"It is, but don't you think a slinky, sexy red one like this, would be more fun?" She virtually shoved the Vogue pattern book under my nose. It certainly was a stunning dress with a daring plunging neckline.

"I don't have the confidence to wear a dress like that." I elbowed her in the side. "I wouldn't be seen dead in that on a first date, but it is very sexy."

"Oh, come on, Elizabeth, stop putting yourself down. You could pull it off."

"Never!"

"How long will it take you to make the dress you like, and what material are you planning on using?"

"I was thinking of emerald taffeta, and I guess it will take me about two weeks." I grinned then, out of the blue, I remembered a film I wanted to see. "Hey, *The Godfather* is being released next week. Let's go. I want to see that flick."

"Ja, great idea." Amelia had her eyes focussed elsewhere, but she asked casually, "Can you spare the time?" "I know what you're thinking," I said, smiling.

"Do you? What?"

"That I should be making that sexy little number your thumb is on."

"How did you guess?" Amelia roared with laughter.

Finally, in between discussing movies, styles of evening wear and colours, the green taffeta and my first choice of pattern won. I couldn't wait to lay the material out on the carpet in my tiny little sitting room and pin the pattern to it. It had a simple, understated round neckline with a low back, which was very daring for me. The skirt panels fell away from the waist in gentle folds to the floor; it was gorgeous. A real fairy tale ball gown, something I'd always dreamt of wearing. A week later, Amelia came to view the first fitting.

"Hmm, I love it," she shrieked. "Stunning. Great choice."

She whistled as I modelled it carefully, trying to avoid being poked by pins.

"When I need an evening dress, I know where to come. I hope he's worth it, and if he is, you can make the sexy little black number next." Amelia chuckled playfully.

Family Christmases were always special times for our family, but this year was a bit different. I left the farm on the morning of 30 December to return to Bloemfontein. I didn't dare tell my mother why I wanted to spend New Year in the city, though I was quite sure she'd guessed; there was nothing I could hide from my mother, and she never asked.

The big day was upon me. I was nervous; I couldn't sit still and aimlessly wandered around my flat, unsure of what to do with myself, wishing Amelia was with me to pass the time. Butterflies played havoc in my tummy, and there was an odd metallic taste in my mouth brought on by nerves. At four that afternoon, I jumped into a hot bath filled with bubbles and lay back popping them with my toes as I tried to relax. My mind was filled with visions of what he may look like – as girls do. In the end I decided all I wanted was a polite man with decent manners and a sense of humour. His looks were not a priority, though a bit of eye candy would be a bonus.

Seven o'clock was ticking closer. The bath water had long gone cold and when I'd finally finished titivating myself, it was five to seven. Swirling around, viewing myself from every angle for the last time, I knew I looked good. My private flaunting session was suddenly interrupted by loud raps at the front door. I jumped. My heart skipped a beat then thumped wildly against my ribcage, making it difficult to breathe. I felt absurdly panicky; Amelia would have laughed her head off if she'd seen me like that. Taking a deep breath, I picked up my bag, clung to it like life support, and my mother's words came to mind: "Humour is the lubricant of life, my dear child, make sure you use it."

Trying desperately to stay poised, I opened the door. In front of me stood a tall, devilishly handsome man who oozed sex appeal from every pore. My knees turned to jelly in an instant.

Why hadn't Oom Paul told me he was the best-looking man in the city? He was immaculately attired in a navy blue suit, a white handkerchief peeped out from the breast pocket of his tailored jacket and the whiteness of it caught the glint in his dark brown eyes as they twinkled confidently. Dressed to kill. My lips parted to say hello but not a sound left them; I was too stunned by the sensory input standing at my door. I gulped and swallowed. He was mouth-watering, even the cute little dimple on his chin didn't go unnoticed.

"Umm… hi," I girlishly managed, doing a superb job of messing everything up, so I burst out laughing.

"Dion." He introduced himself without response to my laughter. Instead, he bent down to take my hand and kissed it.

I noticed, as he stood up again, his brown eyes shone with amusement. He was forgiven.

"Good evening, Elizabeth." His voice was deep and cultured.

I shivered; there was just way too much exquisite masculinity standing in front of me, and I had no idea how to deal with it or how to conduct my reaction to it. I was just a simple farm girl who'd never been on a date before.

"I'm sorry." I smiled bashfully and took a deep breath to feed some vital oxygen to my brain.

"Don't apologise," he purred annoyingly, shattering what remained of my withered confidence. "It's a pleasure to meet such a beautiful, happy lady. You look stunning."

He was as self-assured as I was introverted, which was very intimidating. I laughed again while trying to pull my shaky hand away from his grip.

"Shall we?" he asked politely, pointing to the waiting car and I wondered how my shaking body would get there.

My legs vibrated like a banjo as I struggled with the key to lock my flat. Every ounce of poise I'd practised in front of the mirror was gone. I felt him slip his arm through the crook of mine and my pulse quickened as he guided me down the stairs and opened the car door, graciously lifting the remaining taffeta skirt into the car. I caught another whiff of his cologne; he smelt wickedly good too.

"Beyond my wildest dreams," he said as he took his seat behind the wheel. "You are gorgeous." Compliments slid easily off his tongue while my mouth dried out rapidly.

"Thank you," was all I could manage. I couldn't wait to tell Amelia what he looked like.

We made our way to the hall and joined Oom Paul and his family.

"Wow-wee." Oom Paul whistled as Dion led me to the table. He pulled my chair out and I sat at the table setting where my name card was. Dion sat beside me.

"You look stunning, my girl," Oom Paul said proudly. He always called me "my girl" as if I was one of his daughters.

"Thank you," I said again.

It wasn't long before he was teasing me, enjoying watching how my cheeks changed colour with each gentle jibe. Admittedly, the teasing helped to ease my nerves and gradually I began to relax. If this was blind dating, it wasn't so bad.

A butt ugly bloke would have been easier though, but I wasn't complaining.

"Penny for your thoughts," Oom Paul said.

I blushed furiously. I couldn't possibly share my thoughts and definitely not for a penny. I smiled coyly.

Everything inside me was responding nicely to the occasional sip of brandy and ginger ale. Little by little, the alcohol numbed my nerves.

Dion and I danced endlessly, wowing the group with our foxtrot, our bodies pressed tantalisingly close as whirls of green taffeta swung around my legs. While we danced the slow numbers, Dion sang along to the music. He had the most stunning singing voice. I could feel his breath against my neck, raising the hair along my spine and arms and soon gooseflesh covered my body.

"You have a magnificent voice," I said as we swirled around.

"Thank you. I love music. Singing and playing the piano relieve the stresses of work."

"It should be your profession, not your hobby."

He smiled at my suggestion, but didn't answer. I guessed he'd heard that before.

Then, the clock struck midnight. The evening had passed so quickly. He pulled my body closer to his and kissed me passionately for the first time. I'd never kissed a man like that before. I was only dreamily aware of other couples gyrating happily to the music and singing along to the traditional singsong of "Auld Lang Syne". People were hurling streamers across the room and enjoying the celebration, while I was celebrating a heavenly kiss that took us joyously into January 1972.

Blinking out of a semi-dazed state, I heard Oom Paul booming voice, "Happy New Year" and it was getting closer, so I released Dion from my grip.

"You two seem to have hit it off! Happy New Year." Oom Paul kissed me warmly and slapped Dion on the back and gave the thumbs-up signal.

Our first week together was a busy whirl of blissfully romantic dinners, a movie at the drive-in cinema and lunch on two occasions. I was ecstatic. My whole world had dramatically changed. Did it get better than this? I'd met the perfect gentleman; he was everything I'd ever wanted, all in one package. Tall, dark, handsome, funny. He had lovely manners, he made me feel like a million dollars, he could sing beautifully... what more could I want?

By the end of the week, I felt ready to explore a little more, perhaps invite him to my flat. But I was like a green horse; I had no idea which direction to turn or what to do and I didn't want to ruin what was developing by being clumsy.

At the end of the following week, I had lunch with Amelia. I couldn't wait to tell her about my new beau. I'd not seen Dion all week; he'd been away on business. I was aching to see him.

Curious to know how the last two weeks had been with Dion, Amelia rattled off a string of questions, hardly taking a breath or stopping to sip on her milkshake. We shared everything and this was no different. While I chatted, her smile kept changing with my varying tales of lust and innocence. Then I told her, my face heating from a rising blush, about what happened when Dion dropped me home after the New Year's Eve dance. It was, for me, an excruciatingly embarrassing moment and I was still feeling it.

"Oooh, tell me, tell me," she urged.

"Well, we got back to my flat around two in the morning. I was so nervous that I stood with my back to the front door, ready to say goodnight then disappear inside, when he pulled me to him and squeezed me so tight, I farted. It wasn't a little oops, it was a whoosh of air escaping boldly and gratifyingly." I laughed, my face burning like it had that night. "And, there was no dog around I could blame."

Amelia couldn't contain herself!

"Did it stink?" she squealed with mirth.

We suddenly realised everyone in the restaurant was looking at us.

"Sorry." Amelia covered her mouth as forty pairs of eyes pointed our way.

"No! Thankfully it didn't stink. Oh God, imagine..."

We were both giggling and the couple at the table next to us were straining to hear what we were saying. Most of the patrons in the restaurant were still looking at us, some were grinning, some just staring.

"What did you do?"

Amelia exploded with loud hysterical laughter again. She couldn't stop herself as visions of my discomfort came to mind. The couple next to us couldn't resist and asked what the joke was.

"Don't you dare tell," I warned Amelia; her infectious laughter had everyone smiling now.

"Oh my God, I would have died," she stammered through hysterics. "Not even a dog around to blame. I love that."

She guffawed and the people next to us began to laugh along with Amelia's rapture.

"So, what did you do?"

"I burst out laughing, what else could I do? It was also the perfect time to say goodbye. I hastily retreated into my flat shouting my goodbyes and thank yous and closed the door. I dealt with my embarrassment where he couldn't see me."

"Well, it didn't put him off."

"Oh no. In fact, he teases me about it now, and I still blush. I think he mentions it to make me blush. We've had dinner twice, we've been to the drive-in, watched the Bond movie *Diamonds Are Forever*, and this week he's been away."

"No sex yet?" Amelia teased.

"No! Amelia! But, to be honest, I wouldn't mind, but I'm too scared." My cheeks flushed again.

"So, when am I going to meet this sexy dude?"

"Soon. We're going out to the farm this weekend. I want Dion to meet Mom and William."

"Oh, wow! That's quick. Well, if your brother approves, you're home and dry." She whistled.

We finished our meal and arranged to meet the following week.

Her parting words as we hugged were, "Good luck with your mom and brother."

We blew kisses to each other and went on our way.

Thankfully, Mom was suitably impressed. I couldn't read William's thoughts; he never readily voiced his opinion. William's advice was essential to me. I'd badger him later. I needed his opinion.

He did approve. He called me at work to let me know just as I was leaving to meet Amelia for lunch.

"My, my, you sure have a glowing look on your face. There's no doubt you are in love, Elizabeth," Amelia said, complimenting me easily. "I'm looking forward to meeting this handsome beau of yours."

"Well, not long now. I can't wait to see Dion, and I'm looking forward to watching *Cabaret*. Should be a good movie. After that, we'll grab a bite to eat."

"Have you done it yet?"

"Amelia! No!"

"I'm just teasing. Remember those randy girls in the res last year?" She chuckled.

"Yes, they were terrible. Sex ruled."

Dion arrived looking as stunning as ever. I saw out of the corner of my eye Amelia give him the once over. She approved, raising her eyebrows a few times before she raised her thumb and smiled.

The music from the film set the mood; Liza Minnelli and Michael York did it for me. I squirmed in my seat while Dion held my hand and tickled my leg. I couldn't concentrate. I imagined Dion singing the same songs to me and I visualised myself ripping the buttons off of his shirt and pushing him back on the couch as soon as we got back to my flat. Just like in the movies. That was a fantasy! I couldn't pull that off, even if I'd wanted to. Virgins didn't behave like that! But I couldn't ignore the delicious desire burning inside me. Tonight, I didn't want him to be too much of a gentleman.

After supper, we couldn't get back to my flat fast enough. I slammed the door shut and prayed I wouldn't fart! We were quickly entwined in each other's arms. Slowly, we edged towards the sofa as we kissed. No dramatics as I'd visualised. This was better. We'd even skipped the coffee bit, but there was something I had to tell Dion first, so I pulled out of his grip.

"Dion," I whispered, afraid to ruin the mood. "I'm a virgin and I'm scared."

He pulled a little further back and looked at me tenderly.

"Wow, and I'm deeply honoured," he whispered, kissing me tantalisingly on the side of the neck, whispering that he'd take care of me as he ran his fingers through my hair that sent shockwaves rippling through me.

Suddenly, I was covered in delightful, tingling anticipation. We moved from the couch to my bed, and slowly Dion removed my clothing. My breasts were tight with ecstasy, and I found it hard to deal with such intense physical yearning. I'd never imagined it to be this heavenly.

Dion began gently kissing my tummy, tickling my navel with his tongue, then he stopped and looked down at my slim body appreciatively. The dimple on his chin deepened with desire. His chest and arms showed beautifully toned muscle formation. I sucked in my breath, holding on to it as his trousers dropped to the floor. My chest was tight with desire and anxiety. He leant forwards and gently gripped my nipple between his teeth, provocatively nibbling at me while my body convulsed towards him instinctively. As slowly as he had promised, he gently nudged at my opening and my body trembled in delicious, fearful anticipation of becoming a woman.

During the Easter weekend, Dion and I decided to live together. He was still living with his parents on their smallholding outside of Bloemfontein.

"Isn't that a bit quick?" Amelia and my mother asked, surprised by our haste.

I was sure this was the man I wanted to spend my life with no matter what anyone said.

We found a flat and settled into our cosy little nest. I'd never felt so happy. We loved the small home we'd created. The weekends passed in a musical muddle of singing, guitar strumming and passionate love-making. Dion was my first love in every conceivable way.

Then, one weekend in September, he surprised me by whisking me away to a game lodge for two nights. While we sat beneath the setting sun, hidden in a game hide watching game come down to drink, filling their bellies with water for the night and listening to the sounds as dusk descended, Dion whispered, "Will you marry me?"

"Yes, of course I will," I said, squealing with delight, disrupting the tranquillity and splendour of an African night.

Eventually, the animals drifted off. In that blissful silence, beneath a velvety African sky filled with sparkling diamonds, we celebrated our commitment to each other.

Chapter Three

We had our wedding on the farm and William walked me down the aisle. It was a small garden wedding, surrounded by a few special friends and family. It was the type of wedding I'd always wanted.

A blissful eighteen months passed, then some unusual changes began to occur. I couldn't work out what was causing the sudden eruptions and changes in Dion's behaviour. His moods swung like a pendulum. Sometimes I felt like I was living with a stranger. Perplexed by these weird personality changes, and wanting to help, I chose the moment with care.

"What's changed, Dion?" I asked calmly and kindly.

He seemed to be in a good mood. I waited quietly for an answer and watched his expression begin to change. It was like watching a chameleon stalking its prey and I was the prey. His face altered in colour from his natural tan, through the orange spectrum and ended with a deep angry crimson. His cheeks puffed up too, just as a chameleon does. What frightened me was, in an instant, his face went from crimson to a chilling deathly white. *How on earth does that happen?* I thought, feeling the silent fear in me. This wasn't the man I'd married. His eyes were dark lifeless pools now.

"Nothing has changed." The deep red returned to colour his face once more.

I had never witnessed anything quite as macabre. I also knew that any civil discussion wasn't going to be possible, plus he'd had four brandies by then. I instinctively knew it was time to keep my mouth shut.

During the last few uncomfortable months, he'd shown that a woman deeply in love was not the most brilliant judge of character! My fairy tale wasn't panning out quite the way the books portrayed. In that moment, I would have happily become a pumpkin. I was not only acutely frustrated by trying to decipher his peculiar behaviour, I was frightened of him now. This so-called fairy tale was morphing into a terrifying thriller, which I didn't know how to handle, or whom to turn to.

I noted it was always after the fourth drink that Oudemeester (a South African brandy) turned Dion into an ugly monster and though I wanted to ask, "Who are you?", I didn't dare.

The following day, when he was sober, he was either defensive or apologetic. Somehow, I had to convince him that his love for alcohol was not only changing him, but it was also ruining our marriage, even threatening to end it, which was not what I wanted. I wanted my Prince Charming back.

I loved him, the real Dion, the one I had married, not this monster born to Oudemeester. The quandary continued, for in our culture, his behaviour was considered taboo. Talking about it wasn't done. It was the sort of conversation one only had in private with someone who could keep it confidential. Being an alcoholic, or displaying any form of mental health issues, was considered a problem that only afflicted the poor or the lower classes. I certainly didn't want to tell my mother, least of all my brother. Though I trusted Amelia, I didn't know how to begin describing what was happening.

Besides, still spellbound by his sober charms, I lived hoping it was a passing phase brought on by the stresses of his job. He'd mentioned the stress repeatedly over the past few months. When he wasn't drinking, he'd sing to me as I prepared supper, then all resistance would crumble and I'd forgive him. He knew just what buttons to press. He would move in behind me while I stirred what I was cooking, nuzzle my neck and sing to me. In seconds, I'd have no idea what I was cooking. Supper would be abandoned until later, much later, or not eaten at all. Those days were blissful, and not for a moment did I suspect that the beautiful serenading and confessions of undying love were becoming a cunning disguise.

One evening, another opportunity opened for me to discuss the drinking issues. While we sat curled up on the couch, I carefully led the conversation to the problems.

"Please stop drinking, liefie," I said using the Afrikaans term of endearment. "I'm worried about you," I pleaded. I knew I risked ruining the mood, but I had to express my concerns.

He exploded.

"Don't you dare bitch about my fucking drinking, do you hear me?" Spittle flew from his mouth like an angry viper.

Though I'd prepared myself for retaliation, this venomous reaction not only shocked me, it terrified me. He'd never hissed at me with such poison before. I noticed his jaw was quivering and his hands had balled into fists.

"Dion, that's not necessary," I said, watching his fists. "Only cowards hit their women and if you hit me, consider our marriage well and truly over."

I was struggling to maintain composure. The word "coward" seemed to trigger an angry, uncontrolled rage and he growled at me. I didn't dare respond or move. I loathed this sort of confrontation. Tears pricked my eyes. Reaching for the brandy bottle on the coffee table in front of me, I grabbed it and smashed it on the floor, shattering the bottle and the atmosphere. I stormed off to bed.

As the months progressed, Dion's personality changes became even more dramatic. My sixth sense rang alarm bells in my head, cautioning me that Dion was dangerous. I kept finding myself excusing his vile behaviour. I still loved the old Dion and this new monster was destroying everything we'd built together.

On occasions, we'd have wonderful conversations. Then he was sensitive and apologetic. For days, sometimes weeks, all was as it had been when we first were married. Often, he'd even admit to behaving like an animal after the fourth drink, but it didn't stop him. Our social life had dwindled away too. Our friends had become bored listening to Dion carry on, often with ugly criticism of them and others, at social braais (barbeques). Consequently, invitations became rare. I was living a continuous apology.

After an ugly, hostile confrontation between Amelia and Dion during our last braai together, she vowed she would never come to another. It broke my heart, but neither did anyone else ever come again. Isolated and alone, Amelia and I met in town when we wanted to see each other. She never told me what had prompted the outburst, but I guessed he must have been strongly suggestive, which was probably the case, or darn right rude and insulting, which was also probable, neither of which she would have tolerated. Amelia was volatile with admirably strict principles. He, on the other hand, didn't give a damn about principles. He also had the morals of a shark, perhaps worse. Nor did he care that our friends no longer visited. The feelings of others were not his concern. Providing *he* was happy, nothing else mattered.

Not everyone saw through him. He was a suave operator when it came to business and he knew it. His business lunches became a social whirl: a pre-requisite for the orders he secured, or so he said.

"All part of the window dressing," he'd say.

Having sexy little company secretaries attend the luncheons, armed with the company credit card was also part of that so-called window dressing. When Dion's silky smooth tongue began operating, and the ladies became more mesmerised by his charms and good looks, they didn't mind how much he spent to secure the deals he was after. His explanation of how he lured his clients gave him a real sense of power, not to mention an abundance of perverse satisfaction. He loved telling me how he clinched those shady deals. Personal pride and self-belief shone in his face.

"I can see how much you love it, but it's not very ethical," I suggested, then added, "Why is all the drinking such a necessary component to seal the deal?"

"My liefie, closing the deal is much easier when the buyer has had a few 'doppe'." (Afrikaans slang for drinks.) He smiled ruefully. "They spend easily then. It's an ego thing. Sometimes they may spend half their annual budget in one order, but that depends on the discounts I dangle under their noses. My monthly sales figures soar, which does wonders for my commission earnings," he said boastfully, suddenly realising he had walked straight into something he wasn't sure of how to wriggle out of.

"I'm sure it does. You've never shared that with me before, or any of your commission earnings," I said matter-of-factly, twiddling my fingers through my hair, something I did when I was feeling insecure and out of my comfort zone.

His body language told me he was feeling the same insecurity. He obviously had no intention of sharing his commission earnings with me, ever.

What made perfect logical sense to him was utterly immoral to me. He couldn't see that. I knew there was no point in causing another heated exchange of words, but I found his sales techniques deplorable.

He quickly covered up his financial contribution blunder by saying, "There have been some good commissions, but none big enough to change our financial future."

The lie was just too casual and too blatantly obvious.

"But more than enough to change our marriage by putting it into savings instead of spending it on Oudemeester, coke and beer?"

He shifted around, then suggested playing my favourite songs on the piano, which he did for a while, which pacified the mood, then he came back and we continued chatting.

"Why have you never shared with me what commission you get?" I asked carefully.

He was in an unusually approachable mood, despite being a bit uneasy. He didn't answer, instead he got up and put some gentle music on the gramophone and joined me in the kitchen.

"You're right, babe. I'm sorry. The next commission cheque I will give to you. Deposit it into our house savings."

I nearly fell over. I wasn't expecting that answer. What a refreshing change of attitude! He was wearing his best apology face. I was going to do my best to keep the mood, praying he wouldn't change his mind.

"Thank you, liefie. It will help your health, cutting back on drinking. Excessive alcohol intake is known to make a person depressed. Plus, a boost to our house savings will be great."

"Aagh, ja, babes. It will be good to buy our own home. And ja, I guess you're right, I'll cut back on the drinking for you." He didn't sound convinced and finished up by saying, "It's all about targets and I always go beyond mine, liefie."

The atmosphere was a happy one. How I wished it could go back to being constant. I took advantage of the moment and suggested we rekindle our love and celebrate our third wedding anniversary by taking a few days' leave, spending a little of his commission on the celebration, and to my surprise, he agreed.

During our getaway, I learnt just how hefty Dion's commissions were. I was horrified. Over the past year, he'd drunk more than a deposit on a modest home. But what concerned me more was this indicated the drinking problem was more serious than I'd thought.

I wondered how he could have been so thoughtless, so irresponsible. I wasn't going to ruin this unusually idyllic time together. I'd tackle it later.

It wasn't long after our romantic getaway that the mood swings and character changes shot up a gear. I had to turn to someone. I turned to Dion's father for help. I felt that by being sensitive and keeping the problem within our family circle, it would be respected. I got on well with my father-in-law, and he also knew Dion's weakness for alcohol. I prayed he could offer me some guidance. I was desperate for advice. I badly wanted to talk to my mother, but I didn't know how to broach the subject with her.

"What's up, my girl?" he asked, hearing the quiver in my voice.

I explained tearfully while he listened, allowing me to finish without saying a word. Though I felt better having got everything off of my chest, he offered little advice other than promising to speak to Dion. If he ever confronted his eldest son, it didn't make the slightest bit of difference.

Now I needed to seek professional advice from someone who understood the workings of an alcoholic's mind, and whatever else was going on inside Dion's head. I hadn't spoken to Oom Paul for a long time, so I called him to ask if he knew of anyone professional I could turn to. I could hear he found what I had to say challenging to comprehend, or believe, but he was sympathetic, suggesting I call Alcoholics Anonymous and ask them for advice, or go to our minister.

"I've tried that. I went to Pastor Geldenhuys and what he suggested I put to Dion was worse than hell when I actually put it to him. Dion wanted nothing to do with Pastor Geldenhuys after that and never attended Sunday ministries with me again. He doesn't believe he has a problem," I moaned, feeling helplessness shroud me once more. "I'll try AA. Thank you, Oom Paul."

I didn't. I was too embarrassed to call them. Then I thought my boss might be able to offer some sound advice. It took me days to pluck up the courage to speak to him.

"Elizabeth, get your doctor to give him a prescription for an anti-depressant, and I will dispense them for him." His dismissive attitude rankled me. He didn't give a rat's arse about my problem and spoke down to me as if I was a nothing. Though I was young and naive, he hadn't learnt there was a fire within me; I protected those I loved.

"Mark!" I snapped more rudely than I'd intended. "Those are also addictive. He already has an addiction." Luckily, there were no customers near who might have overheard my rudeness.

"It's up to you, Elizabeth. Depression often leads to alcoholism."

I could see he was stunned by my bold, rather impolite response to his careless suggestion, but he went on.

"Why don't you ask him to try it out for a month and see if things improve? If it doesn't help, then he needs to get professional guidance from Alcoholics Anonymous."

The mention of AA again.

"He's a borderline alcoholic who doesn't believe he has a problem. He's so full of his own self-importance, he won't go to AA. The drinking and mood swings are getting worse, and the more he drinks, the nastier he gets, but depression? I don't see that. In fact, the next day he thinks it's funny. If I get anti-depressants for him, he will hit the roof, or me."

"Elizabeth," Mark said sternly, "Once the depression is under control, he won't have the same desire to drink excessively. Depression is definitely there, believe me. You might not think he suffers from depression, but I guarantee he does. Find the right moment to tell him." He was walking away from me as he spoke, but I was so desperate I followed a few paces behind him.

"But... um... it's not just the alcohol," I said quietly, desperate to have someone to listen and support me through a situation I could not decipher or even articulate. "He has frightening personality changes, even when he is sober." I suddenly felt excruciatingly insecure.

35

Pathetic desperation sounded in my voice and must have irritated Mark. He stopped, turned around, stared straight at me and said, "You're a typical woman, always wanting the man to change. It's time to grow up, Elizabeth."

Seething, hurt, but not yet defeated, the fire within had just been ignited.

"I beg your pardon?" I spat furiously. I was no longer the meek employee, but a caged tigress.

The argument continued as I followed, but soon he closed his office door. Ten minutes later, I walked out the pharmacy doors and out of a job. Dion was furious when I told him. All I was trying to do was help Dion.

"I don't need fucking anti-depressants, Elizabeth. There's nothing wrong with me," was his snarky, sharp response.

How I wish Mark had been there to hear it. It was exactly what I'd thought his reaction would be. I began to wonder if the fight was worth it, but a chance to get my old husband back was my goal, so I pressed on.

"You have to address your drinking problem, Dion. Maybe if you do take anti-depressants, as Mark suggested, even for a month or two, you may not feel like drinking. Surely, it's worth a try?"

Dion shook his head, raised his eyebrows and went on drinking.

Our lives swung from good to bad. When it was on the backward swing, it was hell and I was ready to give up on him. When it swung the other way, times were wonderful again. It was an unpredictable future though.

On the forward swing, Dion was mostly his old self, but the problems had gone far beyond just alcohol consumption. In my innocence, I believed it was entirely up to me, as his wife, to help him. I'd made a vow and I took it seriously: "In sickness and health…" I adored his sweet, good side and I'd do anything to get it back – permanently.

Alcohol-induced schizophrenia may be a label used nowadays, along with bipolar and other new terminology that puts people in boxes, but not in the seventies. Dion's symptoms were more obscure and not openly discussed. Help was very hard to find, plus there was something more sinister hiding in the depths. It wasn't just alcoholism.

I put on my happy face and found another job in another pharmacy closer to our flat. I walked to work, no more bus fares. I was happy about that.

Determined not to be beaten by Dion's maladies, I went in search of a diagnosis within the confines of the library during my lunch hour. There, I could spend time researching discretely in a quiet space, finding out more about what multiple personality disorders were all about and trying to pinpoint which category Dion fell into. I dug up some alarming material, but there was precious little I could do with it, other than allowing it to clog up my mind with his frightening afflictions. His symptoms were not considered a "disease", but a social or personality flaw. Well, I'd established that without the aid of the library!

The scary truth was everything about Dion and his mood swings matched the description of multiple personality disorder, schizophrenia, sociopath, psychopath and narcissist. What was I to do? I could tag on alcoholism if I wished; all of which would leave him vulnerable to addictions. Who could I get to help me understand the complexities of what I faced?

I turned to Amelia, but after we had some laughs about it, she said, "Honey, he's a fucking head case. He loves himself more than anyone else, and believe me, my friend, he knows exactly what he's doing. Chuck the fucker out. You can do better."

There was a lot of truth in that, but I wasn't ready to tackle life alone. I still wanted my old Dion back and naively I believed it was possible. I didn't want anyone else and though I prayed, God wasn't handing miracles my way. Dion went on drinking. I went on researching. I finally understood the need to seek professional help instead of jumping from one friend to another. My life was going to be a dangerous living hell if I didn't, and finding the solutions was up to me. My prayers became urgent, grief-soaked and more needy than I cared to admit.

I was still deeply in love with my husband and now I realised his personality complexities were way beyond my comprehension. Beneath his charming, irresistible exterior lurked a calculating monster. Dion had two distinct personalities. One turned me wild with passion and giddy with love; the other was a nasty, violent beast that frightened and infuriated me. It was this personality I was living with more regularly. In the blink of an eye, he could switch from one to the other. When his mischievous brown eyes turned to eerie dark pools, something far more significant than terror filled me.

My dilemma was being able to provide an articulate explanation of this strange behaviour to someone else who would believe me without seeing Dion's metamorphosis. It was also about summoning the courage to do it. When I wanted to speak to Dion, I had to pick the right moment. A week after my research, I found that moment.

"Liefie, I need to get you some help. I can't live this roller-coaster life anymore. I don't understand what has happened to you. I want the old you back," I said, keeping my tone as loving and as warm as a kitten wanting its food.

He exploded, of course. I should have known.

"Fuckin' hell, what is it with you?"

Idiotically, the loving, warm kitten morphed.

"You know what's eating me, Dion. We've discussed it endlessly."

"It's only your opinion," he responded with nasty sarcasm. That was like a blow to the solar plexus. "Christ, you're not going to go on about my drinking, are you? *My* so-called problem is all in *your* head." There was a nasty sneer on his face. This time, the tiger came to my aid.

"Fuck you, Dion du Toit."

I swore. Something I rarely did in those days, but this time, it felt incredibly good to say it with anger.

"I'm doing this for you, plus I can't go on like this. It's not just your drinking that's a problem, and you know it." It was time to release all my pent-up frustration. "One minute you're eating me alive with desire and the next you're spitting fire at me, damning me for being alive and in your life. Alcohol exacerbates the problem. But why, in the name of everything holy, can't you remain as just one personality, the one I fell in love with?"

As I said that last sentence, a sadness touched me deep inside and doused my fire. I began openly sobbing. I was struggling to explain my feelings as rivers of tears poured down my face. I couldn't let him know about the research I'd been doing in the library; he would kill me.

"Don't be ridiculous, Elizabeth. I've never heard such bullshit in my life." I could see he was holding onto his temper. "I'm fucking sick of your accusations. I am neither an alcoholic nor a psychopath. I am one person, Elizabeth, only one person." He emphasised his belief by violently and deliberately digging his index finger into his pectoral muscle and finished up by saying, "You don't see two of me, do you? Or have *you* been fucking drinking?"

I was flabbergasted. Such an idiotic, noxious retort. He ranted on, hardly giving me time to breathe and think. So many of our evenings were spent this way now – arguing or me silently reading while Dion got drunk.

"Don't be childish. You know I'm referring to all those crazy characters inside that complicated head of yours, not you physically," I stated calmly, but then I saw the monster crawling out of its cocoon: his eyes had darkened.

I backed away and disappeared to bed, filled with misery and desperation. Where was God when I needed Him?

Later that night, the "pussy cat" climbed into bed and cuddled up to me, pushing himself into the small of my back, waking me with his arousal, whispering shallow apologies in my ear while kissing the back of my neck, anticipating a positive response. He'd reminded me repeatedly he could fix my irrational female complaints. I was going to show him that sex didn't always work. I lay rod still, pretending to be asleep. I felt the change in his breathing, but I wasn't giving in. He was leaving again in the morning, and he'd be away for a few days. He'd have ample time to give our conversation some thought if he had any sense at all. Eventually, he rolled over.

The days without him were bliss. We'd even had two, almost loving, telephone conversations and he admitted, in the quiet time with his own company, he'd given some thought to what I'd said. My heart did little flick-flacks in my chest and I smiled. Not a triumphant smile, but one of hope, and I suddenly realised I was looking forward to seeing him.

Later that Friday evening, when I got home from work, he was standing at the front door.

"Hello, my liefie. Stressful week? You look exhausted," I said, stepping towards him.

I kissed him hello then dumped the shopping I was carrying on the kitchen floor before turning back to face him, thinking a hug was in order, but the wild look was in his eyes.

Oh God, help me, I said silently and stepped away.

I hadn't expected this; I'd been so looking forward to having him home – the weekend was probably going to become dangerously volatile if he had anything to drink.

"No. I'm just fucking tired," he swore. "Where were you?"

His irrational question prompted a snarky response from me. Surely, it was obvious where I'd been.

"Where do you think, Dion?" I answered, pointing at the bags of shopping lying on the kitchen floor, all of which I'd just lugged into the house without help.

He glanced with disinterest at the shopping on the floor. "I'm fucking hungry and dinner isn't ready."

I could scarcely believe what I was hearing.

"You fucking chauvinist. It's only 5.30 p.m. and I've just walked in. I work too, you know, and I don't piss my earnings up against the wall."

He took no notice and went on swearing at me like a mad man, pacing around the kitchen gulping down one beer after another. I didn't respond. I finished unpacking the shopping and quietly got on with making supper. It was safer not to engage in confrontational conversation or make any further sarcastic statements. While I was cooking, I had a thought.

"Liefie, perhaps you shouldn't have changed jobs. This one seems to stress you terribly," I said, hoping that a sympathetic tone would diffuse the mood, but there was an unmistakable, nauseating threat about him tonight that nothing I said or did was going to change.

"Don't be fucking ridiculous. You know how much I love my job." He shook his head. "I don't understand you. It was your suggestion I take the job. Just to let you know, in future, I want dinner waiting for me when I get home on a Friday evening."

He stood in front of me, defiant as ever.

"You can't be serious… That's impossible, and you know it. If you're that hungry, why don't you have lunch later or make yourself something to eat if you get home before me?"

Our marriage was like my to-do list: housekeeping, cooking, finances, doctors, research, tolerance, patience.

"Fuck that," I swore under my breath.

"Cooking is a woman's job," he snapped, popping the cap off of another beer and throwing the bottle opener on the counter.

I came apart.

"What?" I yelled. "I'm not your slave. With each passing month, you treat me more and more like I am one."

He was goading me. I knew I shouldn't take the bait, but I couldn't help myself.

"Some of the best chefs in the world are men," I continued. "We're living in the 1970s, Dion, not the 1940s. Things have changed and will continue to change. Get off your fucking high horse!"

A brooding silence remained between us.

Eventually, he said, "Make a plan."

Make a plan. Right.

The following morning, Dion woke with the anticipated violent hangover. He'd really hit the bottle after I'd gone to bed. I heard him scratching around in the bathroom as I lay in bed, grinning wickedly. Not every binge brought on a headache, but last night's one had.

"Where are the headache tabs?" he called out. I detected a slight quiver of desperation in his voice; he urgently needed to reduce the throbbing above his eyeballs.

"In the wall cabinet," I called back, but I'd hidden them, hoping a nasty hangover with no pain medication might provoke some thought on giving up drinking.

"There's bugger all in the cabinet. Where else have you got some?"

"All the meds we keep are in there. If there aren't any, they're finished," I shouted back and I heard him groan.

Unfortunately, he had a remarkably short memory of painful hangovers, but he had a back-up plan, like most addicts do: a box of paracetamol in the cubbyhole of his car, tucked away for emergencies. For the rest of Sunday, we scarcely uttered a word to each other.

On Monday morning, we went our separate ways – another week apart. When I got to work, I asked my boss if it was possible to reduce my working hours on a Friday. He frowned, and for a moment, I thought he was going to ask me why. Fortunately, he agreed without needing an explanation.

I turned Dion's demands to my advantage. This extra time meant I could meet Amelia for lunch every Friday, appease my chauvinist husband, and do the weekend shopping.

Ironically, from that Friday onwards, he was never home by 5.30 p.m. for supper.

Chapter Four

Was this how a real grown-up marriage happened? I found myself asking this question more frequently. I didn't feel like a "proper" grown-up; I was only twenty-four. I had crept out of the happiness coma I'd been in for eighteen months with a nasty awakening. I didn't want to be all grown up and began to question who I was. Had I turned Dion into this monster?

Was I to blame? A question I asked myself repeatedly for he kept shouting, "Don't blame me." I was sure it had nothing to do with me, but he made me feel it could be. He had set me up perfectly and continued to manipulate me, making me feel like I was the problem in our marriage.

Amelia kept me believing in myself, and when I got to our favourite restaurant on Friday, she was already sitting there, her back to the window. I tapped the window. She turned and smiled, but it wasn't her normal radiant smile.

"Hey, how's my oldest and dearest friend?" I asked cheerfully, wrapping my arms around her shoulders.

"I've been fine. Well…" She hesitated. "Actually, that's not true. I was going to call you, but you beat me to it."

I smiled at her. It wasn't often I saw Amelia down in the dumps.

"I'm ravenous! God, it smells good and garlicky in here today."

"It does, doesn't it? Shall we have the normal house wine?" Amelia asked.

"Ja, for sure. I must be home by 3.30. Don't ask." I raised my eyebrows and grimaced.

"Why?"

"Dion insists I have his supper ready at 5.30 every Friday." I felt a bit sheepish admitting I'd surrendered to his demands, again.

"Fucking dog. The way he treats you, I'd tell him to go screw himself." Amelia scowled. "He's the reason I was going to call you today."

"Oh, what's he done to you now?" I sensed I was in for bad news.

"Not to me." Amelia shuffled uncomfortably holding her wine glass close to her mouth, looking at me over the rim as if it gave her protection from what she was about to say. "I don't know how to tell you what I must tell you. You're the dearest, kindest, most considerate person I've ever met, and telling you this is not going to be easy, but know I've got your back. Just hear me out."

I took a large swig of wine.

"He's sleeping with Zandri." Amelia spat the words out quickly, like they were poison in her mouth.

Her words stung. My world turned upside down in that moment. I nearly choked on my wine. Amelia put her hand over mine as I spluttered.

"What?" I eventually breathed out. "Are you sure?"

I didn't want to believe it. I'd accepted Dion was a flirt, but screwing his brother's wife was far beyond my comprehension and absolutely inexcusable.

"Oh, Elizabeth, how I wish it wasn't me delivering this shitty news. I'm so sorry. Your heart must be breaking right now. You've gone ashen white."

I swallowed hard. I didn't want to burst into tears in the restaurant. There were tears in Amelia's eyes. We were holding onto them.

"It's okay." I tried to smile. "I'm glad you've told me. Coming from you, I know it's true. The son of a bitch. How did you find out?" The questions tumbled from me now. "I've had the alcohol abuse to deal with, his changing personalities, now infidelity with a very sick twist. I can't take it anymore. It's so hard because I still love him, that old Dion."

"I know how you must be hurting right now. I hate seeing you in this miserable marriage, my friend. I'll say it again, Dion doesn't deserve a person like you."

"He says I'm to blame for everything, Amelia, and the harder I try, the worse it gets."

"Don't go on trying then. He's going to bring you down with him, Elizabeth, and I'd hate to see that happen."

Deep down inside I knew she was right.

"I won't let that happen," I whispered. "The bitch."

It all began to hit me harder. I wondered then if anything would ever be as it was in the beginning.

At the start of the meal, I'd been ravenous, now my appetite had all but gone.

"What are you going to do?" Amelia asked as she watched me slowly push a little salad onto my fork.

I looked at it, decided I couldn't eat, lay the fork down on the plate and took a swig of wine instead. Anger was now diluting the pain.

"I don't know, but I'll come up with something. You know, thinking back, I always thought Zandri was after Dion. It's a pity Dion isn't like his brother Phillip. He's such a sweetheart; he doesn't deserve this either."

"Oh my word, Elizabeth, that is so typical of you, always thinking of others' feelings before you consider your own. How about looking after you for a change? Forget about Phillip's feelings for now," Amelia said, then added, "I know what you should do. Just kick the fucker out, as I've said before." Her red-headed temper was showing, but perhaps she was right, maybe it was time for me to face reality.

I smiled feebly – a smile of mixed emotions all trying to express themselves at once. Sadness and hurt first, amusement at Amelia's thoughts, then anger and pain. I always loved Amelia's forthright manner.

"Kick the fucker out." I repeated her words. I needed time to digest all this agony. In less than a minute, the energy and enthusiasm to help Dion had gone. I wasn't going to allow all his personalities to destroy me. I needed to take Amelia's advice.

It was time to head home.

"If you need help, a place to sleep or a shoulder to cry on, just shout," Amelia said.

I nodded my thanks, thinking I would probably take her up on her offer in a couple of hours. We gave each other a tight hug and I tearfully said goodbye.

In the safety and privacy of my car, I cried rivers of bitter tears. As they dried, sadness was replaced by anger, then every other emotion born of the pain of infidelity came hurtling in. It all began to fall into place: being away more than usual, and now no longer home on Friday evening early. She was probably cooking his dinner now.

Revenge was not the answer, of that I was sure, though the thought was tempting.

I parked under the jacaranda tree on the edge of our driveway. It was my favourite tree. I loved the purple flowers, until they all dropped, covering the driveway and my car with a purple carpet that came alive with bees in search of nectar.

He wasn't home yet, and after what I'd learnt, I didn't expect him.

He drove in thirty minutes later. I was so unprepared I wished he hadn't come home at all. Standing in the kitchen, watching him through the window gathering up his jacket and briefcase off of the back seat without a care in the world really irritated me. I took a long deep breath – not that it guaranteed to help my disposition or clear my head. It was still foggy with conflicting emotions, and no amount of oxygen helped heal my broken heart.

"Hi." He leant down and pecked my cheek, then he took a step back and said, "You look like you're ready to kill something."

"Not something, Dion. Someone," I said and watched the frown deepen the lines between his brows. "How long have you been screwing your sister-in-law?"

I couldn't bring myself to say her name. I also hoped, by using her relationship to him instead, it would make his infidelity sound more disgraceful.

Damn, now the tears were back.

His eyes bored into mine while his hands visibly gripped harder on the handle of his briefcase, an action that hadn't gone unnoticed by me. I stood still, my jaw set. I was ready to retaliate as I carefully scrutinised his body language with lasers in my eyes. He stood like a statue in front of me; that spelt guilt. Finally, he spoke.

"I have no idea what you're talking about, Elizabeth."

Of course not! What did I expect?

"I think you do. You're sleeping with your sister-in-law, aren't you? Your silence hasn't fooled me."

I could feel my pain deepening as I looked at him. As hard as I tried to hold back the tears, they kept on coming. Knowing my husband was having an affair was painful enough, but with his sister-in-law made it a hundred times worse.

"There's not an ounce of truth in what you've heard, Elizabeth. Surely, you know I wouldn't do that to my boet."

Oh, but you'd do it to me! I thought silently and stared at him while he put his briefcase down, headed straight to the fridge and grabbed a beer. It was the "Dutch courage" he was going to need after I'd finished with him.

He stood looking at me expectantly, then took a swig. I wanted to behave like a wild woman scorned and belittled by a ruthless, heartless rogue. The urge to attack him with bunched fists was overwhelming. I maintained control and didn't move an inch.

Then I said very, very slowly, "That's what I'd hoped, Dion, but it's not that way, is it?"

I kept my focus on his eyes. It was shamefully apparent he was lying, holding his cheeks and lips tight, forcing a faint grin and the dimple on his chin deepened. Before he could answer with more infuriating lies, I spun around and ran out of the house.

I walked around the garden, trying to sift through the myriad of thoughts: some clear, some confused. I breathed in the fresh air of the early evening hoping it would help connect my heart and my head; they'd come detached over the years, but anger merely suffocated them. Once I had calmed down, I walked back into the house. Dion was still sitting on the barstool at the kitchen counter. I passed him, saying nothing and put on the kettle.

"Does… does Phillip know?" I asked, focussing on the kettle.

"Does Phillip know what, Elizabeth?"

"Oh, come on, Dion. Didn't I give you enough time to think up a new bunch of lies?" I asked sarcastically. A few tears ran down my cheeks. I wiped them away quickly, determined to remain steadfast in front of him despite the agony of this despicable betrayal. "We need to talk, Dion."

"There's nothing to talk about, liefie."

I spun around. "Don't 'liefie' me, Dion. There's plenty to talk about. You can go on denying your disgusting, immoral actions, but let me warn you, if you don't end it with a phone call tonight I will confront her at the top of my voice on Sunday morning outside church so the whole congregation knows the scandalous things the two of you have been up to. There won't be any forgiveness, trust me."

The monster within leapt to his defence; there was just enough alcohol in his system to support a nasty reaction. Dion jumped up, grabbed both of my arms firmly and stood rigidly stiff in front of me, holding on to my arms forcefully.

"Ouch, you're hurting me, Dion. Let go of me!" I yelled at him, looking directly into two dark eyes as they glared into mine.

We held each other's scowl. Dion knew, without any doubt, I would do what I'd promised. I felt his confidence withering as he slowly let go of my arms, then I handed him something else to ponder.

"I'm going out now. Fix your own dinner while you think about church on Sunday."

"You can't just walk out, I haven't eaten," he said, shock evident in his voice that I would consider such an action.

I headed down the passage shaking my head. The cheek of him. I packed an overnight bag, and as I passed him on my way out, I thought he might try to stop me. Thankfully, he didn't. He remained on the barstool staring into the space in front of him.

"Ignore me and you will see hell play out in front of you on Sunday and God won't be there to rescue either of you. Decision's yours."

Chapter Five

A few weeks after the Zandri affair ended, Dion found a job in Kimberly, the famous diamond mining town in the Northern Cape, far away from the tramp in Bloemfontein. After continued begging, I agreed to give our marriage another chance.

Settling into Kimberly was surprisingly easy. The whole affair and my response to it had given him a more significant fright than I'd thought. Once we were settled and the painful memories lessened, we spent hours chatting. Our conversations were deeper and more meaningful than ever before, though they too happened gradually. He'd done the honourable thing by moving away and wanting to try again. We were in a place where we could concentrate on each other.

It was tough not having Amelia close. Perhaps that was for the best – she'd tried very hard to talk me out of going back to Dion. For now, Dion was all I needed. I loved the man I married. I wanted to help him, and I needed to learn to forgive him. While I was dealing with all that, I also prayed the monster, his monster, not his sister-in-law, had stayed in Bloemfontein.

While idly looking through the local newspaper, I found a position advertised for a pharmacy assistant. Though I wasn't particularly excited about working in a pharmacy again, I thought it would be a good place to meet ladies in the community, so I applied for the job and got it. The pay was better than Bloemfontein and I didn't have to work on Saturdays.

The company Dion worked for had rented us a comfortable house with a swimming pool, which was set in a lush garden surrounded by lovely old indigenous trees, and semi-tropical shrubs had been planted along the borders. It was a beautiful place. The perfect environment in which to heal my broken heart. I spent Saturday mornings lounging around like a lizard basking in the sun, getting an excellent tan while reading my favourite novels. Life was rosy once more and our relationship was progressing back to a comfortable place. Dion was almost his best self.

My skin had turned a beautiful brown, but after only half an hour of sunbathing, it was too hot to go on. I closed my eyes and listened to the musical serenade of the birds in the trees for another ten minutes, then went inside. Dion would be back from work in an hour. I hoped the sales manager position for Music & Instruments would afford him the opportunity to showcase his remarkable musical talents too. My hopes were realised just a few short months later – he was a hit in Kimberly, smashing all the company's previous sales records and with the commission earnings, he invested in (with my permission!) a second-hand white baby grand piano, which took pride of place in our living room. Even a "baby" grand was a mighty piece of furniture to move, weighing in at around 500 pounds. We knew it would have to be re-tuned once we'd set it in place, which cost more than the removal company's bill, but it was the most exciting investment we'd made together. Not that we'd made any others before. Dion had drunk all the spare money.

Most evenings after dinner, we'd share memories of special times while he caressed the keyboard passionately, singing along, and sometimes creating his own stunning music. I kept thinking such self-taught talent was being wasted in a sales job. I was sure that if Dion was able to find financial backing, he would have soared through the ranks to join the famous singing sensations of the day, but for now, he wasn't interested and, thinking back, it was just as well. Becoming a small-town sensation was enough for the moment and a perfect place to show off his musicality. His deep, beautiful masculine singing voice was soon becoming well known and as it was our much-needed home therapy, it was also bringing joy back into our relationship.

One memorable evening, he'd finished playing "Gentle on My Mind" by Glen Campbell, an old sixties favourite of ours, when he turned to me, gently cupping my face in his hands and looking into my eyes.

He whispered, "I'm so sorry for putting you through such hell, my liefie."

It was said with such tenderness and sincerity, how could I not forgive him? The critical "sorry" word was so rare from his lips; I believed him this time. Had the Dion I loved and adored returned home? The passion from our musical interludes took us from the piano to the bedroom and brought with it another celebration.

Some weeks later, I discovered I was pregnant. I couldn't wait to tell Dion and raced home from work at the end of the day.

"Babe, I am pregnant," I shouted as I danced across the lawn to greet him, barely giving him a chance to get out of the car.

"That's wonderful news, sweetpea." A smile of unbridled joy spread across his face as he picked me up and whirled me around, kissing me. He carried me into the house where Splodge, my precious, newly acquired kitten, was meowing as if he too was caught up in our excitement.

"How far gone are you, my skat?" he asked as he put me down.

"Nine weeks, I think. I'll make an appointment to see the doc next week."

"This is so exciting. What a way to start the weekend." He winked at me, turning my legs to jelly and my tummy tingled delightfully. I'd long forgotten those wonderful feelings. Oooh, he was so sexy.

Perhaps that was part of the difficulty getting over the affair? I didn't want to share the sexiest man in town.

For the most part, I was incredibly proud of how well he was doing in Kimberly, even though a tiny part of me was still a little nervous, but I kept reminding myself to cast the niggles to one side; we were starting a family now. The tiny seed of our love-making began to grow; emotions and hormones bounced all over the place joining in excitedly. Our relationship grew, until a near disaster struck five weeks later when I threatened a miscarriage.

Dion was in the country visiting clients, but as soon as he got the message, he drove through the night to get home to be by my side – this was another unusual Dion response.

The doctor booked me off of work for a week and insisted I was to remain bed-ridden for at least four of those days. Without hesitation, Dion took three days off and did absolutely everything for me. I couldn't remember the last time I'd been so spoilt, with little Splodge often curled up with me until he got restless and entertained us with comical high jinks, throwing around the feather toy I'd bought him which had us in hysterics. I got up on the fourth day and Dion went back to work. On Friday evening, he came home armed with Dr Benjamin Spock's book, *The Common Book of Baby and Child Care*.

"There are no Afrikaans versions in print, my liefie," he said as he handed it over.

Over the following months, I read it from cover to cover, wondering if I, or anyone else for that matter, would ever fit the role of the "perfect mother".

"You learn as you go. Keep common sense alive and know the first baby is the guinea pig," Mom had said, and her words seemed to resonate more easily than those of the famous doctor.

The rest had done me good. I went back to work refreshed, but without much enthusiasm. I was thinking of giving up my job, but I was hesitant to discuss the idea with Dion. It turned out I didn't have to worry.

"Just five months to go. Why don't you stop work, sweetpea?" he suggested.

I was surprised, but ecstatic.

"Can we do this without my salary?" I asked, pointing at my growing bump.

"Of course, we can. I got paid my commission. It's way more than I expected. That alone will see us through the next six months without using your maternity pay."

"You're brilliant. Thanks. I'll resign tomorrow. Yippee," I shouted ecstatically and hugged Dion. "I can spend time doing up the nursery."

This was another first: the first time Dion had willingly shared his earnings. We were making progress. Conversation was comfortable and relaxed and though I often didn't see Dion for a couple of days during the week while he visited customers out of town, suspicion was a thing of the past.

A few weeks later he asked, "Babe, how would you feel about going to the company Christmas party?"

"I'd love to, but let me check with the doctor first." I smiled. "The last time I saw him, he commented that rest and swimming were the best things for me." (He had warned that my historic thrombosis issues could worsen during pregnancy and the elevated leg positions I'd be able to lie in at home, as unladylike as some were, were highly recommended.)

"Of course, liefie. There's plenty of time. I must let them know in a few weeks, for catering purposes. No rush."

"If the doctor says it's fine, I'd love to go, but then we can't stay out too late, which I know is a shame, but baba is more important, hey?"

"Of course. We come home whenever you want to." He rubbed his hand gently over my tummy, grinning proudly.

After supper, Splodge burst into life again with a masterful performance and had us both in fits of laughter. As quickly as he'd started, he lost interest and flopped down next to us, exhausted. It surprised me how much Dion enjoyed our adorable fluffy ginger and white tom kitten. He'd got his name from his colouring: stunning white splodges all over his ginger body like someone had thrown white paint at him. Dion was not an animal lover.

We toppled into bed, our tummy muscles stretched from laughing at Splodge's antics and settled contentedly into each other's arms, holding each other in silence for a long time. I rolled onto my back while Dion rested his ear against my bulging tummy, listening for a faint heartbeat and beamed when he felt the flicker of a tiny kick.

Dion was leaving on a country trip the following day.

I hated being alone, but I had Splodge to keep me company. I felt safe in Kimberly. Decorating the nursery kept me occupied. I swam every day, and said yes to the Christmas party invitation after my check-up. I had the scan just after the seventh month of pregnancy… I was carrying a little girl. We agreed to keep it secret as none of the family were visiting until after her birth, so I could complete the nursery in colours for a girl. I decorated it in pink, white and cream.

Leon van der Merwe, Dion's boss, popped in to see me during the week Dion was away. After all this time, I'd not met him before. Leon was a small man with a tremendous attitude and an overloaded ego. I took an instant dislike to him as he sat across from me drinking tea, discussing Dion's musical and sales talents. A roadmap of purple veins crisscrossed his cheeks and bulbous nose; a face that alerted me to a lifestyle of heavy drinking. I sat opposite him wishing he'd never come round – his whole demeanour spelt trouble as far as I was concerned.

I politely thanked him for coming and before he left, he asked about the staff Christmas party.

"Are you able to come to the Christmas function?" He tried to pretend it was an afterthought, but I knew it was the sole purpose for his visit.

"I'm not sure if we'll be there," I lied.

"Oh. That would be a pity. It would be nice to have you both there. We want Dion to sing a few numbers for us."

I knew there was an ulterior motive for his visit.

"Don't make definite plans. If I'm not there, Dion won't be either. Goodbye, Leon." I didn't want to be rude, but couldn't help myself. He got the message.

It was the evening of the party. I had bought a pretty powder blue maternity evening dress and when I was ready, we left the house. Dion had refused the invitation to sing at the party, which I was happy about; it meant we could leave when I was ready or found sitting on hard chairs too uncomfortable.

A delicious traditional Christmas dinner was served. All the usual fare: roast turkey, glazed gammon, legs of lamb with all the trimmings and more. The table decorations sparkled as candles flickered in their holders down the centre of the tables and the hall was filled with jovial Christmas noises of crackers being pulled and laughter as people read out the joke strips from inside them. I felt good. Dion and I had some lovely slow dances together before dinner, but after dinner, the music became lively and energetic; everyone keen to work off their indulgence. I did one fast dance with Dion and couldn't manage more, so he danced with work colleagues.

As I sat watching and the minutes ticked by, I began to feel a rising anxiety replace the happiness I'd felt earlier as I caught glimpses of where Dion was on the dance floor. An hour later, I tried to catch his attention but couldn't. Just as I was about to head onto the dance floor and haul him off so we could go home, Leon passed me.

"How about a dance? You can't sit there all alone."

"That would be very nice, thank you," I said.

It would get me onto the dance floor, and I could talk to Dion about leaving.

I followed as he led the way through the dancers and on passing Dion, he patted him on the shoulder, saying, "Hey, she needs to head home after one dance."

In an instant, the monster sprung into violent action. Bellowing loudly, he grabbed the back of my dress and possessively wrenched me to him with such force I nearly lost my balance. Driven by an inexplicable jealous rage, the ogre was back with a vengeance.

The dancing stopped. Everything stopped. Somewhere in the distance, I heard a woman yelling, then I realised she was racing towards me, coming to my rescue. The chaos happened so quickly.

"Stop that, leave her alone," the woman screamed as she scrambled towards me, pushing others out of the way.

I didn't know the woman, but she pulled me from the grip of my husband and guided me quickly to the ladies' room, leaving the men to try to calm the fire burning inside Dion.

He'd reached that tipping point; I should have known better than to go onto the dance floor with Leon, as innocent as it was. Now I was terrified life would spiral downhill once more. I couldn't deal with that in my last trimester. What had been a glorious evening for everyone, ended abruptly. I was so embarrassed.

The journey home was frighteningly stressful as Dion bounced the car from one pavement kerb to another, weaving into oncoming traffic, trying to negotiate the way home with one eye open, alternating with the other. He'd had far too much to drink by then.

We got home alive.

I was seething. During the journey home, I warned myself not to say anything, but as I wearily dumped my handbag beside the bed, I heard myself ask, with a note of sarcasm, if he was sleeping with the woman he'd been dancing with for so long.

Before I knew it, I was flying across our bed. I slipped off the edge on the other side and hit the floor hard. My nose started bleeding from the force of the punch that had sent me flying and the metallic taste of blood was running down the back of my throat. I pushed myself upright. I felt dazed and disorientated. I cupped my hands over my nose to catch the blood and noticed blood was dripping from my forehead too. There was blood everywhere; I had to get to the bathroom.

Standing up slowly, my eyes filled with tears and stars, blood and defeat. I staggered to the bathroom and holding onto each side of the basin to steady myself, I watched, mesmerised by the blood dripping onto the white porcelain while my sobs beat in time with each dark red droplet as it fell. Then I felt our baby kicking objectionably. I prayed she would stay where she was until her due date. Then I felt my precious Splodge rub his warm body up and down my calves, entwining himself between my legs as he purred and meowed to comfort me, which only made me cry more. Then I looked in the mirror and noticed the gash. It ran from my left eyebrow, across my forehead and ended in my hairline. It was a nasty cut.

My nose was swelling and changing colour as fast as my eye socket was bulging outwards. My face had quickly become an ugly canvas of blues, blacks, yellows and deep reds. I dressed the cut as best I could, thinking it should be stitched, but how was I to get to outpatients.

Dion was passed out when I eventually got my face clean, stopped the bleeding, downed two painkillers and tearfully, but carefully, slid into bed, making sure I didn't wake the bastard. Mercifully, I fell into a deep, emotionally exhausted sleep. When I woke it was midmorning; he'd left for work earlier.

Looking in the mirror was a painful reminder of what had happened. My mind filled with all the old questions, bringing with them familiar fears from the recent past. The things I'd hoped we had left in Bloemfontein.

My dear, loyal house cleaner was horrified when she saw me in the morning.

"Eish, missus!" she said, raising her hands to cover her mouth.

I told her I'd fallen. She had no reason not to believe me, for only the day before our marriage seemed perfect.

I spent the morning digging deep into my thoughts and feelings, contemplating whether or not to contact my mother and the doctor. Two things prevented me from calling her. Firstly, she would insist I come home immediately and secondly, walking out of my marriage just two months shy of giving birth to our first child was not what I wanted to do. Mom's intolerance and vehement disrespect for any man that hit a woman, especially in my condition, would be difficult to stop her from sending William to collect me. I didn't have the strength to argue. Besides, I certainly didn't want her to see my face all cut and bruised. I peeled off the plaster and to my relief, it didn't need stitching, but the possibility of a premature arrival of our little girl as a result of the fall concerned me.

I endured a few stressful days while treating my face with ice packs, and waiting in vain hope that Dion would call from wherever he was staying. I had covered the cut with a clean plaster and massaged the area with healing ointments.

By Thursday I still had not heard from Dion. The swelling on my face was much the same. My active baby (I didn't think of her as ours anymore) was growing as rapidly as my anxiety; I seemed to have swelled quickly in the last four days. No threatening labour, much to my relief. I was sure I'd go full term now. By five that evening, I knew I couldn't delay the inevitable much longer. Just as I was about to phone Mom, she called me.

The brewed and stored emotion of the beating and the week alone erupted like a tsunami when I heard her voice. It was time to let the matriarch take control. As I predicted, she was outraged and ordered me home. This time I listened, leaving a short note on the coffee table for Dion, hoping he would be home Friday evening.

Chapter Six

Mom and William were furious when they saw me. I think William was ready to put an end to Dion. He insisted I lay charges of assault. He'd take me to the police station.

"Sorry, sis, but the evidence is all over your face. Divorce the swine," William said. "He doesn't deserve you."

Exactly what Amelia had said.

"I will have to go back, boetie. I must sort this out myself and have my baby there."

"Why? What on earth for?" William responded logically, but when he saw I was close to tears again, he put his arms around me. "I will always be there for you, you know that."

I nodded.

Dion called after he'd found my note and insisted I return home the following day. I refused, pointing out that he'd started the drama.

"I'll come home when I'm ready, not when you demand it, Dion."

"I want you home tomorrow so we can discuss this," he snapped.

I put the phone down and went home the following Friday with Mom and William as chaperones.

Dion was waiting on the front veranda, his chest puffed out with anger. I could see the expression on his face as I drove in. Then he saw who was in the car that followed closely behind me and his bravado disappeared. Under normal circumstances, William was an absolute gentleman in every sense of the word until a member of his family was hurt.

Dion was acutely aware of this.

William had suppressed his anger all week, and I knew my return home was not going to be a happy one. Dion didn't move. He stood like a marble statue as he watched William stride across the driveway towards him. To turn and go inside was suicide; he had to face my brother. He was shit scared of William, but I felt no sympathy. I watched my brother launch at Dion, grabbing a handful of his shirt front. William shoved his nose against Dion's. I was standing too far away to hear what William said to him, but I didn't need to. He despatched Dion like a ragdoll who staggered backwards a few steps. William came striding back to help carry our suitcases into the house. Mom and I didn't dare look at each other, but I glimpsed at Dion as he found his footing. He knew it was time to behave.

"I won't come in," William said fiercely. "If I get near that arsehole again, I'll fucking kill the bastard, but I've warned him." It was rare that William swore in front of either me or our mother, but under these circumstances, she graciously pretended she hadn't heard. "Call me if you need anything, sis."

William wrapped me in his arms. I felt so safe there; I didn't want him to leave.

"If he touches you again, sis, he's a dead man, even if he is your husband," he called out the car window, loud enough for it to be another warning to Dion, though I don't think he heard. I hadn't told him Mom was staying.

The big "birth" day was fast approaching. True to his word, William called every day to check Mom and I were safe. I'd been monitored carefully by my mother and thankfully all was well so far. Having Mom with me for the last few weeks in waiting was comforting, though not for Dion. We had rarely spoken to each other. Though Mom never asked, I was sure she knew from the nursery furnishing, she would soon be holding her first granddaughter.

During my final check-up and scan, the doctor asked, with apparent difficulty, whether I'd be staying in my marriage after the birth, openly admitting his concern for our safety. I didn't answer. I didn't know how to. I wasn't sure of anything anymore.

My due date was 14 April.

"The first baby's due date is always a surprise. They either decide to make an appearance a week early or arrive a week late. Have your bag packed. It's all going well, so relax and enjoy the last of it." The doctor smiled reassuringly.

"The apple will fall when it is ripe, my child," Mom added and smiled knowingly at the doctor.

"No truer words spoken. Moms are often more accurate than us doctors." He smiled at her while I sat wondering who'd be right.

Hanging on the doctor's wall was a picture of a herd of zebra with their young. The next time I would see that picture I would have my daughter in my arms. The next time I would see the doctor would be in the delivery room. That thought made me nervous.

On Tuesday evening, during the last week of my pregnancy, Dion called, sounding a little more like the old one now our baby was due so soon.

"Have you taken the rest of the week off, Dion?" I asked with a begrudging tone.

"Leon's not budging on leave, liefie."

"Why aren't you pushing him, Dion? This is not just casual leave, and you are due at least two weeks," I argued.

Dion didn't seem particularly concerned and casually gave me the emergency number of the hotel where he was staying. I was furious, but I knew it was pointless going on about it; my words would just fall on deaf ears. At least I had my mom with me, and she was happy Dion wasn't around.

Late into Thursday evening, the contractions began. This child wasn't going to keep me waiting! Though I was excited, I was frightened and sad that I was to experience this without my husband. The stirrings of labour were gentle to begin with and continued that way for quite some time. I was convinced it was a false alarm.

By one o'clock in the morning, I knew it was time to call the hotel. It would probably be more than a few hours before I needed to get to the hospital, giving Dion time to get home.

Mom had calculated three to four hours before I needed to get to the hospital. I hoped she was right. I had no idea what to expect.

The hospital was no more than a fifteen-minute drive from the house. If Dion left promptly from the hotel he was staying in, there was more than enough time for him to get home; he was just over a two-hour drive away. Dion had to get home as Mom couldn't drive me to hospital. She'd been born with a slightly deformed foot, and over the years, it had gradually deteriorated to the extent where she was no longer able to drive. I didn't particularly want to drive when gripped by violent contractions, so I was dependant on Dion getting home in time.

I dialled the number of the hotel, and it rang for a long time before being answered.

"Windy Acres Hotel emergency. Can I help?" said the sleepy voice on the other end.

"I'm sorry to disturb you at this hour, but I urgently need to speak to my husband, Mr Dion du Toit. I'm in labour," I said.

There was a pause. I could hear the man paging through the register. "There's no one booked in here by that name, madam."

"What? Are you sure?" I asked, horror-struck. "Your number is the number he gave me. He said he was booked into your hotel." I began to feel the prickly sensation of fear and panic grip me.

"I'm sorry, madam, he is not in our hotel."

I slammed the receiver down, too angry with Dion to speak. Glancing at Mom's enquiring expression, I had to turn away from her, even though I knew she would never say it: "I told you so!" I grabbed the phone and called the police station in Lime Acres. A duty constable answered sleepily. I quickly explained the urgency of my situation. Like the hotel receptionist, the duty policeman was equally disinterested that I was in labour.

"Please look for him," I pleaded. "I need him home urgently."

The constable sleepily assured me he would do what he could and call me back when he'd found Dion.

Oh God, that could be hours, I thought as I placed the receiver.

Lime Acres, a tiny dusty little hovel of a town in the middle of nowhere, was only popular for one-night stopovers used by salesmen and game hunters. There were a few shops that serviced the farming community, a post office, a bank, a butchery and a police station. That was about it apart from two small country inns, one at either end of the town. They both provided the village with its only source of entertainment. Dion's van had the company logo blazoned across it, so I was sure he'd be easy to find, but by 5 a.m., it was time to get to the hospital; I'd have to drive myself. The contractions were stronger, but nothing I couldn't bear.

I gathered up my toiletries and shoved them into my pre-packed bag while Mom busied herself with filling a flask of hot coffee. She knew me so well. I was a coffee addict; she also knew, being the nurse that I was, I wouldn't rush into the hospital until I *really* had to.

I'd not driven more than twice in the last two weeks. My tummy was huge; the skin stretched, tight and uncomfortable. There were scarcely millimetres between it and the steering wheel. Driving was awkward and I felt alarmingly trapped. Luckily, the journey was not far and the likelihood of any other traffic on the road in the early hours of the morning was slim.

I parked close to the hospital admission's entrance, switched off the engine and looked at my mother.

She smiled knowingly and dug out the flask, asking, "Have you had another contraction?"

"No. Nothing for about twenty minutes. Oh God, Mom. I loathe hospitals when I'm the patient," I moaned, pushing the seat back as far as it could go and settled my head against the headrest, taking in a deep breath.

"We'll go in just now."

I sighed. Mom's maternal pride and love was in full bloom. I could see it in her face and her eyes sparkled with excitement at the thought of a grandchild arriving.

"That's why I filled the flask. I knew you'd have to have a cup before going in."

I closed my eyes and waited for the next contraction. Cupping my hands around my coffee cup, I began to take one comforting sip after another, savouring its delicious taste and fragrance.

"I'm scared, Ma," I said as the minutes ticked on.

"The first baby is always a mixture of fear and excitement, my child, but you will manage. We all do. Once you have that little bundle in your arms, the memory of the pain soon disappears. What do you want?"

I opened my eyes and looked at Mom, confused.

"Ma! Haven't you noticed how I've done the nursery?"

"Yes, I have, but you've never confirmed whether you know or not. I didn't ask for I hoped you'd volunteer the information, but you haven't."

"Oh, Mom, you're so sweet. So thoughtless of me, I'm sorry. Yes, it's a girl. It was confirmed shortly before all the shit with Dion happened."

"I'm delighted you're having a girl." Mom smiled. "It'll be easier to bring up a girl on your own if you decide to leave Dion."

"Oh, Ma." I rested my head on her shoulder. "I wish I had a normal marriage. Sitting here like this really brings it home hard, especially not knowing where he is at a time like this… It shouldn't be like this. Do you think this baby will change Dion?"

"Well…" Her face said it all. "I certainly hope so, Elizabeth, but I'm doubtful. If he doesn't become a proper husband, promise me you'll leave him."

It was so unlike her to encourage a separation or divorce, but she despised Dion's vile actions.

"Ma, I can't promise that. I still love the old Dion, but if he doesn't change over the next few months, I promise I will make the decision then."

We sat quietly for a while, absorbed by our thoughts. Then it occurred to me that I hadn't had a contraction for ages. We'd not been time-keeping, so I didn't utter a word; it could wait a little longer.

"More?" Mom lifted the flask and broke the silence.

"Do I ever refuse coffee?" I chuckled and watched the hot coffee tumble into my cup, filling it up.

Perhaps not the best thing to be drinking just before an impending birth, I thought.

"Ma, it must be at least forty-five minutes since my last contraction. Is that normal?"

"My goodness, has that much time passed? And you shouldn't be drinking all this coffee," she said, verbalising my thoughts.

"Let's wait another fifteen minutes, let the coffee settle, and if nothing has happened, we may as well head home. Do you think it's a false alarm?"

"No, my child, not a false alarm. Stress and anxiety can halt it for a few hours. They'll be back, that's guaranteed."

I was so close to my due date I didn't think it could be a false alarm, but what did I know! We were about to drive off when Leon drove past and noticed my car. He slowed, then turned his car around and came into the car park.

He was the last person I wanted to see. He pulled up alongside us, asking if I was okay.

Instead of offering a response to his enquiry, I snapped, "Where the hell's Dion? He's not at the hotel he said he was staying in."

A glazed look covered Leon's face. I knew that look; he knew where Dion was.

"Even the police couldn't find him in your emblazoned company van. Very strange, in a tiny town like Lime Acres. Can you find him and send him home urgently?"

"I will try to get hold of him as soon as I get to the office and tell him to get here urgently." He nodded.

"Thank you. We're going home now as nothing is happening, but it would be nice to have the bastard home today. You could have at least given Dion this time off."

"He didn't ask for time off, Elizabeth, but I will do what I can."

My lips pursed and I physically crumbled, pained and confused. Mom raised her eyebrows. I looked at her and silently thought, *Should I make that promise now?*

With disbelief, I asked again. "He didn't ask for time off, are you sure?"

Leon was about to say something else. I didn't wait to hear the answer, so I sped off, wheels spinning out of the car park, and burst into tears.

"Did you notice the way he looked at me, Mom? I hate that man. He knows where Dion is. Why Dion didn't ask for leave is what I'd like to know. Even Leon looked shocked at that." I sobbed, trying to focus on the road. "Why are they lying to me?"

"Why do you dislike Leon?" Mom asked, not committing herself to anything else.

"He drinks like a fish, and I'm sure all the nonsense with Dion again is because of him. He encourages Dion to drink and sends him all over the place, playing pianos in hotel bars to get orders for pianos and other musical instrument sales. He's such a bad influence."

"Dion doesn't need anyone to influence him, my child." Mom's chin was set. The tip of it had gone white. Mom had had enough. "You heard what the man said. Dion didn't ask for leave. I think you should have your baby and come home. The man is never going to change. The English expression 'a leopard never changes its spots' is true."

"I'll see, Ma. Let me have the child first. I'm so confused and so torn."

"I know, and I'm very proud of you, my girl. You are handling a dreadful situation with such maturity. That man is nothing but heartache and trouble, I'm sorry to say. You were raised with good morals and ethics. He wasn't."

"Ma!"

"I'm sorry, but it's time to see the truth. I don't know of any other woman who would give their husband so many chances, and now this... it's unforgiveable."

I knew Mom was right. We had not talked much about Dion since she'd been with me. Dion may be a puzzle I couldn't put together, but it was clear to all who knew him that he was just a bullshitting fraud. Why couldn't I see it? If he was having another affair, I'd catch him.

I wanted to keep sobbing, release the pain and disappointment, but I just felt numb. We sat at home waiting for the contractions to begin again.

We waited all morning expectantly. Nothing happened. *Probably because of all the coffee I drank.*

Just after a light lunch, they hit me like a tidal wave from nowhere, fierce, agonising and close together. Moaning loudly as the force of the pain washed over me, I knew without hesitation, this was it. I couldn't drive, I could scarcely move.

It was 2.45 p.m. Where was Dion?

"I'll try driving, Mom. We have to go now," I groaned, holding the base of my enormous stomach.

Sweat had begun to drip off of my forehead and was running down the side of my temples. When the next contraction came, I gripped the car keys so savagely I thought I might bend them. I hobbled towards the front door, gritting my teeth, taking one painful step at a time, and as I stood on the veranda waiting for the contraction to subside, Dion raced into the driveway.

"Oh, thank the Lord." Mom breathed a sigh of relief. "Just in time."

I couldn't remember a time when I'd felt such overwhelming respite.

I yelled, "Open the door and drive." I took the last steps and got in the car.

My waters broke as I was wheeled into the delivery room with a nervous, agitated Dion beside me. He watched his first child being born on the eve of the 16 April 1975.

Storm was born fifteen minutes after I arrived in the delivery room. A good healthy set of lungs was music to my ears; the life-changing sound triggered a rush of absolute joy while tears rolled down my cheeks. Just as Mom had said, the pain was almost instantly forgotten in those precious moments as I gazed upon a pair of perfect little feet. A human so tiny, so perfectly flawless. I was overwhelmed. I glanced up at Dion and noticed tears were trickling down his face too.

The midwife handed our little bundle to me. As I held her for the first time, gazing at her in wonder and awe, I could scarcely believe I'd carried this little miracle for nine months. I opened her tiny hand and examined her perfect long fingers and smiled as the instinctive reflex to grip happened in an instant. A perfect index finger curled over mine with surprising strength and only then did I look up at Dion and allow our eyes to meet for the first time. There was a softness about them, influenced by this exquisite moment, but he had questions to answer. For the next few minutes, all I wanted was to focus on my beautiful baby girl. Her perfect rosebud lips, wisps of curly black hair, long dark lashes and pink cheeks filled my heart with a joy I'd never known possible. The moment was exquisitely mine to savour forever. My baby girl had been through a rough carriage since conception. Without consulting Dion, I named her Storm.

Two days later, we were on our way home.

"She looks like you, liefie," I said to Dion as I settled into the back seat of the car, looking at her sleeping in her carry cot.

"She's as beautiful as you, sweetpea." He leant in and kissed my forehead before jumping into the driver's seat.

Despite the elated emotion, forgiveness wasn't within easy grasp for me. The last months had spoilt the most beautiful moment of my life.

I lay my head back against the headrest. If nothing else, she was at least conceived with love, but for the rest, we'd wait and see.

"I'm so proud of you, liefie," he said, looking at me in the rear-view mirror. "May I hold her when we get home?"

I didn't reply. I noticed he was glancing from me to the road, waiting for an answer.

Mom was waiting for us on the veranda. She was so touched by the arrival of her first beautiful granddaughter. I wondered how she had managed being home alone with Dion for two days. I wished I had been a fly on the wall. She would not have been kind. Her body language in the ward had screamed disapproval. She wasn't going to forgive him. For now, she graciously enjoyed the excitement of the birth of another grandchild.

Dion helped me out of the car and proudly carried the sleeping Storm into the house and lay the carry cot on the couch. He went back to the car to bring in my suitcase, flowers and gifts. Mom had already put the kettle on, but I avoided coffee. I was breastfeeding and peeped in at a sleeping Storm and sat down carefully next to the cot.

"Why didn't you choose an Afrikaans name?" Mom asked. I knew she would ask at some point, and I noted the disappointment in her voice.

"I couldn't find one I liked, and after the tumultuous journey we had together during the pregnancy, the name felt apt." I smiled. "Dion wasn't impressed either, but he didn't dare argue. He caused the storm in more ways than one," I said and excused the pun.

"I hope the name isn't an indication of what the child might live through in her future," Mom said, her disapproval obvious.

"Her second name reflects her Afrikaans heritage. I will never tell her why she was called Storm. Hopefully, it will be a constant reminder to her father to behave."

"Well, that remains to be seen."

Storm stirred in her cot and I lifted her out. It was time for a feed. Mom and I went on chatting while we had the opportunity. Dion would be back from the hospital shortly with a car full of lovely flowers and gifts. I had been very spoilt.

"How long before my nipples harden, Mom? I'm so tender."

"A couple of days and you'll be fine. As you know, be careful what you eat."

"Yeah, the nurse gave me some tips on what to avoid."

While Storm suckled, maternal bonding was tingling and my heart swelled with motherly love. It wasn't long before Dion arrived carrying bowls of beautiful flowers from family and friends.

Amelia had sent a pure white orchid. Written on the card, she'd scribed: "To my most treasured friend, I'm thinking of you cuddling your beautiful daughter. I wish I could share the moment with you. Miss you terribly. I chose the white orchid: a delicate, exotic and graceful plant, which typifies your wonderful personality and represents love, luxury, beauty and strength. Love you lots. We must get together soon."

Her message touched me deeply. I missed her so much.

"What brings on the tears?" Dion asked. "She's a beautiful, healthy baby girl."

"I know. They're tears of joy." I didn't dare say that Amelia's white orchid had triggered regret that I hadn't taken her advice years ago.

Soon, the house was filled with flowers. The gifts he'd put in our room. Dion awkwardly settled in the lounge. Mom and I gazed at Storm as she suckled on me.

"I've got today and tomorrow off," Dion finally announced. I almost felt disappointed.

"Oh, that's nice. Why didn't you take days off before Storm was born?" I snapped, more than asked.

"Leon wouldn't give me time off."

"Bullshit!" I barked and upset Storm. Her eyes opened wide, then she went on suckling and Mom left the room. "He saw Mom and I sitting in the car when I first went into labour. I asked him why he hadn't given you time off, and he said you hadn't asked for any."

"I did ask. He said I had to meet my targets."

Lies fell off his lips without conscience. The ease of his spoken untruths sickened me. I went on with my planned interrogation.

"Where were you on Thursday night?"

"Ja, I'm sorry, liefie. I haven't had a chance to tell you what happened. The owner of Fontein Hotel, south of Lime Acres, ordered a piano and offered me a room for the night. I'd played until late. With that order, I broke last year's record." Dion beamed as if I should be delighted to hear how well he'd done, instead of being with me when I started labour. He seemed more excited about that than the birth of his first child.

"Is that all you care about? Why didn't you call and give me the Fontein Hotel telephone number? You knew the importance of me being able to contact you at such a critical time." I felt my bottom lip quiver. The hurt caused by his dismissive and careless attitude was almost worse than his lies. I was glad Mom had left the room.

"No, of course it's not all I care about, but it gives us more money to spend on Storm. That I care about." He knew how to say the right things at the right time, but his expression didn't match his words. I wasn't going to argue. Time would tell.

"So, why didn't you give me that number?" I asked pointedly.

Dion shifted and looked away without offering an answer, like a practised politician, he offered some other bullshit. Silence prevailed.

I lay Storm down in her cot and buttoned my blouse as visions of Dion dressed in the outfit he used for piano presentations: black tails, white shirt and royal blue velvet bow tie, floated in my mind. I imagined him seated at the piano, perfectly manicured, nimble fingers dancing across the keys while ladies gathered around my handsome husband, desperate for his attention. Ladies deprived of entertainment for months, going crazy, swooning over him. I had to forcibly drag my thoughts back to the present.

"Is there anything you want me to get you from the shops?" he asked, desperate to get away from my questioning.

Having Mom to stay kept Dion on his toes. Surprisingly, he immersed himself in doing all the right things for his daughter and me. The nappy bit left him terrified. Worried he would be gifted something he couldn't deal with. It broke the tension while I teased and watched him try, but the aromas of a full nappy found their way up his nose and he visibly gagged and ran out of the room.

"I'll do anything with her, but not that," he'd said apologetically.

He came home every night after work, despite Leon's complaints. Gradually, the tension eased. Mom went home. As soon as Mom left, and without consulting Dion, Leon booked gigs for Dion at inns and hotels, booking them far from home again.

"Callous and inconsiderate. All the bastard cares about is reaching the company targets," I seethed. I was furious.

Dion was nonplussed.

Once the owners of the hotels and pubs heard Dion play and had tallied up their takings for the night, another piano or organ was sold and Dion was booked again. Leon traded on that. Dion loved the attention, and what he was paid to do was an extra gig. Baby Storm and I were of no consequence. Dion du Toit was a lucrative attraction. For nine long weeks, we rarely saw him. I'd had enough. I was exhausted, lonely and depressed. I called Leon. I was sick of arguing with Dion. I was never sure he was telling me the truth, but Leon was a liar like Dion.

"He's our top rep, Elizabeth. He's brilliant. His reputation has spread across the province. I'm sure you're very proud of him. Pianos and organs are selling faster than we can get them in."

No matter my lament, it didn't seem to matter. Leon was focussed on one thing and one thing only: sales. I needed to hear myself say what was on my mind.

"Let me remind you, Leon, he's married to me, not your bloody company. I want him home, not gallivanting around the country. My daughter doesn't even know she has a father because of you."

"He's too popular to stop booking him out, Elizabeth," Leon stated thoughtlessly. This response wasn't worth answering politely; he didn't understand that dialogue.

"You inconsiderate fucking creep. You don't get it, do you?" I swore and I didn't care. "I want him home this weekend."

I slammed the telephone down with force. It had barely settled on its cradle when it rang again. I never answered it. Instead, I fell into my armchair and sobbed. An hour later, the phone disturbed the peace with its shrill ring. I thoughtlessly answered it.

"I'm not interested in speaking to you, Leon. It's like pissing into the wind. The consequences are not quite as unpleasant but

equally as pointless." The retort flew out of my mouth unexpectedly and I wasn't going to apologise. Just as I was about to put
the phone down, he quickly spoke.

"I'm sorry, Elizabeth. We'll sort his hours out."

"When?" I screeched. "And where's he been staying?"

"I'm not sure, but I will get him home for you. Don't worry."

"You're his boss. You must know where he's staying. I'm not
an idiot, Leon. Refrain from treating me like one."

"I'll find out and call you back."

"Don't bother, just get him home."

I slammed the phone down in a rage. Oh, how I loathed the
patronising arsehole.

Dion came home that evening.

I wasn't in an attractive mood. Every angry, painful emotion
had scratched at my innards for three long lonely months. The
emotions had brewed a chaotic mix of post-birth hormones,
post-natal depression and resentment; a dangerous potion, and
there was nothing I could say that I would regret. After venting,
it was an evening of stilted conversation. I had been prepared
for continued battle, but somehow Dion managed to steer the
conversation cunningly away from what was pertinent. I was too
angry and hurt to find the words to steer him back to a place of
vulnerability. I was spent in every way.

When Storm woke for her feed in the early hours of the
morning, Dion didn't stir. He went on snoring throughout her
feed. He was still in a deep sleep when I finished feeding Storm,
affording me the opportunity to dig through his briefcase to
satisfy my suspicions. I hesitated a moment. It wasn't something
I'd normally do. I opened it up as if it was contaminated. Guilt
for snooping and the sharp sword of infidelity lodged together

deep in my heart. I tucked the note into my gown pocket and spent the rest of the night considering my next move.

He and Julie Malan were going to pay. Her telephone number and address were written in what I guessed to be her hand-writing. There were a few little hugs and kisses across the bottom of it. The address where I was sure to find her was a farm just outside Lime Acres. The dotted line in my mind was now forming a picture.

I said nothing to Dion when he woke and said goodbye as casually as I could. He was trying to tell me he'd be in the country tonight. It was to be his last night away. The information lodged somewhere in the recesses of my mind as he pecked me on the cheek.

"Where will you be staying tonight?" I called after him.

"I'll check where Leon's booked me and call you later with the details, liefie." He stopped, turned and came back to hug me.

I stood, cold as a statue. I didn't want him close to me. He'd just unwittingly confirmed that Leon made his accommodation bookings. Another nail in his coffin.

"What's wrong?" he asked, aware he'd just hugged a motion-less form as cold as ice.

"Nothing, I'm just tired."

He shrugged off my answer. "I'm probably staying at Fontein Hotel again, but I'll let you know. It's the most convenient place for me to operate from."

"Oh, yes, I'm sure it is," I answered sarcastically.

He frowned.

Once he'd left the house, I arranged with Miriam to sleep in our house that night, telling her I had to leave very early in the morning. She'd take care of Storm while I was away, and I'd be back about mid-afternoon.

I expressed enough milk for Storm's three feeds with a little over just in case I got back late. Miriam would mix in a few teaspoons of baby porridge and give that to Storm; she loved her porridge and it would keep her full. Miriam nodded, obviously troubled by my mood, but she asked no questions.

I was laser-focussed when I left the house at three o'clock in the morning. The bittersweet taste of revenge in my mouth, 9 mm pistol loaded, safety catch "on", ready and waiting in the cubbyhole, and off I went. My knuckles glowed white in the darkness of the cab's interior as I gripped the steering wheel as tightly as my jaw was clenched. An aching throb in my head kept time with the whining motor, which was now at full throttle. My thoughts were only on what lay ahead as I drove on recklessly, pushing harder on the accelerator.

The skies were starting to lighten; dawn was twenty minutes away when I arrived at the farm. I'd got there earlier than I'd calculated. It was cold in the car, and I shivered involuntarily, sniffed in the fresh, moist winter air and focussed on the red brick farmhouse draped in bougainvillea. It had finished flowering a few weeks back, but there were still some vibrant purple flowers on it, but mostly the dry ones that still had to fall. Like the woman who'd taken my husband was about to do.

I quietly got myself out of the car and left the door ajar. With the pistol cocked and ready, I ran across the lawn to the back door and knocked loudly. The sound echoed around me in the silence of the breaking dawn. It wasn't long before two ladies greeted me cheerfully as one of them pulled the door open, obviously expecting to see someone else at the back door at this time of the morning.

Their cheer vanished as rapidly as my murderous intent. I stared, dumbfounded, at the two ladies who quickly slammed the door, screaming hysterically. Rage and revenge suddenly drained from me as the horror of what I'd intended on doing came hurtling in. No longer numbed by hatred, everything became flawlessly clear for the first time.

Blurred by the hurt, hatred and revenge of the last few months, I suddenly realised I had no contingency plan. I felt my body give way to uncontrollable quivering and my right arm shook as I tried in vain to unload the pistol. I knocked again.

"Fuck off," came a loud retort.

"Get away, you lunatic," said the other. "What do you want here anyway?"

I wondered if that was Julie speaking.

"My husband, Dion du Toit."

A guilty silence filled the air, then I heard other footsteps approaching the door and stop.

"Put that fucking gun away, Elizabeth." Dion's voice boomed from behind the closed door. "Or I will call the police."

"Call them, Dion. Please, call them. Tell them to get here quickly. A murder is about to take place."

Hushed silence surrounded us for a moment. My mind went blank while inside the house there was panic. My body shook violently from the cold and the shock of what I'd been about to do. All my strength had suddenly deserted me. Fuelled by adrenaline, driven by vengeance for too long, I stood at the back door emotionally exhausted, weakened and confused. I turned and staggered across the lawn, fell into my car, slammed the door, threw the pistol into the cubbyhole and switched on the ignition. Only then did I take a deep breath to regroup.

I slowly turned the car around and headed home, guided by instinct. I remember none of the journey home. What I do remember is the exaggerated relief of arriving home safely without leaving a murder investigation behind me and a child who would have been brought up by a lying monster. I stumbled through the door into the welcoming arms of my loving, caring maid, Miriam.

Though she knew none of what I'd attempted to do, she could see I was about to collapse. With quiet wisdom, she knew then it had something to do with my lying, adulterous husband. She knew all about adultery. Miriam led me to the couch and sat me down with the promise of a hot cup of tea. Her thoughtfulness reduced me to a sobbing heap of broken bits.

Storm was mercifully still asleep.

"Oh, my missus," she whispered, understanding the pain of infidelity. It was a part of her culture. I always wondered whether she felt the same way I did, or was it just accepted. "You must sleep, my missus. I will take care of Storm for the next few hours."

I was asleep before Miriam had even made the tea.

It was Dion who woke me. I looked up at him through swollen eyes and panicked. I hadn't fed Storm. Why hadn't Miriam woken me? I jumped out of bed, almost knocking Dion over as I rushed through to the kitchen to find Miriam had taken care of everything. Storm was giggly and cheerful and as happy to see me as I was to see her, while I wiped the sleep out of my eyes.

"What did you feed Storm?" I asked Miriam.

"I put water in milk and a little porridge after milk. Happy Storm." She beamed.

She'd sacrificed the care of her own family while keeping a vigilant eye on Storm and me. The depth of my gratitude was all-encompassing, but I failed to find the words I felt.

I didn't want Dion anywhere near me. I hated him. I hated what he'd done to me. I vaguely heard him saying he was sorry, then I heard myself growling at him like the wounded lioness I felt I was.

"Your apologies mean fuck all, Dion du Toit."

"I know how hurt you are, but let me explain."

"Explain what? There's nothing to explain. One woman is not enough for you, I see. You need two at a time."

I wrapped my hands around a scalding hot cup of coffee, then I remembered the note in my dressing gown pocket. Quickly putting the coffee cup down before I dropped it, I pulled out the folded piece of paper, threw it at Dion, picked up my coffee mug and walked away.

"Let me talk, damn it. Before you barge out of here. You owe me an apology," Dion shouted.

"I owe you what?" I swung around to face him; the audacity of his comment had stopped me in my tracks.

"You heard me."

I didn't trust myself to respond. I needed the security of the kitchen where I'd find Miriam with Storm. I stood beside Miriam. He had followed, trying to explain how kind the twin sisters had been to him, mumbling on about how they'd prevented him from driving drunk and they had insisted on feeding him a hearty bowl of stew when they got home and offered him their spare room.

"Do you honestly expect me to believe all that crap?"

I flicked the kettle switch to top up my coffee with boiling water, more to keep myself occupied than the need for more coffee.

Miriam took up her position next to me with Storm on her hip. Baby Storm had a worried expression on her face. Her lips curled upwards, and her chin quivered as if she was about to cry, but Miriam soothed and reassured her.

"You're making it sound like everything is my fault. I'm the one who has put up with your womanising, inking, lies and bullying. How dare you ask for an apology. An apology for what?"

"I haven't ever intentionally wanted to murder two innocent people before," came his sanctimonious response, which sickened and enraged me more.

"Because I haven't gone off and had repeated affairs, that's why. You were ready to murder Leon when he led me across the dance floor if you remember. Don't you dare provoke me, Dion! Innocent ladies? That's a joke. Which one ordered the piano with hearts and kisses on the bottom of the note?" My voice had reached a pitch so high it left my throat dry and husky. "Let me repeat, you deserve no apology. The only thing you deserve is to be castrated."

I'd been tempted to put a bullet through my head on a few occasions, stimulated by post-natal depression. The only thing that stopped me was my beautiful baby girl.

Dion tried to reach out to me again on Sunday, but I was unreachable. I refused to talk to him. After he left for work on Monday morning, I packed all I could fit into my car, strapped Storm into her car seat while Splodge hopped into the car and curled up on the front seat. I headed off to live with my mother on the family farm, 160 kilometres from Kimberly.

I had done a lot of driving in the last few days!

Chapter Seven

I was in a good mood for the first time in months. The farm was my favourite place. A place where I felt internally at peace with myself and entirely in tune with everything around me. It was a place where I knew I was truly loved.

I'd filled the car with fuel, had the windscreen cleaned and the oil checked, then we left the city. Storm was strapped into her car seat and Splodge was still asleep on the seat next to me, purring softly while his ears twitched every so often. Our journey was going to be a happy one, back to where I belonged, back to a place where I could cleanse away the recent heartbreak and sadness. What had been my happy place as a child was to become my healing retreat now. This time I wouldn't be sitting beneath the wild cosmos growing in our fallow fields like I did as a child. Sadly, it was the wrong time of the year. My mind drifted back to when I sat watching, with delight, the butterflies and bees busy doing their work in the cosmos. It was there, hidden in that wonderland of pink and white, where everything lived side by side in perfect harmony, that the pain of Papa's death had become less troublesome to me.

The kilometres rolled on smoothly towards the farm, and as they unravelled, so did the tension in my shoulders. Something Dion never appreciated was the beauty of nature, and now without him around, I could soak it up as I travelled. The Dion who'd once made my dreams come true had now shattered them.

There was more to life than this pain though. I'd left behind a man I'd learnt to despise as equally as I loved. I struggled not to lose my grasp on hope and purpose. I had to admit I was too young and too unwise in the ways of psychological complexities to help Dion, but the desire was still there.

Would I find the answers to my future in the fields? Would the butterflies and bees bring them to me, show me the signs I was looking for?

A few weeks of precious quiet time on the farm would be perfect to let me sift through the confusion and find the path to the next chapter of my life's journey. It was the ideal place to think while pushing Storm down the sand roads in her pushchair, introducing her to the magnificent wonders of nature at the tender age of five months old. The air was clean and unpolluted, and the natural swaying of grasses and flowers in gentle breezes and insects all claiming their share of the bounty would not only soothe me, but would hopefully fascinate Storm.

These were the things that mattered; they were the things that grounded me.

I didn't want to think of single parenthood. It held no appeal, but nor did going back to this altered man, a man who was so unlike the man I'd married. The one I was still in love with. How could I throw that away? "He" was still there; it was finding a way to make him stay that had me flummoxed. If I did decide to try once more, would it be worth it? Nothing made sense right now. I would untangle my thoughts and emotions one day at a time, harmonising with the music of the winds, the songs of insects and birds, the dust storms and the setting African sun.

Out on the open road, traffic racket and city noise far behind me, I wound down the window and fresh air blasted its way past my face, and with it, the lovely pungent smell of damp long grass and wild herbs growing on the side of the road. The radio was playing some good music and soon I was singing along, the humiliation of another affair behind me. Thank God, I'd not pulled the trigger! Those thoughts still brought beads of sweat to my brow.

Recent rains had washed the dust off of the countryside. It was refreshingly clean and crisp, reflecting a palette of soft wild African greens. The mid-morning temperatures had climbed to thirty degrees Celsius and were rising off of the wet earth, making the air close. The dams were full, and the sky was a bright, vibrant blue; it was a perfect day. Home was not far off. Soon I would be reunited with my family.

We were a close family, unified by tragedy and hardship. I'd grown up with only some of my siblings and a strong mother and guided by the warmth and happiness of our staff. We'd all missed Father's presence, especially my brother, who'd shouldered more responsibility than any teenage boy should. The unavoidable circumstances had forced us to grow up faster than our friends, but we had the priceless gift of the great outdoors. William had taught me a lot. In fact, he'd turned me into quite a tomboy. As a young girl, I preferred to wield hammers and screwdrivers than play with dolls and learn to cook. William possessed a wisdom far beyond his years, a wisdom I was going to call on now.

Storm began to stir, interrupting my childhood thoughts. We were on the quiet gravel road now, so I pulled up beneath the shade of a large acacia tree and switched off the engine. The silence of the African bush always sharpened the senses. I'd forgotten how blissfully quiet it was. Unbuckling Storm from her car seat, I lifted her up and settled her onto my lap. She was hungry and fidgeted as I unbuttoned my shirt, loosened the front of my bra, and released a painfully engorged breast. Her feed time was way overdue, but she'd slept well, and I hadn't wanted to disturb her. It must have been the peace, quiet and fresh air that had made her sleep longer.

I marvelled at the euphoria that accompanied breastfeeding and had a glorious release of hormones that accompanied Storm's suckling. My mind was sharper as I sat listening to the birds in the tree above while Storm greedily fed.

In little over half an hour we were on our way again. Splodge had settled after yelling for water and mewing frantically, which Storm found particularly funny. She chuckled with delightful liquidity, making me go all gooey inside.

During the last leg of the journey, my mind drifted back to life in Kimberly, the famous old diamond mining town. It suited Dion. Though we hadn't been there long, it was long enough for Dion's reputation as a musician and singer to spread fast. With help from Leon, he was invited to play the piano and sing in many of the quaint historical pubs and hotels in the town, where young hopeful miners with dreams of wealth had drunk before him. Kimberly came alive at night and had I not been pregnant and threatened miscarriage, perhaps I would have enjoyed more nights out with him. Many of the old pubs replicated the energy and vibe of yesteryear when diamonds were discovered in 1871. The area had erupted then, with a mad scramble for claims; anything went down. Hard-working diggings consumed the miners during the day, which was followed by hard drinking at night, and just as it was in my time, there were plenty of loose women to satisfy the primal desires of man. The purpose for our move had been to get away from one woman, and now our marriage had become a symbol of the town's history: blood, sweat and tears, hard drinking and endless womanising. There was no doubt Dion considered himself the Barney Barnato of the seventies. And he possessed the debonair good looks of the diamond tycoon. However, there was a significant difference: they didn't share the same wealth, and there was a sad absence of diamonds, but both men thrived on the attention lavished upon them by adoring women, status and booze.

I was close to home now, bumping over the dirt road. Splodge had moved to my lap and was kneading my leg and purring while inflicting immense pain with his needle sharp claws in my thigh. My thoughts hurriedly left Dion and Kimberly as I tried to move him.

Chapter Eight

Rural black women in South Africa know precisely how to unleash torrents of unashamedly good cheer and excitement at seeing someone they love after a time apart. This was just what I needed. A simplistic, authentic, heart-warming welcome of ululation while ushering me in to stop beside them.

Word had got around that "Missus Elizabeth" was bringing her new baby for them to meet. I parked beneath the shade of a large white stinkwood tree in the centre of the driveway. They bombarded the car, giggling and laughing, swaying merrily, serenading with high-pitched African yodelling excitement, dressed in bright ethnic print uniforms, waving their aprons around. Their happiness was infectious, but Storm wasn't sure how to interpret the merriment. Her bottom lip quivered with uncertainty and her eyes were wide open and unblinking. Five happy, apron-clad, black women with an abundance of love in their souls and the warmth of the earth in their hearts peered into the car at her. I loved looking into their shiny black faces, smeared with Vaseline, beaming toothless smiles that shone like the moon against a dark sky, but Storm looked on with an anxious infant stare on the verge of tears.

Ester, the head lady, reached in and shamelessly grabbed Storm, passing her around like a trophy. Overwhelmed, Storm bawled her head off while the ladies cajoled and mocked the infant joyfully. It wasn't long before the tears were gone, and Storm began to enjoy the well-intended love and laughter and pressed out a smile.

A call from Dion inevitably destroyed our quiet Friday evening. I'd been on the farm a week. I knew it had to come. I couldn't hide from him forever. He was spitting mad I'd left. The fact he'd only found my note on Friday was proof he hadn't bothered to call home during the week, for Miriam would have told him I wasn't there.

"What the fuck are you doing on the farm?" he yelled down the phone.

"If you'd called home once during the week, you'd have known. Goodbye, Dion."

I put the receiver down, and it rang again seconds later.

"I'm here because I can't sit around waiting for you to come home while you screw around with every willing slut in and out of town."

This time I slammed the phone down before he had time to answer, but he persisted and rang again. The shrill sound of the telephone ringing again spiked my blood pressure and my mood. Taking in a deep breath, I left it ringing for a bit longer before picking it up.

"Elizabeth, listen to me. You're jumping to conclusions. I'm not sleeping with Julie or anyone else. That's the truth."

"You don't know the meaning of truth, Dion. I don't even think you can spell it. I can't trust you. You promised you'd never be unfaithful again after Zandri, but you can't resist, can you? Another promise you made was that you'd stop drinking. My understanding of a promise and commitment are worlds apart from yours. Your promises are said because they sound like the right thing to say at the time, not because you mean any of them."

There was silence on the other end, then he asked, "When are you coming home?" The question confirmed he'd listened to nothing I'd just said.

"I don't know if I'm coming back." Hearing myself say that hit me harder than I'd anticipated. Tears of futility and sadness smeared my cheeks.

"I was not sleeping with Julie. How many times do I have to tell you?"

"Get it into your head, Dion. I don't believe a word you say. You had her details in your briefcase, written in her hand with hugs and kisses along the bottom of the piece of paper I threw back at you. You and I both know she wasn't looking for a fucking piano."

This time, I gently placed the phone back in its cradle, and when it rang for the fourth time, I left it ringing.

Though Mom was busying herself with Storm while I was struggling with Dion on the phone, she'd heard snippets of the argument and when I turned to her, falling back onto the couch, I noticed a mixed expression on her face, but she didn't comment.

They say cats have a sixth sense. Splodge displayed his by jumping on the couch and spreading himself across my lap, as if to say "well done" and purred like a steam train. He possessed me, as cats do, quietly ruling my life without asking, but I adored him. Though he had the intuition of a cat, he behaved more like a loyal dog. He went everywhere with me, quite happy wherever he was as long he was with me or protectively loving Storm.

I remained on the farm for ten days and revelled in the gentle quiet of the countryside. I refused to speak to Dion when he called. I binned the letter he'd written to me.

"My child, you can't go on like this," Mom said. "You need to speak to your husband and sort things out, one way or another. If he calls tonight, try to have a civil conversation with him." She was worried by my refusal to deal with Dion.

"I know, Ma, but I don't know what the solution is. Only a small part of me wants to go back."

"Ignoring him isn't going to solve it or help answer your questions. He's not going away. Unfortunately, he's your husband."

Mom was not often annoyed with me, but this whole episode was wearing her down as she watched me go into a place where no one could access. She didn't want me to go back to Dion, but it was up to me. My deliberate procrastinating irritated her now, probably because she'd never seen me this indecisive. I knew I could not solve this by a telephone conversation; I had to work this out in our home.

I got up from the chair, lowered Storm into her pushchair and disappeared down the road that led to the farm dam. I sat and contemplated, trying to gather a practical perspective on my situation while moorhens, herons and Egyptian geese watched over me. I envied them, monogamous or not, their lives were simple and without complication. *How wonderfully simple life would be if I was a bird*, I thought aimlessly for a moment.

That night, I spoke to Dion after resetting my thoughts at the dam. "I will be home tomorrow night," was all I said.

Chapter Nine

An eerie sense of foreboding raised the hair on the back of my neck as I stepped through the front door into familiar surroundings. It felt like there was someone behind me, right behind me, so close I could feel the mysterious breath blowing down the back of my neck. It was a frightening sensation. I suddenly wondered whether I had made the right decision by coming back.

Then Splodge reinforced my thoughts by digging his claws into my forearm, leaving a deep red scratch that bubbled globules of blood. I screeched as he ran off, and a shiver went down my spine. Splodge crossed the floor in a flash, his hackles bristling indicating danger or a dangerous threat. He was eerily unhappy. He'd been okay before we left. Small droplets of blood were now dripping down the side of my arm, then I noticed Splodge's hackles were down and he didn't appear quite so tense. I wasn't a believer in ghosts or the supernatural, but the sensations Splodge and I had just experienced upset us both. Thankfully, Miriam changed the mood with her cheer, scooping Storm up in her arms, kissing her chubby cheeks while Storm, instantly recognising Miriam, giggled and gurgled.

Miriam and I unpacked and tidied up, but intuition kept nagging at me insistently. It wanted me to listen, but listen to what? When Dion got home, I was curled up on the couch.

Splodge was sleeping next to Storm, who was propped up against me while I read, and listened to ABBA.

"I'm so happy you're back," he said as he walked into the lounge, leaning down with his arms spread as if to embrace us all.

Splodge was having none of that. He shot off the couch and disappeared into the kitchen, waking Storm, who started to cry. Dion was mildly taken aback by his daughter's reaction; Splodge disappearing that quickly had gone unnoticed by Dion.

"I love you, liefie. My life is nothing without you in it," he said mournfully. "I know you don't trust me or believe what I tell you, but I can't live without you. These last three weeks have been a living hell."

"I love you too, Dion. But not the Dion you are now. I love the old one. The one I married. I hate the one you are now," I said simply. "You've hurt me badly, and though I might find it in me to forgive you, I can't promise anything. I can't and won't live with your drinking, lies and continuous infidelity. You have a lot to prove. Right now, I'd far prefer to be on the farm surrounded by salt of the earth, sincere people who genuinely care about me. I've only come back to see if we can sort out the issues amicably. Whether I stay or not remains to be seen."

There was an honest, anguished expression on his face. One I'd not seen before. Though I wasn't ready to believe him, I also wasn't prepared to divorce him immediately either. What he needed to know was that I wasn't just going to melt into his arms. He'd created this disaster and it was up to him to fix it, but Dion du Toit loathed being threatened.

"It looks like you'd be more comfortable with just that bloody cat and your daughter as company," he said, with stinging bitterness.

"They've earned the right to my affection, Dion. If you want me back, you have to earn it too."

He didn't respond.

Once I'd fed Storm, Miriam bathed her for me and put her to bed, singing an African lullaby to her as she drifted off to sleep. I knew I had a difficult evening ahead. Splodge was a welcome distraction. I could hear him mewing for his favourite meal: sardines. After scooping out the smelly fish into his dish, I rustled up a farmhouse omelette for Dion and I. Splodge gobbled up his sardines and meowed for his bowl of milk, purring with gratification.

Now, why aren't husbands that grateful when we feed them?

Our conversation was stilted and uncomfortable during supper. I felt awkward, and I wasn't going to start a conversation. Dion relieved me of that.

"My life spiralled out of control," he began, "The orders poured in, I revelled in the limelight, which went to my head, and all I could think about was money and more money. You're right, liefie, I scarcely know my daughter, and I nearly lost you."

He reached forwards and kissed my forehead, which I pulled away from. The old tenderness still didn't provoke a need for forgiveness, but it did relax the tension a little.

"I'm not yours, Dion. I never will be. We're two individuals sharing a life. You do not own me. I can't return to our marriage like it has been these past years. I'm not even sure how to even begin with the forgiveness process. The only way I can see our marriage working is if you give up drinking, commit to us as a family and come home every single night. Start sharing your thoughts and your income and put in quality time with us. I can't switch off the pain you've inflicted like a light. I'm still hurting.

I'm still angry. I don't think you understand the extent of what you've done to me."

I looked away, unable to hold his gaze. I was unprepared for the sadness I saw etched on his face. Maybe my walking out had made him think, though I doubted it for that recklessness was still in his eyes.

I knew the danger in their depths, and just then, I felt the familiar, mysterious trickle of breath down my spine, and the hair on my arms stood up. Although there were fine lines of fatigue etched at the corners of his eyes, there was still something sinister lurking there. I needed living proof that the stress showing on his face was because he genuinely loved us and felt guilty for his misdemeanours and selfishness. Loving him was indeed painful and complicated. Mom had warned me love was not effortless, but I was sure she wasn't referring to this kind of situation. My husband was no ordinary human being.

"While you were away—" Dion continued, but I interrupted when I got up to put our plates in the kitchen sink. I could see that irritated him, but he kept his cool for once.

When I got back and sat down again, he said, "I answered an advert for a general manager's position for a privately owned music store in Bethlehem. It's well paid, and I won't have to travel much."

"That's just running away again, Dion. *You* are the problem. Until you change your habits, the problem will go with us, so what's the point of moving? I thought you said you were doing well. I haven't seen a penny of that money."

"Well…" He paused. "I went for the interview and got the job. Do you want me to take it?"

He took my face in his hands and kissed the tip of my nose.

"We only move if it's what you want," he whispered, the master manipulator at work once more.

"It's not up to me, Dion. You can't keep running from you. Didn't you hear what I just said?" I responded irritably. "You're just moving the problem to a different location!"

"It's a good offer, a better salary, a house and virtually no travel. Will you give me a chance to repair what I've broken, even if it's a different location? I promise to work on me and our marriage together."

I looked down, fiddled with my fingers and couldn't respond for a few minutes while Dion, uncharacteristically, remained quiet. Was this an early breakthrough?

The thought of starting again in another rural town was daunting, but without Leon's influences, maybe we had a better chance. Dion would have to learn to resist temptation, for he'd still meet the likes of Leon along the road of our lives and Bethlehem wouldn't be any different. I didn't know how to cope with what he'd thrust at me. All he wanted was for me to say yes and agree with him on everything. He'd carefully planned it all while I was on the farm, even down to taking the position before discussing it with me, hoping I'd have no option but agree to go with him. I closed my eyes and rested my head on the back of the sofa.

He started humming softly. "Somewhere over the rainbow, way up high, there's a land that I heard of once in a lullaby…"

It was almost impossible not to be pulled in by his charms, especially as a part of me still loved that side of him. Personality number one was what I called the Dion I adored, who was now in "flawless performance mode". He went on humming, then I felt him take my hand, and he began to sing for my heart once more.

"Someday I'll wish upon a star and wake up where the clouds are far behind me. Where trouble melts like lemon drops..."

I opened my eyes and surrendered to my tears, letting them stream down my face.

"I love you," he whispered.

"Oh, Dion, I love you too," I said, sobbing.

"It will never happen again, I promise."

"Don't promise, Dion. I'd rather you show me you mean what you say."

Everything inside me felt tender, torn and damaged, then I heard myself begin to answer in a quiet murmur.

"I want to believe you, but I'm scared. It's not just about other women. It's the drinking and all the other personalities that emerge when you've had a few too many drinks or you're in a vile mood."

His gaze had turned to one of love, tenderness and depth and it burnt gently into me. There were tears in his eyes too while he gently wiped mine away. It was the most poignant moment we'd had in a very long time. I was watching the lovely side of my husband, but I also saw his dependency on me, and that scared me.

We went on discussing our future a while longer then he moved to the piano and sang for me. Splodge and I remained on the couch, comforting each other. Every note, every word he sang, lodged deep within me, and when he finished, we moved to our bedroom where he hummed another of my favourite tunes into the back of my neck. I fell into a deep contented sleep.

Chapter Ten

The House of Music, for the era, was a very grand shop – absurdly out of place, I thought when I saw it. It was situated on a principal street corner in a sleepy little "dorp" called Bethlehem. The town primarily served farmers. I wondered who the shop's target market could be.

There was little relationship to the biblical "Bethlehem" other than the area was commonly referred to as the "breadbasket" of South Africa. The town was nestled in a broad basin in the heart of a wonderfully fertile farming area, but I still wondered how it could sustain such a fancy music shop, one that could make a decent profit. It fascinated me, for although it served the surrounding smaller towns too, there were only so many people who would buy guitars, pianos, organs and drums. It all seemed crazy to me. But here we were in one of the coldest places in the country.

The town was founded as far back as 1864 and it had grown fast. Its fertile lands were quickly sought after by early settlers. With an above average rainfall and temperate climate, it was perfect for a wide variety of different crops and cold enough in the winter months for a variety of fruits to be grown successfully, especially apples and cherries. Its natural beauty, sandstone cliffs and steep mountains made the area a charming place to live, but

I still couldn't work out the need for such a lavish music shop! I hoped it would prove me wrong. And so it was agreed, swayed by musical melody, that we'd move to Bethlehem and begin a whole new chapter in our lives.

When I walked into the store for the first time, I could scarcely believe what I was seeing. In front of me lay a spacious, elegantly designed showroom. It provided the perfect platform for displaying a vast selection of beautifully polished instruments. For farmers? I still found it particularly odd. Several pianos and organs stood proudly on display and dominated the shop. Dion couldn't resist taking a seat at the organ, and he began playing my favourite hymn "Jerusalem". Of course, passers-by were drawn into the shop like flies, eager to see who was singing. Dion's voice was crystal clear, the most beautiful masculine voice one could imagine, and it was now being accompanied by the pristine sound of a brand-new organ. In Bethlehem of all places.

Gleaming, in a splendid display behind Dion at the organ, were guitars, flutes, clarinets, cellos, violins and the sax, the sexy sax, and more, all twinkling like polished gems as if they too were mesmerised by the hymn. Soon, the shop was full of people as they squashed in from the street. It was quite a show.

When he finished, the crowd clapped loudly and started singing out, "Nog, nog." (More, more in Afrikaans.)

It was a unique and memorable introduction to Bethlehem. Soon Dion became the talk of the town, in much the same way as he had in Kimberly. The difference? The customer went to the shop and there was no nasty Leon.

Proudly displayed in the main shop window were newly introduced colour televisions. Also sold in this shop were long playing records, gramophones, radios, stereos, pretty much anything to do with music. Televisions were instruments of much controversy in South Africa at the time. We quickly learnt that many of the folk in Bethlehem frowned upon the introduction of television, suggesting it tainted the community. Especially vocal was the congregation of the large NGK fraternity (Nederduitse Gereformeerde Kerk. In English, the Dutch Reformed Church).

I had to admit, and only to myself, this job suited Dion. Perhaps he'd made the right decision. All he had to do now was stick to it and take responsibility for his life and ours.

Splodge approved of the new house and roamed around the perimeter marking his territory, satisfied that intruders would know this was his spot, then he returned to the couch and watched us unpack, as cats do. The company had rented us a modest three-bedroom home with a lovely garden that attracted bird species I'd not seen before. Fortunately, Splodge was far too lazy and well fed to worry about catching them. He did catch the odd rat or two when he prowled the area. We had a spectacular view from the lounge and veranda looking out across the hills to eternity; it was where we sat at the end of the day.

Storm adjusted quickly, thanks to the input of Miriam, who'd moved with us and was delighted with her new spacious little flatlet built onto the back of the house. We'd only been in Bethlehem a week when Dion brought home the first surprise: a colour television. I was like a child at Christmas and couldn't wait to switch it on and discover what it was all about. "Television" was the buzzword across the country at the time. There was great excitement about this new form of entertainment. Bethlehem residents were deeply divided though, and there was considerable radio and newspaper outrage about its launch, especially amongst the Dutch Reformed Church-dominated communities, as Bethlehem was. In some small rural towns, the sale of television was banned.

I couldn't think of anything more exciting than curling up on the couch on a cold winter's evening, dancing flames spreading warmth throughout the room from the fireplace, a monster bowl of popcorn on my lap, watching colour television until the test patterns came up at midnight. It was also not something I could imagine getting sick of. It didn't interfere with my faith, but the ladies at Bible study were horrified by my attitude, so I left the group. The older folk thought televised media was, in their opinion, undesirable and unacceptable. They were deeply concerned that the type of imported media from the USA would show "race-mixing" and it became known in town as "the devil's own box".

"What?" I said to Dion as I read that bit out from the local newspaper. "You better be careful some of the locals don't attack you in the shop."

"Ridiculous. I'm sure that won't happen. We've already sold six this week. Seven if you include ours."

"Really?" That was good news.

My thoughts went to the ladies at Bible study who'd accused me of being immoral.

Soon there were hundreds of immoral families living in Bethlehem, loving their in-home entertainment. The hypocrisy was ridiculous and went on for months, but as the shock wore off in the rigidly "moral" communities, everyone wanted one, even the local ministers who had been so outraged by their introduction.

We loved our television, and I was certain the good Lord wouldn't mind us watching. One of our favourite programmes, launched in 1976, was called "The Villagers". It was a hilarious sitcom that cleverly depicted ordinary life in a reef gold mine village of the era in South Africa. It was great entertainment; we never missed an episode, but then my days of being graciously unemployed came to an end. I was bored. I also needed to top up my empty savings account. The new energy felt great; I was healing. I was rejuvenated and ready to face the world once more which pleased my worried mother.

I found a job, more quickly than I'd anticipated, working in a clothing store. It wasn't a job that offered much satisfaction; the boss was a complete pig, and I wondered how long I could stick it out after I'd endured a month there.

In the morning, I'd generally begin the day in the accounts department, then in the afternoon I served customers and tidied the store or, when the boss felt like it, he ordered me to chase up customers who'd neglected to pay their monthly accounts. It was most unsatisfying, but there were lots of cuddles and kisses with Storm when I got home in the evening. Those soothed away the frustrations. I was working for a man with an ego that even superseded Dion's.

I'd felt guilty putting Storm into daycare so young, but I needed the income. I always felt insecure when my savings were depleted, and though I was happier within myself and our marriage was good, something niggling deep within always warned me to be vigilant. My husband changed faster than night and day. Dion's promises seemed to be intact, though he hadn't entirely convinced me.

Then he joined a local band.

Chapter Eleven

Practice sessions began once a week. The strumming of guitar strings and tapping of piano keys mixed well with the alarm bells ringing in my head. I was struggling with riotous contradictory feelings. I was happy for Dion to show off his singing talents and do what I'd encouraged and hoped for him, but unhappy with my own burdening fears. Fears which I couldn't shake off for obvious reasons.

It was complicated. He was complicated. My thoughts were complicated too, and my lousy job gave me time during the day to brood. Dion had been so perfect since we'd moved, and I wanted to keep the delicate balance undisturbed.

Wrapping Storm in fleecy blankets, we set off in my old car – another thing I had to save for. My "skedonk" Datsun was due for retirement, but it always got me to where I needed to go. Storm and I headed off to watch Dion during a practice session.

As I pulled into the driveway of the dentist's luxury home in my skedonk, it suddenly seemed even older as I parked next to gleaming new expensive cars. My little Datsun was a car with character, and I loved her.

As I lifted Storm and her bag of baby necessities out of the car, I heard Dion singing "Morning Has Broken", a favourite Cat Stevens song of ours and my heart swelled with pride. God, he had a beautiful voice. I knew he was doing the right thing. Apart from being beautiful, smooth and deep, his voice was an intoxicating aphrodisiac that lit a fire deep within the pit of my stomach. More often than not, I cursed it.

"The Rogues" was the name they had given their band. It was very apt, but I liked it. It wasn't long before the band was in popular demand and miraculously, Dion was still behaving like a perfect gentleman months later. Mom checked on me regularly and boetie called once a week.

Storm loved the music and stood holding onto my knees and bobbed to the beat, giggling and chortling. Life was good. The demand for the band to play at functions grew, so the group practised three to four times a week, making it impossible for Storm and I to attend each practice session, but watching Dion sing once, sometimes twice a week, became my drug.

"Hey, Dion, you're fuckin' brilliant, bru," Gert, the drummer, shouted when they finished singing one of Elton John's magical songs in preparation for a gig in Johannesburg.

Gert was so excited. Everyone was excited. The mood in the room was contagious. A few Afrikaans love songs followed, and the end of the practice evening was testament to another brilliant session. They were good, and they complemented each other well.

Back home, I cuddled up to Dion, our naked bodies pressed into each other, and we kissed deeply.

When I finally pulled away from him, I whispered, "I'm so proud of you. I love you so much."

He covered my mouth with his and kissed me hungrily again.

"You're irresistible. You keep me going. Thank you for standing by and encouraging me." His gaze was laden with desire and he hummed softly, "You make me feel brand new."

It was impossible to resist the soft, sexy tones and now my desire for him had reached even greater heights. We lay in each other's arms, exhausted, and it wasn't long before Dion was softly snoring while I lay sated, relaxed and marvelled that he'd finally thanked me for something.

The opening song the band sang to usher in the new bride and groom was a Rita Coolidge one: "Your Love Has Lifted Me Higher and Higher". This was the first Johannesburg wedding they'd played at, and they were a huge success. From that wedding the word got around that the Rogues were exceptional. The bookings rolled in, and a month later, I discovered I was carrying our second child.

Chapter Twelve

It was a pregnancy we'd not planned, but we were both thrilled. I kept the occasional feelings of hesitation to myself – brought on by memories of the turbulent pregnancy with Storm.

"A new life, a new miracle, how divine," Dion blurted out happily while we sat together in a quiet little restaurant after one practice session and toasted the pregnancy. It was the first alcoholic drink Dion had had in months; the first I'd had in years!

The following day, I called Mom. She wasn't overjoyed by the news, but she wished me well nonetheless. Then I called my closest sister.

All she could say was, "Oh God, Elizabeth, that's just another devious way to force you to stay with him. Why you live with that bastard, none of us can understand. Good luck, sis."

I had much the same response from William too. That was that. My family would not celebrate, and though it hurt, I understood their sentiment.

Five months into my pregnancy and hardly showing, I decided it was time to notify my nasty boss. He was a big man, all too aware of his masculinity, who aroused a deep primal fear in me. I'd never trusted him, and I was nervous about advising him of my pregnancy. He treated women with unreserved disrespect, which made the situation even more uncomfortable. I'd arranged a meeting with him and stood in front of him. He never offered a seat, and after informing him I was five months pregnant, he stretched back in his large leather executive chair and silently gazed at me, running his eyes slowly over my body, stopping purposefully at my crotch, then my breasts, as he visually undressed me. I knew precisely what was going through his twisted mind and my skin crawled.

"I'm afraid," he began, a disdainful smile creased the edge of his lips, "You are not entitled to maternity benefits and the company is under no obligation to offer them."

"Why not? That's disgusting sexism, Mr Freeman. I work hard here, and you know that."

The business world was dominated by men like him in the late seventies and it was considered ultimately rebellious mentioning anything to do with sexism. He considered women subservient and there was no doubt he expected me to grovel before him.

"It has nothing to do with sexism, Mrs du Toit," he spat angrily. "It is not compulsory by law, and I don't offer it to any of my female staff."

"Excuse me, Mr Freeman, though you may not have noticed, you only have three female staff, two of which are too old to have children. I have been a loyal member of staff, doing two people's work for months without recognition or thanks or extra remuneration."

He gave me a look of disinterest. I was so angry, I stormed out of his office, sat at my desk, wrote out my resignation and marched back to the schmuck's office and dumped it on his desk.

"What's this?" he asked, looking at the folded letter I'd dropped in front of him.

"My resignation, and the employment agency is going to know about this. I won't work for a chauvinist like you for another minute."

I swung around and left, striding across the showroom floor for the last time. I'd been unconsciously holding my breath, and my chest was about to explode. Once I was outside, I stood for a few moments to gather my wits before heading to Dion's work.

I'd never liked the arsehole from day one; my first impressions of Mr Freeman could not have been more accurate. Standing on the pavement outside the shop, I felt an overwhelming sense of freedom. Happiness pumped through my veins at a rapid rate now I'd gotten over the humiliation. The only issue... I had to tell Dion. I went to the employment agent first. Once again, my loyalty and feminism were thrown in my face by another ungrateful, sanctimonious dickhead, who was shit scared of Mr Freeman and wouldn't take on my case.

I was paid my salary and leave pay, but not a cent was added as a bonus for the extra hours I'd put in during stocktake, or anything else I'd gone the extra mile on. It was a lesson in character assessment and when to go the extra mile and when not to.

Every dog has his day, I thought while I walked through town, mulling over my explanation to Dion. Though the band was doing well, the shop wasn't. He was disappointed in me for just walking out, but at least he wasn't angry.

A month after walking out of my job, Dion got a verbal warning for arriving at the shop reeking of alcohol after an extended lunch break. I was spitting mad. If he lost his job, we'd lose the house too and the whole fucking rollercoaster would begin again. By then, I was just into the last trimester. I also didn't know he was drinking again.

Panic now replaced baby nausea.

"You promised no more lies and no more drinking," I said with fiery, frustrated cries when he told me of the warning. "When did you hit the bottle again?"

He remained silent, looking uncharacteristically embarrassed, then I realised it wasn't his conscience troubling him, it was the fact that his office had a glass front, and his staff were watching us argue. In my anger, I'd forgotten that we were visible to all who were in the shop.

"You do realise you're giving me full permission to fuck off out of your life, forever this time! I warned you. Do you want that?"

"You bitch, don't threaten me in here," he said, and my sister's words flashed through my mind as he said it.

"I don't deserve this, Dion. I never have deserved any of the crap you have dished out, but especially now. Are you going to make this pregnancy as bad as the last one?" Resentment was rising in my throat like a bitter poison; I could feel it burn. The monster was back.

"Just fuck off out of here. We'll talk tonight at home." He stood up to usher me out. I stood next to him with my nose almost pressed up against his as I glared at him.

I said quietly, "Adjust your attitude before you get home."

I turned and slammed his office door to make a point, and the glass partition rattled precariously.

When Dion got in, he was still seething from being humiliated in front of his staff and customers.

"Don't you ever embarrass me like that again," he yelled, slamming down his briefcase as he turned to me.

"That's a joke, Dion. You don't need me to embarrass you in front of your staff. Being drunk on the job, in your position, does it for you."

Suddenly, those soft brown eyes I'd seen for months were dark eerie pools that always unnerved me. He was angry, but fully aware he'd stepped over the mark.

"We can work this out, Elizabeth," he said back-pedalling rather suddenly.

"No, we can't. It's too late, Dion. I warned you last time. In fact, how many times have I warned you?"

"What do you mean, 'it's too late'?" A slight tremble of panic sounded in his voice.

"Oh, for God's sake, Dion. It's too fucking late. It's impossible to live a rollercoaster life of uncertainty. I'm moving back to William and Bessie's until after the baby is born, then I will decide what to do and where I want to live. You have this house to live in if you manage to hold onto your job," I said conclusively.

Chapter Thirteen

Vivienne arrived on her due date, born in the Bloemfontein Hospital maternity wing, without her father present. It was the shortest day of the year, the winter solstice in the southern hemisphere, 21 June 1978, and it was a bitterly cold day.

Giving birth to Vivienne was difficult. Though I left the hospital after three days, I wasn't feeling well. Four days later, William rushed me back to hospital after a desperate plea from Miriam.

"Baas William, come quick. Missus is dying, please hurry, baas."

I was admitted to the intensive care unit, close to losing my life from septicaemia as I'd retained some afterbirth. The sepsis took hold quickly, leaving me seriously ill. I remember looking at the doctor. Absurdly, he wasn't next to my bed, he was walking down the passage. He was leaving me. They couldn't save me. I could hear him talking to a nurse in the passage, but I couldn't string together exactly what he was saying. I felt weightless and acutely aware of everything that was going on around my bed, even what the nurses were doing.

One moment I sensed the most beautiful awareness of floating in absolute freedom. I felt no pain and no fear, just wholesome, pure, accepting, all-encompassing love which felt marvellous, then I was pulled away from that magical universal space and it was dark again, then suddenly something mystic was enticing me back to that carefree realm. I remember thinking how nice it would be to stay there, floating in amongst a rainbow of colours and light, peaceful and divine, surrounded by nothing but love.

During those hours between delirium and clarity, I couldn't make sense of any of it. All I knew was I wanted to go back to that fairy tale place. Those moments didn't last, for suddenly I was fretting about my two children, smothered with haunting thoughts of them being raised by a drunken, lying, psychopathic father and I was right back in the present. It was those thoughts that pulled me back and kept me firmly rooted to this earth.

Doctor Daan had also been fretting. Worried he might not save my life, he suggested that William call Dion; he was to get to Bloemfontein as soon as possible to say goodbye to his wife and meet his new daughter.

I'd been hooked up to an oxygen ventilator, pumped full of antibiotics and had a fever and infection that threatened my life. Though I never felt that exquisite freedom again, the hallucinations coming out of it were terrifying. Apparently, I'd woken, screaming hysterically. The one nightmare that tormented me was a vision of the two girls lying together on filthy beds, skin and bone, dying of starvation and covered in flies, while their father sat watching them, drunk and disabled from excessive alcohol consumption. The nurses had said they had to hold me down to inject a tranquiliser. It was those grizzly images that made me hang on to my life. For two more days, nursing staff watched over me until finally, the fever broke, and the nightmares disappeared with the illness.

Vivienne was brought to me five days later and William and Bessie brought Storm to visit once I'd moved from the ICU to the general wards. Seeing them both stopped the fitful nights and ghastly visions of them being raised by Dion. I recovered, but the nightmares haunted me for months.

The morning before I was discharged, I lay thinking what a committed nurse I could have been if I'd finished my training, and how valuable that certification would have been for me now. It was one of the many times I felt regret about not completing my nurses' training, but this was not the time for regrets. As soon as I was well enough, I would go job hunting again. I would begin a new life on my own with my two girls.

"Good morning, Elizabeth, how are you feeling today?" Doctor Daan breezed into the ward and stood at the end of my bed.

"Feeling better, thank you, Daan, just terribly weak."

"I'm not surprised. We thought we'd lost you that first night. I kept wondering how I was going to explain that to your family, especially your brother. One of my dearest friends, as you know."

"Yes, the nurse told me."

Daan moved around to the side of the bed and looked down at us both. "Beautiful little girl," he said, smiling at Vivienne. "How would you feel about seeing a psychologist to help you deal with the trauma of your marriage and the nightmares?"

I looked up at Daan, a man I'd known and trusted for years. "Why?" I asked.

"Your nightmares revealed some troubling issues. The nurses called me in when you had the first one. Fortunately, I happened to be on duty. It took three of us to hold you down. I think you were trying to kill Dion." Daan laughed. "I had to sedate you for twelve hours. I suppose you are not aware of that?"

"I remember one nightmare very clearly. That was bad enough. I don't want to remember more. I'm going to carve out a new future now, Daan. I'm not going back to Dion." I looked at him briefly, then added, "Those nightmares actually gave me the will to stay alive."

"Do you know you asked, um... well, should I say you violently demanded that we stop Dion from seeing you or your children. You're holding onto a lot of pain, aren't you?" He rubbed my forearm with the palm of his hand. "I recommend you have a chat with a psychologist who will help you deal with your fears and your pain."

I couldn't stop the tears. As soon as anyone offered sympathy, I crumbled. Daan continued to hold my forearm comfortingly and waited for me to calm down before going on.

"I'll make the appointment, if you agree."

I nodded and wiped the tears away with the back of my hand.

"You're free to go home. William is collecting you and the nurse will give you the remaining antibiotics that you *must* finish." He raised an eyebrow at me like a threatening father.

"Thank you, Daan."

It was early afternoon when William arrived, bringing Storm with him.

"Mama," she shrieked happily, putting her arms out towards me as William lowered her onto the bed.

"I'm so happy to see you, my little princess."

I kissed her cute rosebud lips and hugged her again. Her big, liquid brown eyes sparkled with happiness while her dark auburn curls bobbed in time with her excitement. The purity of

120

love expressed by a child is so wonderfully unique; she melted away all the anxiety and tension I'd been feeling, and my eyes welled up again.

"Why are you crying, Mama?" she asked, looking concerned.

"They are tears of happiness, my angel."

"Oh," she said. "Why do you cry when you're happy?"

"Not all tears are sad ones, my darling," I said as she shook her head, confused.

"How's Bessie coping with being on the farm alone?" I asked William.

My sister-in-law had always been nervous about living on the farm and loathed being left alone, even for just a day, so William was keen to get home before it got dark.

"She's coping fine, sis. She's looking forward to your home-coming."

"I can't wait. Let's get out of here."

I couldn't remember ever feeling so physically weakened; I was even too nervous and too weak to carry Vivienne. The nurse carried her to the car for me and secured her into the carry cot while Storm looked on, excited to have her little sister with her.

"Daan wants me to see a psychologist," I told William on the way home. "I'm not sure I want to. You know my feelings about psychologists."

"It might help you get over the trauma," William said.

I relented and went a few days later, but after that first session, I swore I'd never go back to another. It wasn't about going forwards but a traumatic digging up of the past which I could not deal with then.

I got through it myself, and six weeks later, I found myself sitting in front of a radiantly healthy-looking woman having a job interview I wasn't even qualified for.

Her good health illuminated my weakened state. That made me feel weaker at that moment, but her abundant good health made me determined to get stronger as quickly as I could. Based upon my CV and the initial interview, I'd made it onto the shortlist and waited nervously to be interviewed by the chief accounting officer: Derek Pienaar.

I needed this job badly. I couldn't go on being supported by my brother; he had his own family and I wanted to be independent again.

I was ushered through to Mr Pienaar's austere office, and I suddenly felt very frail, vulnerable and insignificant. I sat down in front of him, the chief accountant of one of the largest grocery chains in the country. I couldn't believe my luck, but I was scared my ill health would put him off.

Derek Pienaar was a short man with a round friendly face, rather spoilt by a thin strip of moustache, which underlined his nose and gave me the urge to chuckle. It could not have been a more appropriate moustache for an accountant. Pale grey-blue eyes reflected his kindness; he had a warmth about him that made me feel comfortable and relaxed. The exact opposite of Mr Freeman. I liked Derek immediately and felt very at ease while I answered his questions. Then he stretched his arms above his head, still holding onto his Parker pen, and his expression changed. My tummy tightened with anxiety. I needed this position so badly.

"I believe you've been very ill."

"Yes, sir. I nearly died shortly after giving birth to my second daughter. Though it may not look like it, I am well on the road to recovery." I didn't know how convincing I sounded, and I knew I looked anything but well, but I was ready to get back to work.

He smiled, but he didn't look convinced.

"You have an excellent work record, my dear, with glowing references." He sat upright in his chair again. "Are you a quick learner?"

"Yes, I believe I am. I will certainly give you my best."

"I have no doubt. How much experience have you had with accounting? Can you do a trial balance?"

"Not much, sir, and to answer your question about a trial balance, no, I haven't prepared books to finish off there. I've just done debt collecting and a bit of basic bookkeeping in my last job."

"Yes, Mr Freeman told me you were the best worker he'd ever employed."

I couldn't believe what I was hearing. My mouth dropped open.

"What? Did he really say that?" I asked, amazed. "I'm ashamed to say I was rude to him, but he did deserve it. I didn't think he'd ever give me a reference. Well, if his reference gets me this job, it will be in place of the bonus he refused to pay me."

Mr Pienaar chuckled loudly.

"Yes, he did say you are a gutsy lady!"

"Did he call me gutsy? Stroppy feminist, I can hear him say. After he cheated me out of maternity leave, stocktake bonus and overtime when he knew I desperately needed the money, I had nothing to lose but to give him a thoroughly well-deserved piece of my mind."

I surprised myself by telling Mr Pienaar all about the experience. His gentle, quiet, self-assured manner was enormously reassuring. Maybe I'd given away more than I needed to. *Que sera, sera*, I thought. Even though I had everything to lose if I didn't get the job, it was a bit late now.

"Well, Elizabeth," he said, looking down at his watch, "I've kept you here quite long enough."

He rolled the Parker between his fingers and took a deep breath. I feared the worst.

"When will you be able to start?"

A rolling relief ran over my entire body, tingling in my toes finally. I could have reached over and kissed him.

"Oh, thank you. Thank you so much," I said, excitedly. "When would you like me to start, Mr Pienaar?"

"Spring day. First of September, if that suits you?"

"It certainly does and thank you very much." I beamed.

"Welcome to the team," he said, pushing back his chair and coming around his desk to quickly pull my chair back.

Having not been treated like a lady for a long time, I was rather clumsy in my weakened state.

"In the meantime, get some rest."

"Thank you, I will."

An old-fashioned gentleman he certainly was, restoring my belief that there were still gentlemen in this world. Despite being old enough to be my father, being treated with respect was incredibly refreshing.

I had time to sort myself out, gain some physical strength and, hopefully, some weight. There was a bounce in my step for the first time in ages. I wanted to sing out loud. The relief of being able to support myself and my two children made me cry. Those tears of happiness again! I just had to depend on my darling brother for one more thing: the deposit on the cottage and the electricity supply.

The girls and I moved from the farm to Bloemfontein during the last week of August 1978. The cottage was a delightful little space, separated from the main house by a tall hedge. The garden was perfectly adequate for Storm to play in and for me to maintain. Surrounded by a couple of well-tended acres that were all fenced, it was almost like living on a farm. It was cheap enough, plus we were safe. I rented Miriam a room walking distance from the cottage. Splodge approved of the move too and explored the garden, marking his territory as usual, then he settled back in his favourite position: spread out on the couch.

I was earning the best salary I'd ever earned. My old Datsun had to last six more months, then I could trade her in. William had offered to buy me another car, but I couldn't accept any more help from my wonderful brother; he'd done so much for me already. Aside from that, I loved my old skedonk. It was a part of me. She still ran on the smell of an oily rag, she wasn't expensive to maintain, and she never let me down. Besides, there would be no financial assistance from Dion for anything, so I couldn't commit to more monthly payments.

"I'll retire you soon," I said, patting her bonnet as we unloaded the final loose bits. Those bits that accumulate and one never knows what to do with, but they still go everywhere with you! One day they may come in handy.

The owners of the property offered to help if I needed anything doing or help with collecting children and child minding. They were dear retired folk and so typical of warm rural types: people who understand what tough times are about.

The move left me exhausted. Miriam was a godsend. The perfect surrogate mother, who relieved me of so many worries, and the children adored her. We settled into our new way of life easily, as if it had been this way forever. Storm rarely asked about her father, and Vivienne didn't know she had a father.

The cottage felt like home, though it was sparsely furnished. Dion still had most of my possessions. We were happy, and it was cosy. Until I had the energy to sort out the divorce, claim my half and get my treasured personal possessions back, what we had would suffice.

A buzzing in my ear woke me from a deep sleep. Disorientated and startled, I sat bolt upright, then realised it was the alarm clock, a sound I wasn't accustomed to. I flew out of bed. Time to go to work again. Hoorah! However, I wasn't so happy when I put on one of the two-piece suits I had. I was horrified by my reflection; I looked awful. No wonder Mr Pienaar had asked if I was able to start work so soon. The navy blue linen suit hung on me like a flag at half-mast. The only way to hold the skirt up was to put a thin belt around the top of it and fold it over the belt. I'd shrunk from a healthy, curvy thirty-four inches to a skinny, grey-looking twenty-eight inches. Being six-foot, I looked anorexic. I turned away from the mirror. I couldn't bear looking at me. I was a bag of bones. I did my face and hair and was soon on my way to work. I felt a spark of energy, but it didn't last long. I got in early, made some coffee and sat at my new desk, when Mr Pienaar interrupted my thoughts.

"Ah, there you are! Welcome, welcome. How are you doing?" he asked warmly, glancing over me briefly.

"Better on the inside than the outside." I smiled at him. "All my clothes are miles too big for me."

"Well, I must say you look better than you did a few weeks ago. I want you to know that if you feel tired, do let me know. No point in exhausting yourself in the beginning. There's an awful lot to learn. You can always slip off an hour early to begin with. When you've finished your coffee, dear, pop over to my office and we can start."

I gulped back my coffee, gathered up my pens and notebook, and joined Derek in his very plush office.

"Come in, come in," he said, happily showing me to a chair.

A long table ran the length of one side of his office and on it were piles of files and papers stacked up the length of it. Just the sight of the mountains of paperwork was intimidating.

"My dear, before we begin, please call me Derek. Mr Pienaar makes me feel far too old!" He laughed heartily.

To me, he was old; he was thirty years my senior. I considered fifty-eight ancient! Moving another chair next to mine, we started to plough through the stacks of files. Before I knew it, it was time to go home. I had to recheck my watch; the day had flown by. Derek was an excellent tutor, and by the end of the week, I felt alive and useful for the first time in a very long time. I was starving by the time I got home.

Derek popped his head around my office door one morning when I'd been with the company for a month. He asked me to join him in his office. I was terrified he'd decided I wasn't up to scratch.

"Have a seat."

I sat bolt upright on the edge of the chair in preparation for bad news and crossed my legs at my ankles.

"Now why are you looking so tense?"

I fidgeted then smiled. I couldn't speak.

"Relax, you're doing extremely well. I'm delighted to have you work alongside me. It's time to start believing in yourself again, Elizabeth."

I nodded shyly. He was right. What a relief. I could still afford to support my children.

"Throw out all nasty thoughts of the past, my dear. You have a great mind, you're a strong woman, and you will go far here."

They were the most important words I'd ever heard. My self-esteem had been pulverised by Mr Freeman and my husband.

"You have grasped the job well and you have an excellent accounting aptitude. I'm very impressed."

The warmth of his tone and what he'd just said were the best anti-depressants ever. The stars were shining down on me for once – I'd forgotten what it felt like to be valued.

"Thank you."

"It is you I must thank. The burden of those piles of files is no longer a headache for me. My last assistant died in a tragic motorcar accident, and I just haven't been able to get through the backlog since. Just look what we've managed to get through." He pointed to the table, which was almost clear. "Elizabeth, I have raised your salary now you've completed your probation. I hope it helps."

Shaken by the generosity, I wanted to weep. I held on, letting go on the way home as waves of relief and gratitude joined hands.

I sobbed all the way home.

Chapter Fourteen

Daily cash checks and balances, general bookkeeping, tallying columns of numbers, learning shorthand and all sorts of other accounting tasks kept me mentally stimulated. At last, I felt like a functioning human again. I looked more like one too! Flesh covered my elbows, knees and ribs.

A new part of my job was keeping a vigilant eye out for theft or any peculiar inconsistencies generally reflected in the daily cash takings. I oversaw new accounts and liaised with security in despatch. The variety was interesting and kept me on my toes. I'd been alerted that cleverly planned theft happened on a large scale in these big superstores. At first, it shocked me just how cunning some of the plans were, but Derek had taught me well. I became a vigilant accounting policeman and was thoroughly enjoying the investigative work.

I'd been working and living in Bloemfontein for four months before Amelia and I met again for a lunch date. She was horrified by what I'd been through, but delighted I'd finally moved away from Dion.

"Hey, how are you doing?" She hugged me.

"Loving life, at last."

We chatted for hours. I didn't want her to go. She was only in Bloemfontein temporarily. She was nursing and living in

Durban. She was not married, but in a relationship and blissfully happy.

"So, when are you getting married?" I asked Amelia.

"We haven't set a date yet, but we will. There's no rush. We thought sometime next year. Make sure you're there." She laughed happily.

"I'll have to bring the children too, but I'd love to visit before you get married."

"We'd love to have you, you know that. I haven't met Vivienne yet."

"I'm not sure my old 'skedonk' will get me to Durbs, but I'm willing to give it a go!" I laughed. "For now, I'll have to be satisfied with regular chats on the phone, won't I?"

"Yup, guess you will. Shame, Elizabeth, what a lot you've been through. I hope this new start gets you back on your feet. You don't need that swine back in your life. You know that now, don't you?"

I nodded. I had accepted I would never have the old Dion back.

My life continued much the same and I'd gained five kilograms. I was happy with my new life – six months had disappeared somewhere.

For a week I'd been investigating a discrepancy, one I'd been flummoxed by and couldn't seem to solve. The deeper I dug, the more complicated it became. It was time to pull Derek's sharp brain in on the problem. I'd been suspicious of despatch for a few weeks, but I couldn't pinpoint the ringleader.

"Is it possible for an Arabella four-piece lounge suite to disappear out of the store, along with two coffee tables and a stereo system without anybody noticing?" I asked Derek.

He looked up at me and said, "Oh, yes, anything's possible, dear. These people are masters at grand theft, you should know that." He smiled. "If they want something, they always find a way. Why? What have you found?"

"You know I've been suspicious that something is going on at despatch? Well, I think it's a bigger problem than I anticipated, and I need your help. It's looking more and more like a syndicate of thieves are at work down there. Look here."

I spread everything out on Derek's desk and showed him what I suspected, how I'd come to tie it all together and with the proof I was holding now, we could catch them at it. I'd been tipped off that a yellowwood dining room suite was ready to go out the door. Being lifted by the same group.

"I think you've cracked it." He beamed. "Well done."

"Yes, but there are some issues I need you to check through to make certain."

He grinned and soon we were both utterly absorbed by the process of piecing the puzzle of an enormous furniture theft operation costing the company thousands.

We were so engrossed in tracing the leads, neither of us noticed Dion standing at the door of the office watching us. He made his presence felt by coughing, and I looked up, straight into the monster's angry eyes. What jolted me was how frightened I was at seeing him again and, in seconds, my inner peace was blasted to smithereens.

How had he known where to find me?

Derek was about to ask if he could help when Dion spun around and stormed out of the office.

"Who on earth was that?" Derek asked, then noticed I'd gone as white as a sheet. He understood in an instant. "Was that your husband? You look petrified, my dear."

"I am petrified. How the hell did he find me?" My hands were shaking so violently I couldn't hold my pen.

"That is not a normal reaction, my dear. You've been through more than you've let on, haven't you?" Derek was clearly concerned. "Let's take a break, have some lunch, and we'll get back to this later."

"No!" I said too sharply and with too much emphasis. "I'll go on here. I'm not hungry."

Derek's expression said it all. "Do you want to go home? Collect the kids and bring them here? What do you want to do?"

"I'm not sure, but seeing him has really shaken me."

"I can see that. Shall I make some coffee?"

I didn't want to go home in case he followed me. The cottage was my sanctuary.

"I'd love some coffee. Thank you, Derek. Maybe chuck some whiskey in it." I tried a little humour.

Derek turned and winked at me. Perhaps he thought whiskey was a good idea too.

Before I left work, I thought it prudent to call Miriam and find out if she'd noticed any strange cars passing slowly by the cottage or going up and down the road. She'd not noticed anything suspicious at home, thank God. I scrutinised the car park before I left the office, then drove all over town, making sure Dion wasn't following me before I headed home.

Chapter Fifteen

The following morning Dion was waiting in the car park at the office. I wanted to turn around and go, but to where?

I parked as close to the office door as I could, switched off the engine, gathered my bag and headed for the office door at speed.

"We have to talk!" he bellowed after me.

I walked faster and put my head down. I knew I couldn't avoid the confrontation, but I wasn't ready, even though he appeared calmer than the day before. Dion was catching up to me as I looked back, and with relief I noticed Derek pulling into the car park.

"When can we talk, Elizabeth?" Dion asked, as I ran through the foyer and jumped into the lift.

The doors closed before Dion could get in with me. However, as the lift doors opened on the third floor, he was standing in front of me.

"I'm not ready to talk to you, Dion. Please leave," I said as Derek stepped out of the lift.

"Leave her alone please," Derek asked Dion politely, but Dion's response was far from polite.

"Fuck you, old man! This is my wife. She ran away from me, and we need to talk."

"I believe she ran away for a good reason," Derek said, standing his ground. He'd taken an instant dislike to Dion. "Can't you see she's terrified of you?"

Derek stood in front of Dion as he spoke, then he turned to me and guided me towards the office door.

"Come on, Elizabeth, let's get to work."

"Who the hell are you to protect her? Her new lover?"

Derek stopped and turned to face Dion once more. "Oh, grow up, young man." He guided me inside his office and closed the door.

Later that morning, Dion phoned. He wanted to meet at Wimpy for an early supper. He wanted to see *his girls*. It wasn't something I could go on denying him even though he paid nothing towards their keep.

"Yes, yeah, um…" I stuttered. "Okay, we'll meet you at 5.30 p.m." I put the phone down to guarantee no more conversation.

I left work early, picked up the girls and told Storm we were meeting Papa at the Wimpy. Although Storm was a bit hesitant at first, she was happy to see her father. Vivienne was indifferent. She was too young and she didn't know who Dion was anyway.

After we'd ordered, Dion explained some of what had gone down in Bethlehem. How much truth was in his story, I wasn't sure, apart from the "being fired and always drunk" bit. That I knew to be the truth. A little later, he asked why I had ordered his removal from the hospital. It was an awkward evening, and I could see Storm getting agitated. I didn't want to regurgitate the terrifying visions I'd had while almost dying. He didn't need to know that now.

"Thanks for supper. We'll get going now and please don't follow me. I'd prefer you didn't know where we live. If you want to see the children, we can meet once a month in a neutral place like this."

"Once a month? That's a bit unfair, Elizabeth."

"No, it's not unfair, Dion. If you were not so attached to alcohol and bullshitting people, your children would be living with you and so would I. You haven't made any effort to contribute to their living expenses either. It's been seven months, Dion."

He raised his eyebrows and, for once, he managed to contain himself as the waitress put the bill down in front of him. I left him to pay, we said our goodbyes and left.

Not trusting that he wouldn't follow, I drove around the streets again before heading home, being advised by Storm that I was going the wrong way. Her comment made me smile; her observation, even at night, impressed me.

Dion's arrival back in Bloemfontein rattled me more than I wanted to admit. Sitting beside Derek at work the following day, my concentration span kept fading in and out. All I could think about was how our security had been compromised by Dion finding us.

"How did your Wimpy supper meeting go?"

"Without a hitch, amazingly. It got a bit uncomfortable when he asked about the hospital, so I never answered. Storm was happy to see her father, but she got a bit agitated when he started questioning me, so we left soon after we'd eaten." I paused and looked at Derek. "His return to Bloem has rattled me. I'm more afraid of him than I realised."

"I can see that, Elizabeth." He'd been watching me struggle to focus.

"I'm sorry. It's all so confusing. I can't make sense of my feelings. I know I'm scared, but there's more. I didn't ask for a divorce last night because I know I'll have to pay. Supporting two children, I don't have the money for that and a new car. And, of course, discussing divorce in front of Storm wouldn't have been fair. Even though she's little, her ears miss nothing."

"Give yourself time, my dear. You have your own life now, don't forget that. So, live it."

I couldn't afford to make any changes quickly anyway. I shoved Dion out of my mind and got back to focussing on finding another sort of criminal.

Later that day, we stumbled upon the weak link in the chain; we found it in "Receiving". We'd broken the syndicate that had been going on for months. It was a terrific feeling. Perhaps I should have been in forensics.

The police were to make the arrests of seven staff members. Later in the week, they were released on bail and attended the company disciplinary hearing. The careful attention I'd paid to bringing an end to the syndicate earned me a bonus big enough to put a fifty percent deposit down on a new car and I very sadly traded the little old Datsun "skedonk" in. I never thought I'd be so sad to say goodbye to a motorcar!

Chapter Sixteen

I never did ascertain how Dion discovered where I worked. I never bothered to ask. The fact was he'd found me. Besides, he knew Bloemfontein better than most people. I was an idiot thinking he wouldn't eventually locate the cottage either and I had to remind myself we were still married. In the eyes of the law he had a biological right to get to know his second daughter and see them both. What he didn't know was I'd invested in a new car. All I could hope for was it would throw him off of our trail for a little while giving me much needed reprieve.

Dion called the office a few times asking me out for dinner, but I refused the invitations, then he called and asked if he could take Storm to a movie.

"She's too young to sit through a whole movie, Dion."

"It's the new Walt Disney flick, *The Aristocats*. She'd love it. Come on, let up, Elizabeth."

I finally agreed to let Storm go. She approved enthusiastically, but I insisted on chaperoning her and arranged with Miriam to take care of Vivienne. Storm loved the movie, and I did too. Who wouldn't? Towards the end, I could see Storm was ready for bed.

"Next time, only the afternoon shows. She has nursery school in the morning."

He nodded. "Would you like to come to my place tomorrow? I'd like to see Vivienne, and perhaps we can have a chat over some lunch."

I stood looking at him in disbelief and before I found an appropriate answer, Storm interrupted.

"Yes, Mama, can we go to Papa's house please?"

I looked down at her, not knowing whether to agree or not, fully aware I couldn't deprive the girls from seeing their father now he was back living in Bloemfontein. He was trying to extend the olive branch. It was me being bristly; he knew where I worked and he now knew about my new car. It wouldn't be long, and he'd know where we lived too.

"Okay. We must get home now. Miriam needs to get home."

Storm kissed her papa goodbye, waving to him as we set off.

Over the following weeks, things went surprisingly well. Storm kept talking about the movie and how she wanted to play the piano again.

"When's Papa coming here?" she asked one night while sitting cross-legged on the kitchen counter next to me as I peeled potatoes.

"I don't know, my precious. I haven't spoken to Papa for a few days."

"Why, Mama?" she asked, pressing her mouth onto the top of her knee, her legs tucked under her pyjama-clad bottom, and I couldn't help marvelling at the way children possess such a unique way of making *everything* seem so simple.

"Well, Papa has got to be a good papa. He must stop getting drunk before I let him come here. We don't want any trouble now, do we?"

She shook her head, but kept her mouth pressed against the top of her knee while she processed, in her innocent mind, what I had just said.

"Are we having chippies and tomato ketchup for supper?" she suddenly asked.

"Yes, we are. With fish and veg too." I pinched her cheek affectionately.

"Yay, yummy! I love chippies. Will the fish be fish fingers?"

"Yes, sweetheart. Your favourite."

After we'd eaten and I'd put the girls to bed, I sat thinking about how I was going to deal with Dion.

We'd been purposefully avoiding the topic of divorce. Friendship was okay for me. As far as I knew, he still wasn't aware of where we lived. I'd collected some of my clothing and personal effects from his house. I told him I'd get the rest later. That should have made it clear I had no intention of going back, though he'd mentioned he wanted our marriage to continue.

For months, Dion carefully guided me towards that place where he knew the doubt would end. One thing he hadn't considered – I knew him well enough now to know all his games. I wasn't going to fall for his lies or gentle manipulations. We'd sorted out a few differences; he was paying towards the children's expenses now, picking up the tab for Storm's schooling too. There was no doubt the fantastic Dion, personality number one, was back; only I knew it was a temporary measure.

I was amazed to hear the band was still going. The Rogues were hugely popular in Bloemfontein. I wondered whether he had done enough genuine work on himself to turn over a new leaf, or was this just Act 1, Scene 3? He'd said the alcohol poisoning, being fired, losing me and not knowing Vivienne had shattered him, but Dion du Toit had a short memory.

I drifted off to sleep on the couch and woke around three in the morning with a stiff neck and a sore back, and though I climbed into bed, I couldn't get back to sleep. I had a shower instead and got on with the usual morning routine and got to the office half an hour early. It was 6.38 a.m. when I sat down at my desk after making my regular cup of coffee. Staring into space, sipping on the coffee, inhaling the scent of a rich Kenyan roast, which I'd sprinkled with chocolate powder, the phone ringing shattered the blissful silence.

There seemed to be an urgency to its ring and given the week I'd just gone through, I wondered whether more accounting forensics was on the cards. Then I heard William's distraught voice as I put the receiver to my ear.

Chapter Seventeen

"Mom was attacked on the farm last night. It's bad, sis. I'm worried she's not going to make it." William's words echoed down the line, shattering my world. Losing my mother… it didn't seem possible.

"Oh God, who would want to attack Mom? Where is she, boetie? What happened?" I asked all at once in crushed disbelief.

"She's in theatre right now, sis. I'm at the police station. Err… sorry, sis, hang on."

I could hear him talking to the cops in the background.

"Aagh, sorry, sis, questions to answer for the police. Um, let me call back in a few minutes. Hang in there."

He put the phone down and my whole body began to shake as my thoughts whirled in panicky chaos.

Who would want to attack an elderly woman and nearly kill her? Everyone loved her; all the farm staff adored her. None of this made sense.

Trying to gather my thoughts and calm myself, I went on sipping my coffee and waited for William to call back. The waiting didn't last long, thank goodness.

"Hi." I snatched the receiver after one ring. "Tell me she's going to live, boetie." My voice was quivering with emotion; no amount of deep breathing could waylay the fears that we might lose our beloved mother.

"Daan is with her in theatre. All we can do now is pray, sis."

"In theatre?" I repeated, struggling to comprehend this ghastly news. "Oh my God, William, what have they done to her?"

Revenge and hatred became genuine parts of my helpless feelings in that moment, surging through me like a runaway veld fire burning in my chest, spreading quickly to my gut, turning it into red hot grief as William explained.

"She was badly beaten up, sis. Torn to pieces and God knows what else." I could hear the restrained anger in my brother's voice. "Mom couldn't talk much during the journey to the hospital. It was one man who attacked her in the orchard after she'd closed the store. Can you get time off work and get to the hospital?"

"Yes, of course, give me an hour. Where shall I meet you?" Panic was still surging through me.

"In the main foyer, sis. Mom will be in theatre for a while yet."

A while yet! Oh God, the hour hand had just passed seven o'clock when I put the phone down and raced through to Derek's office, praying he'd got into the office early.

"God, if you're there, keep Mom alive please," I begged aloud, quickly putting my hands together and looking up to an invisible source, then ran upstairs, half-knocked then pushed Derek's office door open at the same time. He glanced at me with a stunned look on his face as I barged in.

"What's the—" He looked up at my grey-white face. "Not that bastard husband of yours?"

"No, it's my mom. She was brutally attacked on the farm last night. She's in theatre. Please, can I go?"

"Oh, I'm so sorry, my dear. Yes, of course. Let me know if there's anything I can do."

"Thank you. I'll keep you posted," I said as I turned and disappeared down the stairs to my office and called Dion. He'd have to take care of the girls for the next two days. I had no other option. They had friends from school, but I didn't know their parents well. I raced home.

A year earlier, William and Mom had swopped houses. William's growing family needed the more significant farmhouse, the one we'd all grown up in; the cottage was too small.

Mom had been living in a sizeable, four-bedroomed rambling farmhouse, with a wrap-around veranda where William and I used to play endless games as children and where Mom had rattled around in alone for too long, being haunted by memories of our father in every room. It was pointless her living there. Moving her to the cottage had been the most obvious thing to do, and she was happy to move. The main house was also conveniently situated next to all the farm outbuildings, the office and sheds. The swop made William's life easier.

Mom loved the cottage. It was the perfect little retreat for her, but I doubted she would want to live there on her own after this. That thought ripped into my heart; the farm was her life. She was connected to it, not only because she'd farmed it herself for so many years, but my father and brother had been buried in the garden – a special remembrance corner surrounded by banks of white Iceberg roses and agapanthus. So many memories kept flooding into my thoughts as I raced around, trying to arrange my day so I could get to the hospital quickly.

I remembered how Mom had pestered William about running the farm store. She bothered him for months, telling him she was bored.

"I'll grow old fat with nothing to do," she'd moaned. It was so like her, always needing to be busy.

The thought of sitting on the veranda all day watching the birds on the dam, reading, knitting or crocheting would have driven her scatty. Retirement was not a part of her vocabulary, so William gave in, and she started her "job", serving the staff twice a day, opening the little store at nine for an hour and again at four in the afternoon.

One of her favourite little sayings when we were young and doing nothing other than irritating her was: "the devil makes work for idle hands", and she'd put us to work. Even at the age of sixty-seven, she couldn't sit still for long despite her gammy foot, but now, due to some evil, ill-gotten person, she lay critically injured in the theatre, being stitched together by miracle workers. It still seemed hardly possible.

I parked, grabbed my bag and ran across the car park to the front of the hospital, pushed the doors open and saw William. His face was grey and suddenly years older. He was pacing up and down the foyer.

"Oh, boetie," I cried as I hugged him. "Have you heard anything more?"

"It's shocking, sis," he kept repeating. William rarely lost control of his emotions, but I could see he was struggling to keep it all together now.

"Let's sit down."

We sat on two comfortable armchairs, away from the mainstream of visitors. William began to explain what he knew of the attack.

"I shall never forget the desperate expression on Mom's face as our eyes met when I opened the bedroom curtains. That look will haunt me forever, sis."

He pulled a handkerchief out of his pocket and wiped his eyes and his brow. The memory, then the anger and helplessness, brought bubbles of perspiration to his forehead.

"I ran from our room like I'd never run before, screaming to Bessie to phone Daan and arrange for a team to meet us at the emergency entrance of the hospital. Mom was so weak when I got to her, I thought we'd lost her then, but she hung on. Adrenaline had taken over my body. I picked her up and got her into the car."

He paused for a moment as he looked at me. Mom was not much more than a few kilograms overweight, but she was a large-boned woman and quite tall. She probably weighed about eighty kilograms.

"She's tough, sis." He shook his head sadly, as he recounted those moments. "Bessie kept her awake by talking to her, asking what had happened. Her speech had been affected by endless screaming and she kept fading in and out of consciousness. Bessie made her sip on warm water throughout the journey. I drove like a man possessed. It was the worst journey ever. I was literally racing against time." William was shaking as he took another swig of lukewarm coffee.

"The police have been fantastic. They got hold of the army, and troops and trackers were deployed soon after Bessie called, but you can imagine how far Mom's attacker would have got with her bakkie (truck) from six o'clock in the evening to three in the morning when she got us. A helicopter went out at first light too. We'll catch the bastard, that's for sure." William nodded with grim determination.

"Shit, first light? How long have you been here?"

"It's been a long night, sis. A very long night. We got to the hospital somewhere around four thirty. Daan was waiting with a team of trauma nurses, and they raced Mom to theatre. Once she was there, Bessie and I went to admin to deal with the wheels of bureaucracy, you know how it is. Then I raced back to the police station to make the full report. That's when I called you. I was there for what seemed like hours. Because the attack took place out of their jurisdiction, everything had to be confirmed with the Brandfort Police first." William glanced down at his watch. "They should have finished with Mom by now. Let's head up to the theatre."

"Where's Bessie?" I asked William as we got into the lift.

"In town. She's gone to get Mom all her favourite lotions and little treats. I think this is all too much for her, to be honest. You know how sensitive she is. She's probably with Martha now. She'll need the comfort of her best friend for a while. She's been courageous and handled the situation with remarkable calm. I'm so proud of her. She'll be back shortly."

As we approached the entrance to the theatre, Doctor Daan Fouche was pushing through the swing doors, looking exhausted. He was followed by a team of doctors we didn't know, each wearing dire expressions. One glance at Daan's face and I feared the worst.

"A whole team of doctors?" I heaved as I held William's arm.

Daan came towards us, separating himself from the other doctors, waving his thanks as they went on their way and came to stand next to us.

"How your mother is still alive is a miracle," he began. "I've seen some pretty awful stuff in theatre before but seeing what only one savage can do to an innocent elderly lady, someone whom I have known all my life, being torn apart so brutally, was very hard. Looking at her under the scrutiny of blazing white theatre lights made it even more shocking. The cruelty of her wounds made every one of us in theatre weep."

The only words that penetrated my brain in that fleeting moment were the words "still alive"; the rest began to sink in as I looked at Daan's shattered, exhausted face. I knew how bad it was if Daan needed the assistance of a team of specialists to help him save her life.

Daan put his hand on William's shoulder and shook it with affectionate reassurance. They were great friends. I could see the unspoken gratitude William felt for Daan's commitment to saving the life of our mom; a woman he'd known since he was a small boy. Having Daan look after Mom helped ease our fears.

"What are her chances of survival, Daan?" William asked, his chin quivering, just managing to hold on to the last bits of self-control.

"Look, boet, she's badly injured, as you know. She lost a shit load of blood, her pulse was racing towards an early grave and there was serious internal haemorrhaging. However, she's stable now, thanks to the team. If she gets through the next twenty-four hours, she should live."

"Was she raped too?" I asked, horrified. William hadn't mentioned that part to me; no wonder he'd turned grey with vengeance.

"I'm afraid so. Two or three times, with the most brutal results I've ever seen."

I noticed Daan swallowing hard as he looked away. Grief and exhaustion were rapidly setting in after three and a half hours in theatre piecing Mom together.

"How the hell she managed to walk about three or four kilometres in her condition, only God knows. They bred them tough in her day." Daan took a deep breath. "Nobody deserves this, least of all your special mother. I'll keep a close eye on her. I'm sure she's still fighting the man off in her anaesthetised sleep. I must warn you, her wrists will carry the scars for life. I struggled to stitch such thin, fragile skin on the inside of her wrists." Daan paused again. "Listen, I must be off, if you'll excuse me."

William and I headed down to the intensive care unit in silence, each dealing with our own torn thoughts.

"I'm perfectly sure Mom won't give a shit about the wrist scars," William said.

I knew it was his way of managing the hell that was playing out in his mind. I let go of a small smile. An inconsequential statement to help suppress his emotion. My nursing instincts, on the other hand, had taken over my mind, temporarily blotting out the emotional trauma. My immediate worry was septicaemia and pneumonia, now that my brain had registered she was still alive.

"Our poor, precious mother. A dangerous, life-threatening, tormenting ordeal." A sob of relief broke.

William put his arms around my shoulders protectively. We stood there for some time just holding each other. Then I felt another set of arms surround me. It was Bessie. I turned and we hugged, then we sobbed. She'd already shed many tears.

"Has Ma come out of the theatre?"

William and I nodded.

"Have they said how long she'll be in ICU?"

"No, not yet. Probably the next two or three days. I'm going to stay with her, boetie. Mom needs someone near when she comes around."

"Will you get time off work?"

"Yes, Derek said I can take off as much time as I need."

"That's great. Jesus Christ, sis, but what about the girls? Who's going to look after them?"

"Dion has agreed to take care of them."

William's eyes hooded suddenly, like an eagle focussed on its prey. The very mention of Dion's name made his hair curl. I left it there.

William changed the subject. "Well, I won't stop till we catch that son of a bitch, but Bessie and I need to head home now, sis. We'll be back tomorrow afternoon. Keep us in the loop if there are any changes, either way."

William reached forwards and kissed me goodbye, then I stepped into the ICU wards.

Mom was lying silently in her cot. There were pipes leading in and out of every orifice, connecting her to life support machines. Her face, what little peeped out from the bandages, was covered in maddening bruises, swollen beyond recognition. Her hands and arms were also wrapped in bandages while the buzz of the heart monitor reassured me she was still fighting. I gently touched her ice cold, motionless fingertips that peeked out from the bandaging.

Mom had always taught us never to hate anyone, but looking at her, lying broken and fragile, I couldn't help hating the person who'd done this to her and for now, I didn't deny myself that emotion. I needed to feel it to deal with my grief and fury. Mercifully drugged from the anaesthetic and other medicines, I knew she might not hear my whispers, but I said what I needed to.

"We love you, Mom." My whispers were strained with emotion.

She was going to be asleep for a long time, so there was no need for me to stay at her bedside now. I shot home to gather up what I needed for a twenty-four-hour vigilant stint at the hospital, or until I knew Mom was out of danger.

When I got home and told Miriam, she was shattered.

"Oh, my missus, oh, my missus, ay, ay, ay," she kept saying, repeatedly apologising in her humble way.

I shoved my book, toothpaste and brush, hand cream, cosmetics, a flask of coffee and some biscuits into a carry bag, and gave Miriam instructions and a quick hug. Even then she begged me not to allow Dion to take Vivienne and Storm for the night.

"I will sleep here, missus. I'll take care of *my* babies."

I nodded, wondering how I was going to explain that to Dion. Miriam's suggestion made perfect sense, so I called Dion before going back to the hospital.

"I'm so sorry, liefie," he offered as he answered the phone.

I quickly informed him that Miriam was staying over and would take care of the children. As I suspected, it didn't go down well. He insisted on staying with them in my cottage.

"Sorry, Dion. Collect them from school. They can sleep at your place. I'll drop Miriam there to look after them."

I stayed at Mom's bedside for the rest of the day and throughout the night. Caffeine and anxiety were an excellent combination to keep me awake. Just after seven that evening, Mom stirred for the first time. I took her bandaged hand in mine and whispered to her gently. There was a faint movement on her lips as if she was trying to smile and she moved her fingertips, acknowledging she'd heard me, then she disappeared back into the beautiful, deep, drug-induced, healing sleep she'd been in for hours. I was happy. It was the confirmation I needed. She was going to fight through this – she would survive.

I slipped out of the room, popped downstairs to the public phone and called Dion.

"How's everything going?" I asked.

"Fine, the girls are as delightful as ever. Miriam made us supper. How's your mom?"

"A few minutes ago, she half-woke, acknowledged my presence by moving her fingers in my hand and slipped back into a deep sleep. It's such a relief."

"That's great news. Are you still staying next to her the whole night?"

"Yes. I want to be here when she wakes fully. It'll make all the difference to her."

"I'm sure it will. I'll get the girls off to bed shortly. They insisted Miriam sleep in the room with them."

I laughed. That would not have impressed him much.

"Call me at the office if there's anything I can do."

I suspected he would use this tragedy to try to lure me back. After speaking to Dion, I called William.

"Hi, good news. I'm sure Mom will be off the critical list by morning. She responded to my voice by trying to squeeze my hand."

"Thank God. That's wonderful, sis, and thank you for being there with her."

Mom stirred again at around 1 a.m. This time she was far more lucid, but with it came the reality of her pain, and she groaned. I felt every part of her pain shoot through me too. It wasn't much more than a minute or two before she was asleep again, a perfect time for me to put my head down in the family room and catch up on some sleep.

When I got back to her, she was awake. The facial swelling and bruising was awful and her eyes reflected the pain she was suffering. I tried not to show my own shock and pain. Instead, I smiled at her affectionately grasping her fingers. I leant over her, gently kissing her bandaged forehead. Then she tried to sit up, but excruciating pain distorted her face and she fell back on her pillow.

"Don't move, Mom," I said, and propped the pillow up to support her head. "Just rest."

Wanting to sit up and get herself more comfortable was a celebratory sign for me – I felt she'd passed the critical stage. For Mom, it was a horrid realisation of the pain she'd have to cope with over the next weeks, but I knew her determination to live would win the battle. She'd not come out of this unscathed on many levels. She'd handle it in her own time and in her own private way, just as she did after losing Papa. She'd reject any form of sympathy and get on with life. Being treated like a victim would hurt her more. It was going to take the courage of a lion to come through this trauma and the visible scars that were so savagely engraved on her inner thighs and wrists would be a life-long memory she didn't deserve.

When William and Bessie arrived, I escaped home, exhausted, picking up Miriam on the way. Dion had gone to work and was collecting the girls. When I woke the next morning, he was standing beside my bed holding Vivienne on his hip and Storm was standing beside him ready for school.

It took me a moment to process. I couldn't believe what I was seeing. For a moment I thought I was in another nightmare, like I'd been in at the hospital after giving birth to Vivienne. Rubbing my eyes, I sat up and kissed Storm goodbye while Dion tucked Vivienne into the other side of my bed. With Storm standing by I couldn't say anything, but I was seething. Had Storm given her father the address?

"Can we see Ouma?" Storm asked before they left.

"No, my precious, you can't see her yet. As soon as she is stronger, I will take you to see her, I promise. Have a good day at school. I'll fetch you later."

"Mommy, are you home tonight?" Storm asked quickly.

"Yes, I am, darling," I reassured her, and she sighed with apparent relief, which left me wondering what was going on in her little mind. I'd find out later.

Mom's injuries were worse than any of us could comprehend. No wonder Daan had looked like he'd been hit by a bull elephant when he emerged from theatre. Only she knew the unspeakable extent of what had been done to her while we struggled to fight off the demons of revenge, especially when we learnt from her the despicable horrors of the attack. She recounted the attack a few weeks later.

"Mom, you don't have to go through it all."

"Yes, I do, my child. It's my form of therapy." She went on to explain the whole grizzly experience.

The little farm shop was not far for Mom to limp across to in the morning, supported by her walking stick, then back again in the afternoon. It kept her fit and was a place of happy social gathering for the staff, their children and Mom. She'd been generously doing this for the past year. The shop's existence was purely for the convenience of the farm staff, stocking only the fundamental grocery requirements: sweets, cigarettes, tobacco, matches, tea, sugar, bread, a few tinned foods like sardines and tomato relish, bath soap and washing powder. The farm provided the staff with free maize meals (their staple diet), dried beans and salt. The nearest shops were thirty kilometres away, so William's truck shipped the staff into town once a month for their other needs.

Mom treasured the time at the shop. The staff were always proud to introduce her to any new born babies and she loved that. They all adored Mom. Many of them even called her "Ouma" (Afrikaans for grandmother) they'd been working and living on the farm that long.

She sat more upright and held my hand.

"I'd locked the shop at 5.30 p.m.," she began. "I popped the keys and the cash in my apron pocket and set off home. It was always a slow walk, hampered by my blasted stupid foot."

She put her head back on the pillow and closed her eyes; the memories rushing back. I sat silently apprehensive.

The pathway from the shop led straight to the back door of her cottage, passing the entrance to her vegetable garden. A few shallow steps led into the hallway where a key rack hung conveniently above the shoe store cum walking stick stand Mom was so dependent upon. Off to the right was the kitchen, to the left two large comfortable bedrooms down a short passage. Her bedroom had an en suite. Straight ahead was the spacious sitting room, fronted by huge glass sliding doors that lead onto the patio where she sat in the evenings watching the sun go down. She loved listening to, and viewing through her binoculars, the birds on the dam bathing and taking in water for the night. Mom was an avid birder and always noted any new species arriving at the dam. The dining room led off of the sitting room and joined the kitchen.

Mom's routine was probably her downfall in this instance. William and I agreed her attacker must have been monitoring her routine for some days before he made his move. It is said that things always happen for a reason. Walking to and from the shop had kept her fit, and it was her physical fitness that ultimately saved her life.

Mom looked at me with a tiny grin. "Remember the lovely early ripening peach tree I planted years back?"

"Yes, I do, and they're still the best peaches I've ever tasted."

"Well, I'd noticed a couple of tiny peaches appearing on the tree and went to check they weren't being stung. I couldn't wait for them to ripen. Then I picked some carrots to put in my stew. Thank goodness, I hadn't started the stew, or the cottage would have burnt down."

The evening breezes and the endless bird song relaxed her tired shoulders after the difficult walk back from the store. Normally, after an early supper, she'd put her feet up and watch the sunset, soaking up the sounds of approaching nightfall. She did this every evening without fail.

"I was in the vegetable garden. I'd put my stick down beside me and had the wicker basket over my arm. I had pulled down one of the branches that was laden with baby peaches and noticed there was no insect damage yet, but I also wondered how many the birds would leave me." Mom tried to smile again, but it was still too painful to do anything other than grimace.

"Suddenly, I was grabbed from behind and wrenched to the ground. Dazed and caught off guard, I wasn't sure what the hell was happening, but it quickly became abundantly clear the danger I was in when I hit the ground. I was winded and gasping to get my breath back when I caught a whiff of stale wood smoke and dirty, old, masculine sweat. My skin crawled, and the smell alerted a primal instinct to come to my aid in the form of adrenaline.

"The situation was serious. I reached out for my stick and scooped up a handful of sand, which I tossed as hard as I could into his eyes as he stooped over me. Then I swung my walking stick, striking out at his shins, but, of course, it made no difference. I don't even think he felt it, but he responded like lightning to my unexpected fight for survival. Scrawny, nimble and absurdly strong, he hauled me back onto my feet and grabbed my hands, then he bound them together with old rusty barbed wire. I was still trying to get my breath back."

Mom shook her head, closed her eyes and took a breath. When she opened her eyes, she looked long and hard at me. I didn't know what she was thinking, and I didn't want to ask. She went on with her very distressing tale.

"I let go some almighty screams and went on screaming at the top of my voice while I struggled and prayed Ester or someone would hear my desperate cries." Mom started shaking.

"Mom, you don't have to go on."

She ignored me. "I didn't realise it then, but luckily, he'd bound my hands in front of me, not behind my back, but either way, the barbs dug painfully into my wrists and tore the skin. Daan says I will have terrible scars on my wrists now."

I nodded.

"I remember wondering why he was tying my hands in front of me. Later, I realised what a stroke of luck that was. Standing as close as he was to me, he reeked. His breath was the most revolting smell I'd ever smelt. Rotting, putrid, decaying on the inside... I wanted to vomit."

Mom swallowed furiously, remembering the vile smell.

"I glared at him, looking directly into his yellowed, evil eyes, stained from years of living in a smoky hut, drinking disgusting homemade alcohol and smoking dope. I put both my hands out in front of me and tried to push him away, but he blocked my feeble attempt while casually rubbing sand out of his eyes. I was no match for him. He knew it and he taunted me. Then, without warning, he swung his fist into my chest and I fell hard. Without my hands and arms to slow the impact of the fall, my head hit the ground then snapped forwards with such force I bit into my tongue and blacked out." She stuck her tongue out for me to see the damage.

I reached for some water.

"I'd lost my stick by then. My eyes were full of tears from the fall and biting my tongue, which hurt like hell, and I was swallowing blood while trying to get my breath back. I screamed again, a shrill, blood-curdling liquid yell, but the sounds got lost on the breeze."

I had already gathered that the middle-aged black scoundrel had every advantage over Mom. Half of me wasn't sure I wanted to hear the rest, but I knew it was important to let Mom purge herself of what plagued her. Talking this way, in private, just her and I, was her way of clearing the toxins from her system.

"The evil urchin began tearing my clothing, and I kept ripping my vocal cords till I was hoarse. My throat was burning by then. Then he stood over me dominating my helpless form on the ground. I tried to manoeuvre myself away, hitting out at his legs with my bound hands. The barbs caught on his trouser leg, ripping the filth-engrained, ancient fabric."

Mom shuddered, but I could hear the anger in her voice. Gravely handicapped, the sudden exertion must have tired her quickly, even though I imagined the massive injection of adrenaline pumping through her veins would have helped, but not enough.

"He was looking down at me as he stood over me. He had a triumphant look on his face. He straddled my body and started making weird, mumbling sounds like he was in a trance. Revolting strings of saliva trailed down his chin and dropped on my chest. It was repulsive, but I couldn't move. I was trapped between his legs. I yelled at him to let me go."

Mom stopped talking and began to sob, deep ribcage-rattling sobs. I stood up and held her.

"Mom, don't go on." She was so tormented by the memories. I passed her the box of tissues.

"Oh, my child, I have to go on. I have to tell you, then I can bury the attack forever."

"Okay, Ma, as you wish. Can I get you something nice and warm to drink first?"

"That would be lekker (nice)."

I popped out and brought back a cup of hot chocolate for us both. It was all frothy on the top and chocolate powder had been sprinkled over the froth. The first mouthful was delicious. The comforting drink soothed her, and she went on.

"This is the worse part. Panic and horror paralysed me, and I screamed, 'Nee! Nee! Nee!' I was yelling for my life when I realised his intentions." She reached out and held my arm. Her body was shaking. "I kept screaming at him to leave me alone, begging him not to hurt me. It made no difference. I was sure I was about to die a terrible death in the orchard."

The colour had drained from Mom's face. She took another long sip of the hot chocolate. Tears, which had already made a pathway over her swollen cheeks, kept on rolling down.

"He was grinning at me. Can you think of anything more terrifying? Disgusting spittle began pouring out his mouth again. He was relishing the fact that he was in full control of me."

I knew what was next and my poor mother was being so brave reliving it.

"He was crazy, rabid with disease, the most repulsive creature I'd ever laid eyes on." Mom squeezed her eyes closed, she could scarcely breath. "Then he began struggling with the zipper on his torn, filthy trousers. I didn't stop screaming."

She coughed and cleared her throat, thinking back to that moment. "My throat was sore from screaming. The metallic taste of blood, fear and helplessness had dried the inside of my mouth. I wasn't sure how much longer I could endure the torture."

I was gripping Mom's hand while her body quivered.

"A weird, wounded sound rose from somewhere deep within me when I saw his huge erect penis protrude through the opening in his trousers. 'Neeeeeeeee,' I bellowed, then I felt him savagely rip into me, grunting viciously as my screams faded into deep, mournful cries of pain and humiliation. As quickly as the rape happened, it was mercifully over. Will I ever not be haunted by that?"

"Oh... my... God," I wheezed.

My poor mother. Tears were tumbling down my cheeks like rivers as she released her suffering. I was shattered by her recollection of such violence. She wanted to go on, but I wasn't sure I could listen to any more. I suggested she finish the story another day. She shook her head vigorously; she needed to go on to get rid of the demons. Watching the raw pain engraved on her face was one of the hardest things I had ever witnessed, especially from someone so dear to me. My internal rage was hard to suppress. I wondered how much of this William and Bessie knew about. Savagely raped, with her hands bound with rusty barbed wire, at sixty-seven. Nobody should ever have to endure that. Unspeakable things on what I would do with the man if I caught him overwhelmed me.

Mom finished her drink and lay back. The shivering slowly began to subside. Would she ever really get over it? I doubted it. Just then, one of the nurses popped her head around the door and asked if everything was okay. I nodded, but I asked for a sedative. Mom promptly turned it down, saying she needed to finish the story of her horrific ordeal first, then she might take a sedative. Was there still more she had to endure?

"Thank God, my skirt was still on. It saved my butt from being grazed to pieces." Mom even had the grace to flicker a tiny smile that creased the sides of her mouth as she said her skirt saved her butt. "I was dragged along the path, up the steps and dumped in the hall beside the walking stick stand."

The vision of my poor mother lying in a bloodied crumpled heap, dirtied and broken and unable to do a thing to help herself again stirred disturbing desires of what I wanted to do to the rapist. I got up and walked around.

"Mom, I'm just going to the loo," I said quickly and ran to the bathroom, slammed the toilet door and hurled into the toilet bowl.

Bile and hot chocolate were all that was in my stomach, and up it came. I splashed water on my face, swirled my mouth out and dried my face with a paper towel, then I went back to my mom. I sat down next to her and took her hand.

"He started shouting at me, demanding to know where I'd hidden the shop money and he wanted my gun. He'd already ripped all the keys off the key rack and emptied them into his pockets and took off, running through the house, shouting demands in Zulu: '*Nginike yona noma kufanele ngibulale wena!*' (Give it to me, or I will kill you.)

"When I heard the bastard speak Zulu I knew the nasty savage wasn't from our farm, or the district. It was a weird feeling of relief. I could never deal with it if it was one of our staff inflicting the cruelty he did. I could hardly talk by then and my teeth were chattering so fast. I couldn't control it, even clenching my jaw didn't help, but I know now it was shock. I could hear him smashing my precious collection of vases and ornaments that Papa had given me. I wanted to yell out, but he wouldn't have heard me. I sobbed some more."

Mom and I were both crying then. Every treasured piece Papa had given her was broken. Papa's loving energy had been attached to each precious piece, and now they were gone. Shattered into irreparable pieces.

"I prayed, child. Hell did I pray. I prayed that God would remove me from the onslaught, take me quickly. Save me from being subjected to more pain and humiliation. When he came back he kicked my side. I screamed, but little sound escaped. Then he said in English, 'You whities have all the money. *Imali, kuphi, kuphi?*' (Money, where, where?)

"I hoarsely replied in English, 'Because of evil thieves like you, us farmers don't keep cash in our houses.' It was a foolish thing to say, for it only made him angrier. I paid with a powerful punch to my jaw, and I wanted to die. But it wasn't over. My mind was numbed by the punch to the jaw. I heard it crack. Then he pushed me onto my back and searing pain stabbed my jaw and ribs, which were clearly cracked. He dropped onto his knees, one on either side of my broken body and it was then I prayed he would kill me. I couldn't take any more torture, but the swine raped me again, but this time it was more savage than the first.

"He began by tearing into my womanhood with his fingers, ripping at me with his pinkie fingernail: grown long and razor sharp. Then he tore at the skin of my inner thighs. It felt like a dog digging in the earth to uncover a hidden bone. Then he inserted himself into me. Mercifully, I passed out."

Oh my God, so that was the internal damage Daan had referred to when he said he had to do extensive internal stitching. My body was wet with sweat.

"Then he left me lying there in a pool of blood with my arms still bound and my wrists in shreds. I vaguely remember hearing the back door slam and my Toyota pick-up being crashed through the gears as he drove off at high speed. Part of me hoped

I'd die quickly, another part of me knew I desperately needed to get help. That part of the battle I conquered. If I hadn't got myself free of the rusty wire cuffs, Ester would have found me dead on the floor in the morning.

"I had no idea how to free myself of the barbed bondage that had already gouged through the flesh on both my wrists. There was no doubt I faced a horrible, slow death if I didn't free myself and get off the floor."

Mom was interrupted by the arrival of lunch: fish and chips with a side salad, which smelt really good. Besides, it was time for a break.

Miracles did happen, and though the emotion that filled me then was complicated, I was intrigued to find out how she'd got herself across to William's house. Once lunch was over, she explained.

"Luckily, the wire was ancient. I manoeuvred myself towards the walking stick stand, sobbing as I went, and hooked the wire over the decorative knob at the bottom of the stand and worried at it till the wire snapped. Thankfully, William had secured the unit to the wall. I pulled myself upright and felt a stream of hot sticky blood rush down the inside of my legs. I grabbed another stick and hobbled carefully to the phone: the line was dead.

"Very slowly I hobbled to the bathroom, plugged the basin and filled it with warm water, dropped in some Savlon antiseptic and attempted to clean up. The warm water was so soothing. Then I made myself a sanitary pad with a dry face cloth, which I folded over a wad of toilet paper, staggered to the chest of drawers and dug out a fresh pair of panties. By then I was exhausted. I sat on the edge of my bed and inched them up and placed the homemade sanitary pad inside my panties. I hoped this would absorb some of the blood, even stem the bleeding.

"Getting to William's house was my priority. Every bloodied inch of my body hurt. It took me ages trying to pull a light jacket on, knowing I'd need to keep warm as the night temperatures dropped. All I could think of was getting out of the house. I was scared the bastard would come back. Before I left my room, I looked around and wondered if I'd ever see it again." Mom's swollen bottom lip vibrated.

"I was so shaky, but when I got to the back door, I convinced myself I could make it across to William's house. I drank some sugar water and took three painkillers. Standing unsteadily with two walking sticks supporting me, I looked up at the approaching night sky and knew the cover of darkness would come quickly now. Without the guiding light of the moon, my walk to William's would be slower, but safer."

Attacker and victim shared the same road in and out, creating another challenging dilemma for Mom. No one else would be using that road; mercifully, she knew every inch of it. She set off, one precarious step at a time, supported by her sticks. She'd only gone about 400 metres down the road when she heard vehicle sounds far off in the distance, sounds she dreaded but expected, and another surge of adrenaline-filled energy came to her aid. Moving a few metres deeper into the long grass, and with agonising difficulty, she crouched down, praying the grassy spot was not going to be the place where she'd take her last breath. Hiding about ten metres off the edge of the road, he passed her. With immense relief, she realised she'd got herself just out of range of the headlights. He wasn't going to find her in the house, but on the return journey, he would be scouring the edges of the road looking for her. Shooting pain stabbed from every part of her battered body, but she forced herself to remain as still as possible. The silence of the night was startlingly loud as she listened.

It seemed to take forever before she heard her bakkie racing back towards where she hid, passing without the headlights exposing her. Driving at breakneck speed, he would never have located her hiding place, and as the sounds of the vehicle slowly died away, she allowed herself to sob deep pitiful sobs. Just as we were doing together now. I held her in my arms for a long time before she continued the tale of the longest night of her life.

"The sounds of the night were comforting melodies. Frogs croaked and insects chattered. It was the perfect musical ensemble I needed to hear. Even the nightjars called out to me, urging me on as I stumbled down the edge of the road leaving a bloody trail behind me. Blood had seeped through my homemade sanitary pad and was dribbling down the inside of my legs. The physical struggle was huge, and my prayers became pleas to end it all."

It was difficult, as her daughter, to listen to her say she prayed she would die.

"Do you remember that precious carved Swazi walking stick Henry gave me?" she asked.

"Yes, I do."

"It was that one I used the most because it's top was wider and gave my hand more support, but it got so stained from all the blood that had oozed from my wrists that William tossed it out. When Henry gave it to me, we wouldn't have known that one day it would save my life." She sighed.

"Dehydration had become a frightening companion and was another hindrance. Plus, fine sand from crouching down on the side of the road had stuck to the blood and wounds on my inner thighs and it had dried, creating a skin of living sandpaper that rubbed them even more raw than they were. Eventually, I could see the faint glimmer of the outside lights on the veranda of the old house and I knew my ordeal was nearly over."

"How did your foot stand up to all that walking?"

"It didn't. It had been rubbed raw. Like everything else, it was bleeding having surrendered to the journey like every other part of me. Standing unsteadily, I tapped on William's bedroom window. He told me he never heard the tapping to begin with. He was sleeping on his deaf side. But Bessie heard it. You know how she is, such a light sleeper and has always been nervous about living on the farm. She told me she sat bolt upright. Petrified, she urgently tugged at William's shoulder to wake him." Mom grimaced, remembering what William had told her.

"I knocked again and could hear William get out of bed. Moments later, he was peering into the desperate look in my eyes. Poor William."

Finally, Mom rested her head back on her pillow and in moments she was asleep. It was as if revealing the details of the savage attack, and her long walk to get help, had released her of the emotional burden. It was incredible to witness the change in her expression as she slept. It was a lesson I would never forget.

Later that afternoon, Daan popped in on his rounds.

"Mum told me what happened. My God, what a gruesome story. Like you said, Daan, it's a miracle she's alive, but she seems relieved to have got it out of her system. Thank you for saving her life," I whispered.

"Well, when I first saw her, I didn't think I could save her, nor did the team I'd called in to help."

The news of Mom's savage attack sent shockwaves rippling through the community. Both black and white were angry. Everyone wanted the perpetrator found. Local farmers joined forces with the police and the army tracker unit to assist in finding the man that had brutally raped Mom and torn her to pieces, very nearly killing her. The search was relentless, paying off the following week when they found Mom's truck, parked and abandoned, full of dents and scratches; her brand-new vehicle was a mess.

"Mom is going to be furious," William said in passing to a local farmer standing beside him. "That bakkie was precious to her. It was the first new vehicle she'd ever owned, and though she didn't drive it herself, she will be as livid as her driver Joe was."

Thankfully, Mom never saw it.

The search for the rapist continued. On the ninth day, they found him cowering in thick bush next to a river only three farms from ours. The police showed no mercy, and our friends agreed it was the swine's good luck that William hadn't got to him first. Rape, in anyone's eyes, was an inexcusable crime, but done with such savagery to an elderly lady, the darling of the community, enraged everyone.

William and I found the court case almost intolerable; hateful vengeance was not a part of our upbringing, but neither of us could feel anything else. Forgiveness was not something that fitted with what we were feeling in the courtroom that day or what that beast had done to our mother. Listening to the verdict gave way to some of those nasty emotions. He was given life imprisonment – we were satisfied with the sentencing, but none of us would ever forgive what he'd done to Mom. Seven weeks after the incident, Mom left the hospital, still shaken, but on her way to a full recovery. She never went back to live on the farm she so dearly loved; he'd taken that from her too.

William and Bessie found a suitable house for her in the nearby town of Brandfort. Ester, her loyal housekeeper, moved with her, but Joe, her dear old driver, remained on the farm. He collected Mom once a week and took her shopping.

Chapter Eighteen

Only six weeks after Mom's brutal attack, Dion's mother passed away. Mothers were having a massive impact on my life, and the two tragedies united us again (much to my mother's disapproval). Dion had been there for me after her near-fatal attack, and I felt it my duty (I was still his wife) to be there for him during his time of loss.

Timing wasn't a gift I'd been spared during the history of our marriage. We'd both been living separate lives for a long time, and though it suited me, it never suited Dion. Not long after his mother's funeral, Dion's brother Phillip called to say their father wasn't coping well living on his own. Then a month later Hennie sheepishly asked Dion if the two of us would move to the plot. He was lonely and in desperate need of company. I was hesitant, but after endless discussion, I agreed. My family, particularly, were mortified.

My initial positivity and determination to make things work evaporated not long after moving. I was faced with one nasty surprise after another. The first was one I could deal with having been raised on a farm with a generator: there was no mainline electricity to the house. However, the generator he used must have been manufactured at the turn of the century and was on its last legs, screaming for an end to its hard life, deafening us when it was on. When we had visited in the past, we'd never stayed overnight and took modern electricity supply for granted, so it hadn't crossed my mind that we'd be going back into the Dark Ages. The second shock, and this one angered me, was none of our furniture was permitted in "his" house. It was relegated to a rickety old shed that was waterproof but not rodent-proof and thirdly, what I thought was the worst infliction, there was not much clean water. Wrong move.

The death of Hennie's beloved wife had turned, what I thought I knew as, a kind, old gentleman into a grumpy, bitter, old bastard, and I struggled to hold my tongue. When I woke, sore and crippled from sleeping on a bed with an old coir mattress, I didn't keep my mouth shut and ordered the gardener to swop the whole thing for our bed. This obvious violation of his rules enraged the cantankerous old swine and I thought his red puffed-up face was going to explode. I was on the war path after that and checked the children's beds; fortunately, they had reasonably new beds.

Round number two in our battle, which happened a few days later, was indeed about the children. Instead of being over-joyed by the sound of his happy grandchildren bringing cheer and laughter back into his home, they infuriated him. Storm's gregarious character was too lively; Vivienne was messy and far too nosy. He wordlessly tolerated Splodge because the cat fitted in anywhere without a fuss, putting Oupa's Maltese poodle in its place in the first five minutes we were there.

Just as distressing was his housekeeper, Selina, a woman shrouded in a malevolent energy; a woman I was convinced was created in hell and her severe Arabic features, sharp, almond-shaped eyes that viewed me with mistrust and venom, exacerbated an unprovoked hatred. She'd been with the family for years, and though she had been a devoted and loyal housekeeper to Mr and Mrs du Toit Senior, she refused to take one instruction from me. She was determined to make my life on the plot an absolute misery, which she achieved.

I called on dear Miriam. Luckily, she'd gone to her family home for a break before looking for another job after leaving me. I was just in time. She didn't hesitate, despite her previously trying to convince me not to go back to "Mr Dion". Miriam cleaned the parts of the house we occupied, did our washing and ironing, and prepared the vegetables for me for dinner. She did some of the cooking for me on occasions and was nanny to Vivienne. But Hennie always had to have the last say. He told me that even though I had brought Miriam to help me, I still had to pay Selina's salary. I took that up with Dion.

"He's got an absolute cheek, Dion. He's your father, and they are your children too, so you talk to him. But I am *not* paying a cent towards Selina's salary. She does nothing for any of us, is downright rude to me and won't even greet me."

"Calm down, liefie."

"Calm down? Like hell will I calm down. I won't tolerate any more abuse from your father, and I am certainly not paying towards that bitch's salary."

I realised then I had been crazy to agree to this move.

"Besides," I went on, "He asked us to move here, and he's not in the slightest bit appreciative. You don't see or hear what the girls and I have to put up with."

Dion nodded, but he didn't seem to get it or he had gone into selective hearing mode, his default setting.

"Did you hear what I said?"

"Yes, I did, my skat, but I cannot ask Papa to change anything."

"Well, you pay the nasty Selina. Not one cent of my hard-earned cash is going anywhere near her pocket, and that's a promise."

Dion nodded again. That was the end of the conversation.

I was convinced there was something sinister and dark about the relationship between Hennie and Selina, and I felt sure Dion knew some of those dark family secrets I'd not picked up on before now.

Miriam was the angel at my side. Her smile was as big and sunny as her personality. Her lovely characteristics highlighted Selina's mean ones, and admirably, Miriam never allowed Selina's repugnant ways to disrupt her. She just got on with the job as usual.

I discovered the water that fed into the house came from a brackish underground supply and was as utterly vile as the maid that ruled the house. One of Miriam's daily tasks was to boil this brackish water for the kids to bathe in at night. Another massive pot boiled away on the wood stove all day, cleansing it, so the household had drinking water. Then, before Miriam left in the evening, she popped a new pot on the stove for Dion and I to use in our baths. It was the ultimate in discomfort. I'd lived without during my life, but bodily cleansing under a jet of clean water was, for me, not a luxury but an essential part of balancing my psyche This ultimate discomfort in personal hygiene and the despicable attitude of Hennie du Toit and his sidekick made everything around me close to impossible to deal with rationally.

When I got home one evening, Hennie suggested I should "beat some discipline into my naughty children". This was the straw that broke the proverbial camel's back and put an immediate end to my tolerance.

I roared back at him about how ungrateful he was, and he roared back at me, saying, "You are a hopeless, immature woman who has no idea how to bring up children."

An exchange of colourful, creative vocabulary flew from my mouth. He was furious and muttered continuously about the disruption we'd caused in his home, what awful food he was forced to eat and how he loathed the ghastly noisy children. I stopped cooking for him and left his food requirements to the loathsome Selina.

Daily life became a battle of wills – one in which Dion refused to participate. Hennie's grieving was over, if it ever had been that bad. Dion never mentioned his mother and I had unwittingly got myself caught in the middle of it all. I grieved my decision way more than the two men grieved their loss, as if their shallow lives were perfectly calibrated and the children and I had upset the calibration.

Hennie preferred to spend his time with his youngest son, giving us some welcome peace on the plot, but living there was going to end for me and end soon. I hated the house. I hated having to stoke the stove to boil water for a bath over the weekend. In fact, everything about the house was depressing. Not a blade of grass had ever been planted around the house to create a lawn. It stood alone in a desert of red earth; the walls of the house were painted a sand colour, which emphasised the emptiness and exaggerated the gloom and barrenness. The roof was covered in the same dust colour. Everything reflected the loveless environment. I couldn't imagine anything worse than growing up here. It stood as a beacon of despair.

I got home early one evening and found Hennie back at the plot. Greeting him civilly, I continued through to the kitchen. That morning, of all mornings, I'd asked Selina to peel potatoes for me, leave them in water to soak and I'd cook them that evening. Miriam was on a day off and since Dion was still paying her salary, I felt no hardship in asking her, but she'd prepared nothing for me. Ensuring I wasn't rude, I enquired why. She sensed I was annoyed at having my instructions purposefully and spitefully ignored and she stood staring at me, then she put both her hands on her hips and smiled victoriously. I'd reached the end of my tether.

"If peeling potatoes for us is too difficult for you, Selina, then I suggest you leave. Mr Dion pays your salary, and as you will do nothing for any of us, I am letting you know now, we do not need you any longer."

Hennie had been listening and burst into the kitchen shouting angrily, waving his arthritis-gnarled index finger under my nose.

"Selina isn't going anywhere."

I glanced her way and noticed the triumphant look had risen across her face again.

"Well, Hennie, you choose. It's her or me."

"She's going nowhere," he repeated stubbornly.

His words were like a lance penetrating deep into my heart. I'd tried hard for the ungrateful old bastard. I stood in the dark, dingy kitchen, quite shaken by the events and quietly admitted the odds were stacked against me. I was never going to win, but a suspicious thought entered my mind then: had Hennie been having a long-term affair with Selina? He was much too affectionate and protective of her; it was far from an ordinary servant–employer relationship. I left them in the kitchen, headed to my bedroom, dropped down on the edge of the bed and pondered my next move. I was shaking with rage.

Dion wouldn't be home until Friday evening. I wasn't going to wait for him; it would be futile, for he was on his father's side anyway. It was time to leave.

Jumping up, I yanked all of our suitcases off of the top of the cupboards and packed everything in the room that belonged to us.

"What are you doing, Mama?"

I heard Storm's little voice come from the direction of the door and I swung around to face her. She'd listened to the argument and was standing in the doorway looking stunned and frightened – a picture that tugged at my heart. I knew my two children weren't happy, and neither had any affection for their grandfather. In fact, if anything, they didn't like him at all.

"Come here, my precious." I beckoned, putting my arms out for her to walk into, then I wrapped them around her and held her close to me. "Don't say a word to Oupa. I'm going to find a new place to live when I get to work in the morning. Come on, let's go and make supper. I'll pack the rest later."

A happy smile lit up her face.

"Go and get Vivienne and join me in the kitchen."

"Okay, Mama." She skipped off towards their bedroom.

We made dinner for ourselves and ate it in the kitchen. After kissing the girls goodnight, I packed what I could. The following morning we left earlier than usual. Miriam was there to care for Vivienne. She was delighted by my decision, as I knew she would be. After dropping Storm at school, I bought a newspaper, checked for rentals, and found a place that sounded suitable. I called the advertiser at 8.30 a.m., secured the property unseen, begged Derek for a company lorry to move with, and by nightfall, I'd shifted all our stored belongings into our new house with help from the lorry driver and Miriam.

Neither Hennie nor I uttered a word to each other while we loaded and packed. Selina watched from the sidelines with an elated sneer. Dion got home as we were busy with the last load, and he went off at me like he'd been detonated. That took me by surprise. I knew he wasn't happy on the plot, so why the outburst? Suddenly, I felt those nerves again, but I stood my ground; there was no turning back.

"Your father gave the ultimatum. The girls and I happily accepted."

Dion looked stunned. "What ultimatum?"

I didn't bother to go into all the details, but offered him one of two options.

"You can stay with your father or you can come with us. Choice is yours."

I handed Dion a piece of paper with our new address scribbled on it, jumped into my car and followed the lorry off of the property. There was no suppressing Miriam's mood as she took her place in the front seat, while the kids on the back seat were standing up looking back at their angry, rather bewildered father, who stood watching us drive away. With each passing metre of gravel road the car crunched over, a mountain of stress lifted off of my shoulders. Splodge was a happy cat. Even he had become unusually subdued and had given up teasing Dot, the grumpy Maltese.

Dion didn't follow immediately, but later that evening, while I was unpacking and sorting out the mess, he arrived. The monster look wasn't quite there, but I was pretty sure it wouldn't be hard to trigger its full return. He'd found it tricky dealing with my new independence. He wasn't in control of me, and that was a dangerous situation, especially living under the same roof again without his father around.

The more I tried to explain how Hennie had chosen Selina over me, the worse the argument got. I didn't want to start this new chapter on shaky foundations, but I wasn't backing down. The children's happiness came before anything else in my world.

He stepped towards me, threatening me with a warning index finger, then suddenly reached out to strike at my face. As he lunged at me, I brought my arm up, an instinctive protective action. My fist accidentally connected the delicate spot on his temple, knocking him off balance and he fell. I was shocked. The sudden reflex action to protect my face had more power than I realised. I might need to use it again!

It took a few minutes for him to focus and get back on his feet. The danger was he was seething from the humiliation, especially being knocked off of his feet in front of his children and Miriam. He wasn't going to swallow that accidental blow – I was in trouble.

Once he was up, he went directly to the bathroom without uttering a word. Then a short while later, the screeching of tyres were the last sounds we heard from Dion for a week.

By the end of that week, I was apprehensive about his homecoming. I had no idea what to expect, but he was in an unusually good mood when he got back.

Dion had given up on the music industry. He was now working for Nestlé and he arrived bearing gifts of atonement. In the back of his car lay tins of instant coffee and hot chocolate, bars of chocolate and an assortment of other sweets, instant puddings and luxury breakfast cereals. The kids forgave Papa instantly.

Damaged packaging rendered goods unfit for sale in the stores, so it was sold off to the staff at cost. Dion took advantage of the opportunity to obtain this cheap but yummy peace offering.

Storm and Vivienne gobbled a large Bar One each, putting them on a hyperactive sugar high within minutes. They buzzed around the house and garden playing games with each other as if they were powered by Duracell batteries. After supper, Storm dragged Dion to the piano, urging him to play, but it wasn't long before the sugar high dumped her. She struggled to keep her eyes open, while Vivienne was already asleep on the sofa.

With the children tucked away in bed, Dion and I chatted, purposefully avoiding the issue of the unexpected punch and his absence the whole week. The chemistry was surprisingly good, so I didn't dare raise the subject. It had been a long time since we'd made passionate, meaningful love – I gave in to the call of nature.

After a month away from the plot, I noticed Vivienne had recovered from a strange undiagnosed illness she'd suffered while we were living there. We'd had endless blood and urine tests done on her, but they had revealed nothing. She'd been referred to several doctors, none of whom found a cause or gave a diagnosis to her unexplained and unusual illness that had caused ghastly vomiting attacks, high temperatures and fever that burnt her little body up at night.

Vivienne had been a desperately ill little girl; medication had cost a fortune without much relief, and we had no answers. Now it was miraculously gone. Since the day we packed up at the plot, she'd not had another attack, but with everything going on, I'd not paid attention to that fact. This was living proof what a devastating effect a toxic environment can have on children who don't have the vocabulary to express their troubled minds.

I had a sudden thought. Had Selina been slowly poisoning her? She had an aversion to Vivienne. I shook the thought away. I'd also learnt that the week Dion was away was spent with his father, and two months later, he was dead. The old man had a sudden heart attack and I got the blame! I was the one who'd abandoned him. I could scarcely believe what I was hearing. Later that week, I received a phone call from Phillip. We'd not spoken since the affair Dion had had with his wife.

"I'm so sorry about your father, Phillip," I said, offering my condolences.

"Do you know where Dion is? None of us can reach him." His sharp response wasn't expected.

"No, I don't. Have you tried his offices?" I suggested.

"You killed him, Elizabeth. You know that, don't you? *You* abandoned him and left him to die," Phillip said suddenly and without provocation.

"I did nothing of the sort, Phillip. That is a cruel and unnecessary accusation. Your father told me to leave."

I slammed the phone down and sobbed my heart out. I was forbidden to attend the funeral, but I went. I felt it was the right thing to do. The family shunned me; nobody sat on the pew at the back of the church with me, not even family friends, and though it hurt, I'd anticipated the reception.

Later that week, the family gathered for the reading of the will. Money was left to each surviving brother. What shattered the brothers, but didn't surprise me at all, was that 10,000 Rand had been written into the will for Selina, confirming my suspicions. The property was left to the brothers to work out what to do with it.

Somehow, I had to prevent Dion from having his part of the inheritance deposited into his account. He was drinking again, and I knew, without hesitation, he'd drink it all away. Protecting the inheritance for him and trying to arrange it was going to be almost impossible.

A plan was sent to me from the heavens. While I lay awake early one morning I visualised what the plot would be like if it was renovated, surrounded by a garden and vegetables growing in abundance with fruit trees everywhere, clean water and electricity. It would not only be a good investment but a great place to raise the kids. It was far more than I could offer them if I didn't stay with Dion. Despite the initial tension over the death of his father, in fairness to Dion, he was supportive, and he knew how hurt I was; we'd also chatted about his drinking again.

My suggestion came as quite a shock to Dion. He couldn't believe I'd even suggest buying out his brothers and moving back to the plot, but after I'd explained my vision in detail, he enthusiastically agreed. He even let me deal with the lawyers handling Hennie's estate. Eventually, Dion's siblings decided they'd rather have the money than a useless share in a property they all hated and had no emotional attachment to.

Signed, sealed and completed, we celebrated our first home ownership. I was ecstatic.

Youthful dreams and hopes of "happily ever after" were always there in the back of my mind. I knew the "real" Dion; he was being that incredible Dion now and I dreamt of making our marriage work. I would continue to help him over his problems, and I considered *this* move to be the right one.

Dreams and hopes aside, there was not the remotest chance I was going back to the plot before sorting out the water situation. I booked a month off of work to sort it out, which raised some questioning eyebrows. Me, plumbing? Thanks to the skills and training in all things farming, mechanical, building and home maintenance I'd learnt from William, fixing up the plumbing was not a daunting task for me. Besides, William was only a phone call away if I got stuck.

Miriam and I started dismantling the rusty old pipes, ones that had been laid in the early 1940s. They crumbled between the teeth of the pipe wrench as we loosened them from their ancient stronghold. Lots of skin went missing, fingernails got broken too, but we had fun.

As the days passed, Miriam learnt, with lightning speed, the art of wielding spanners, pipe cutters and threaders and our new home was almost ready for the professionals to come in, check our handiwork, make any necessary changes, then connect us to the municipal water mains and sign it off, job done. That was quite acceptable in those days.

Once that was behind us, we gave the whole place a coat of paint, inside and out. Four weeks later, we'd both earned a fabulous new level of fitness, and we moved in. Dion was impressed, but I sensed a little vulnerable jealousy, interpreting my work as just one more display that I didn't need a man in my life and at any given time, I could just walk out. But for me, the work we'd done was about saving money and having a fun challenge.

Miriam and I had loads of laughs, ruining many clothes, but the luxury of clean running water, both hot and cold, was worth it. We'd put a shower into Miriam's unit too. With my savings just about depleted, it was time to let Dion know he'd have to cover the electrical installation costs, which caused a few sideways glances. Dion hated paying for anything.

The following Sunday, William and Mom came to view our handiwork, bringing with them a surprise housewarming gift of a brand-new gas stove and a few gas lamps. I was thrilled; it was a most unexpected gift. They were not partial to Dion and I being together again. It was the children and I they were concerned about, and they made that very clear. I loved cooking with gas, but I couldn't toss out the old wood stove that the coffee percolator sat on, burping away all day, reminding me of my childhood.

Without electricity on call, candlelit dinners lost their appeal after a few months, and the only way to get Dion into forward gear was for Miriam and me to start doing something. I drew a plan on paper of where plug points and light switches needed to go and proceeded to pencil them in on the walls. A week later, Miriam and I began to chase into the cement walls, carving out the space to lay the electrical conduit. Poor Miriam was left to fight with a fine dust storm that covered the house. Dion wasn't amused, but three months later, we'd done the dirty work and electricians came in to connect us to the mains.

"Eish, missus." Miriam's smile was brighter than our new lights as I switched on the overhead one in the kitchen for the first time.

The girls were just as excited when they got home from school. They ran through the house, switching on every light, checking they all worked then they rushed back to hug me. Storm was babbling on about how easy it was going to be to do her homework now.

Eighteen months later, we'd transformed the plot from a depressing dusty dump into an oasis, gorging on our homegrown fresh vegetables every day. The garden was gradually taking on the landscaped form I'd designed – roses were flowering, shrubs were growing well and the flower seeds I'd recently sewn were budding. The lawn looked like a carefully tended fairway and being blessed with an excellent rainy season that year, my Garden of Eden was thriving.

The vegetable garden was one of the girls' favourite places to play. Shrieks of laughter could be heard as they searched through the carrot bed for the fattest ones, hopping about on all fours pretending to be bunnies with carrots between their teeth as they played fantasy games with each other. They named it "The Disney Patch", so we painted a sign for the gate. They were happy days.

Chapter Nineteen

My job as Derek's PA kept me on my toes, and by the time we'd renovated the plot, I was earning an enviable salary. Dion had managed to stay in one job for longer than a year and life had been close to perfect. Although he was still drinking, he'd become more disciplined about it, and the monster hadn't appeared for a long, long time.

I was dreading Derek's retirement, which was looming. He'd not said when he would leave, and he wasn't particularly keen on retiring. I wasn't looking forward to the day when he'd had enough and would pack it in.

One evening, after the girls had gone to bed, I curled up in my big armchair, its wings closing me into a world of blissful comfort and security while I dreamily switched on the TV to check if there was a movie worth watching. I didn't feel like going to bed, and Dion was out. It was just Splodge and I. The peace was idyllic until suddenly it was shattered as the front door flew open.

Splodge scattered as Dion stumbled in, collapsed over the arm of the sofa and toppled off of it, hitting the floor with a frightening thud. He fell so quickly and so hard, my instant thoughts were that he'd suffered a heart attack like his father. I flew out of my chair as fast as Splodge had disappeared and looked down at Dion. He looked dreadful and all I could think of in that moment of panic was to call Daan.

"Hi, Daan, it's Elizabeth. I, um… I'm sorry to disturb you this late, but I think Dion may have had a stroke or a heart attack. Would you mind coming out?"

Without a moment's hesitation, he said, "I'm on my way."

Those were the days when doctors still did emergency house calls, but Daan was more than just our GP. I put the phone down and quickly rushed back to where Dion lay. What an idiot I felt. I should have checked him over more closely before allowing panic to rule me. The son of a bitch was so drunk he appeared unconscious. I was devastated; he'd been so good. As I bent down to feel his pulse, the putrid stench of alcohol and stale cigarette smoke made me want to vomit, but a more potent smell of defeat filled my nostrils.

"What the fuck," I muttered as I stood up, my eyes still focussed on the pathetic heap of humanity at my feet.

How I wished the bliss could have continued. Three incredible years of happy family life on our beautiful plot gave the girls a taste of the best of both worlds. Dion had been sober most of that time. The girls' friends would come and go; they loved the farm life as much as we did, and now this. All gone in one selfish, thoughtless evening.

Twenty minutes later, Daan arrived. I met him at the front door, feeling embarrassed and ashamed.

"Oh dear, Elizabeth, it must be bad. You look like you've seen a ghost!" Daan said.

"I have. The ghost of the past just smacked me in the face, Daan. I'm sorry to have called you. I should have checked him better before calling. He's pissed out of his mind. I didn't think of checking before calling you. He's been dry for so long."

Daan shook his head sadly. "I'm sorry to hear that, Elizabeth, but as I'm here, let me check him anyway and make sure he's okay."

Coming back into the house, the stench of stale alcohol fumes assaulted our nostrils.

"A bad case of alcohol poisoning. Let's roll him on his side. He'll move into a more comfortable position later, but keep an eye on him. He'll have a hangover from hell tomorrow and will probably be as sick as a dog for a few days, but maybe that's what he needs. If there are any changes during the night and you're unhappy, call me. I'm pretty sure he'll survive providing he remains on his side. We don't want him drowning himself if he vomits."

As Daan said that a horrid thought flashed through my mind. How easy my life would be if he did drown in his vomit. It wasn't what I said though.

"He's been so good. I never expected this, Daan. I thought the drinking was under control." I was close to tears, knowing what lay ahead.

"Something must have prompted this. Has he appeared depressed or agitated recently?"

"No, Daan. Though he's been a model father and husband, he's a fucking alcoholic," I sobbed.

"See me at my rooms in the morning, Elizabeth. Let's chat through this and your next move."

"Okay. Thank you. I'm so angry, but disappointed too."

"I'm quite sure you are. It's time for Dion to get professional help."

I raised my eyebrows. I couldn't see Dion agreeing to professional help. Daan left, and I closed the front door behind him, covered Dion with a blanket and went to bed.

Dion was still sound asleep the next morning, precisely as I'd left him and in a feeble attempt to cover for him, I told the girls a fib. The look on Storm's face suggested I hadn't fooled her. There was a deafening silence in the car on the way to school; both girls were unusually subdued. They knew.

I popped into the office and left a note for Derek, then headed down to Daan's consulting rooms.

"Good morning, Elizabeth. How's Dion's head this morning?"

"He's still out for the count. Miriam's at home if he needs anything."

"Do you think we can convince him to see a psychologist when he wakes up?"

"I thought about that last night. I know he's got more issues than just alcohol, but I can't see how a psychologist is going to help him. Don't you think AA would be more effective?"

"Seeing a psychologist may help us discover the root causes of his addiction and personality disorders. I don't want to see you and the girls go through hell all over again. We need to establish why, after all this time, he's suddenly drunk himself into oblivion. We must establish the triggers then we'll have something to work with. Then he can go to AA once he has admitted he needs help."

The logic made sense. I nodded in agreement despite feeling defeated.

"I think *you* will have to call and discuss it with him. He'd never agree if I suggest it, but he's probably feeling sick enough today to agree to anything you suggest. Let him know you did a house call last night. That might shake him."

"Yeah, good idea. I'll recommend he sees Dr Gouws. He's reported to be one of the country's leading psychologists. He has an excellent reputation for getting to the bottom of difficult psychiatric cases. He's worked with the worst."

I smiled, trying to keep the cynicism out of my expression.

A torturous hangover worked in our favour; Dion agreed to the assessment. Daan wasted no time making the appointment before Dion had a chance to change his mind. When Dr Gouws finished the assessment, he sent Dion home to sleep off the alcohol poisoning and booked him off of work for a week.

The following day, I was back in Daan's office when Dr Gouws called. I watched Daan's expression change, then Daan answered irritably.

"There is no question, Dr Gouws. I sent you the right patient," Daan stated.

I turned purple with rage. I was ready to climb over the desk, grab the phone and yell at the psychologist – how dare he suggest *I* was the problem? My emotions felt like a whirlwind in a maize field on a hot day. I struggled to stop myself going from one emotional extreme to another as I felt the anger give way to burning tears. Humiliated again, and now, deeply insulted.

I insisted on meeting Dr Gouws myself, but Daan managed to dissuade me.

That was the level of brilliance we were dealing with when it came to Dion. A master manipulator and the crème de la crème on Dion's list of talents. He was a genius at it; it even surpassed his musical prowess. When Dion felt he was cornered, particularly with a professional like Dr Gouws, the game was on. Instead of fighting his way out, he turned up the charm and performed with more panache and style than any Oscar-winning performance.

He had the person gasping, agreeing with everything he had to say and laughing at his marvellous humour. No one ever believed he was a shallow, selfish devil in disguise with the scruples of a shark. Dion du Toit had managed to manipulate one of South Africa's leading psychologists and cunningly placed the blame on me – a polished act to alleviate his dented ego – the son of a bitch, but it backfired. Dr Gouws was acutely embarrassed and promptly ordered a series of more in depth tests to be done on Dion, finally exposing just how unpredictable and dangerous Dion was.

As I read the report I began to fully understand the enormity of Dion's psychological complications and they terrified me more now than they had in the past. How could he find it so easy to masquerade as the ultimate charmer and enjoy living such a double life? I was far too young to cope with this; I didn't even know where to begin. I always knew he was no ordinary rogue, but I wasn't aware his condition was quite as complex, despite my constant efforts to help him.

"Gifted with intelligence on a MENSA level; a talented, arrogant, egotistical, cunning and sly sociopath, psychopath, schizophrenic, narcissistic alcoholic."

What? Was this my husband they were describing? I had a sneaking feeling even the professionals were not quite sure how to label Dion's character. The investigation exposed a rare glimpse of what lay behind the scenes in the du Toit family's dark secrets. The cracks were getting more profound, the crevices darker, and I wondered what else we'd dig up.

Alcohol was Dion's escape when the gremlins and demons in his head got too much for him, drowning out the noise of the past, dulling the pain, but all the while increasing his anger levels until he passed the point of no return, then he was aggressively in control of everyone; he was invincible in the nastiest of ways and exceedingly dangerous.

"Though we've laughed at Dr Gouws' expense, this is no laughing matter," Daan said thoughtfully, then revealed, somewhat tentatively, what Dion had said about me to Dr Gouws.

"He described you as stubborn and wilful. Committed only to her children and her own needs. Egotistical, selfish and pig-headed."

There was more nasty stuff, none of it remotely fitting my character or how hard I'd tried for him. I sobbed unashamedly in front of Daan; those words ripped into me like a hurricane and tore me to shreds. How dare he!

"Don't let it upset you, Elizabeth. He's covering his arse, it's all his stuff. Besides, his type would never hear of putting someone else first, you should know that. Unfortunately, the gift of a high IQ exacerbates the problem." A frown wrinkled Daan's brow, carving two deep grooves between his eyes; he was not only disturbed by what lay ahead, he was worried about the children and me.

"We'll just have to wait and see what comes of the next procedure before making any decisions."

"How long does that take?"

"He will be admitted tonight and discharged from the psychiatric ward by four o'clock tomorrow afternoon. Dr Gouws will advise us once he has all the results. I'm told he has called in a colleague to assist. As soon as I have the reports, I'll call you. Dion will be permitted to read the reports."

That was not good news. In fact, there was no good news on the horizon.

I left Daan's room with a heavy heart. I collected the girls from school and had to tell them another white lie, which sickened me. Storm was particularly distressed by the news that her papa was in hospital but watching the *Mork & Mindy* comedy show took her mind off of her father.

Pages of medical jargon on Dion's condition were faxed through to Daan; lots of it didn't mean much to me, but it also covered some bothersome childhood issues he'd disclosed that he'd never revealed to me. Dion was made explicitly aware of the consequences of continuing his current lifestyle and was advised to stay off of alcohol for life. Mood enhancers and brain chemical drugs were prescribed, combined with a few other drugs I'd never heard of, also prescribed for life. I didn't like that. Another assessment was required in four weeks. This was to establish how well he was responding to the medication and whether it needed tweaking.

"The patient requires continued treatment. Our investigation will be worthless if he consumes alcohol in the next four weeks of the trials. Should he give in to his addiction within the prescribed four-week period, we will be forced to commit him to six months of confined rehabilitation," Daan read out Dr Gouws' comment.

"He's been off binge-boozing for three years. Those tests haven't revealed the triggers. All they've done is dig up some rather unsavoury bits in his past. That's what I don't like about psychologists. I'm not comfortable with it, Daan. They've also prescribed potentially addictive drugs that have other side effects too. He's already an addict."

Daan looked at me thoughtfully. "Let's take this first step, Elizabeth. It's important to see how he responds to the medication, and then we can assess how he is after the one-month trial.

We need to give it a chance. Cases like Dion's are not solved overnight."

"Okay, but there's something I don't fully understand. Is it being suggested that none of this behaviour is Dion's fault?"

"No, no, that's not what they are suggesting at all. Dion is in full control of his faculties, alarmingly so. He controls precisely what he wants to be in control of, and then when his friend alcohol visits, it makes him calculatingly evil. Unfortunately, you are his primary victim. Although people like him believe there is nothing wrong with them or their emotional state, they need help on a grand scale. Promise me not to go doing the woman thing and feel guilty about anything."

I smiled and nodded, although not feeling guilty was difficult for me.

"All you have to do now is encourage Dion to keep up with his medication and stay off all liquor so we can get the best results."

"I'll do what I can," I said, looking down at the floor. I wasn't convinced.

The month of medication and no alcohol went better than I expected. Dr Gouws still recommended three months in rehabilitation, and to our mutual amazement, Dion agreed. This was what we needed to go through to stay "dry" forever and on an emotionally stable path. He even packed his suitcase and was admitted to the drug and alcohol rehabilitation centre in Welkom without any forceful persuasion.

On the drive home, I wondered why on earth they, whoever "they" were, had chosen a town like Welkom to establish a rehabilitation centre. It had a flat, dreary, dusty, dull landscape, and like most mining towns, the people were like a bag of liquorice allsorts. Diverse people gathered from around the world and were generally hardened drinkers. The positives and negatives of the city aside, *if* confining Dion to a rehabilitation centre worked and I got my "real" husband back, it didn't matter to me where it was. Neither the kids nor I were permitted to visit Dion for the first month.

We waited out the isolation period then set off on a two-hour drive for our first visit thirty days later. Dion appeared to be responding, but during the second month, he became increasingly depressed, so his stay was extended. The next time we visited, he didn't want to talk to us. He wasn't even interested in seeing his children. I expressed my concern to the superintendent who said his condition had been reported to Dr Gouws and his medication adjusted. I didn't like what I saw. I feared they were turning him into a prescription drug addict too.

Dion came home at the end of the fourth month, depressed and unusually subdued. I finally managed to get him to talk to me about what went on in rehabilitation. The stories were grim (if he was telling the truth). Over the following weeks, his mood improved a fraction, but for several months after being discharged, it remained unchanged, but he wasn't drinking, thankfully.

Shopping in town one day, I happened to bump into a social worker who'd worked with Dion while he was in rehab and who was often on duty when the children and I visited. We greeted each other, then she casually asked if I was still with Dion. I nodded.

"Leave him," she snapped venomously.

"Why would I want to do that? I'm not into kicking a dog when it's down." I hadn't liked the girl much when I'd met her at the rehab, and I liked her less now as she rudely continued.

"If I were you, I'd get out now before he kills you. It's just a matter of time, and if it's not you he kills, you can guarantee he will molest one of your daughters. Let me tell you, I've never met such an evil beast in my life. That man is sub-human."

I stood there quite flabbergasted as I glared at her. But the element of truth in what she had said had penetrated my brain. When I did finally respond, I surprised myself by loyally defending Dion. She ranted on as to why I should leave the union as soon as possible.

"I'll be the judge of that," I snapped at her. I desperately wanted to get away from her. Her issues with Dion had nothing to do with me, or did they?

As I walked away, I heard her say, "stupid woman", leaving me asking myself a string of new questions.

There was no denying her words shook me.

I also knew that while Dion had been in rehab, she would have seen the worst of his character. That was my justification, but despite knowing that, I was indeed deeply rattled.

Chapter Twenty

After living for years with someone who could morph into a terrifying freak in moments, I was close to burnout and had to finally concede Dr Gouws was right.

Perhaps even the vicious carer from rehab had been right – he *was* evil, or was he? The sensible part of me was telling me it was time to make radical changes again. My intuition was telling me he had a mental illness that was still misunderstood, but that afternoon, I made up my mind and announced my intentions to Dion as soon as he walked through the door, even before he had time to head to the fridge. I even neglected to say hello in case my train of thought and intention was interrupted.

"It's all over for me, Dion. Your drinking, character shifting and the bullshit that tumbles out of your mouth has finally come to an end. I'm not listening anymore, and I want a divorce!" I blurted at him, suspending his calculated journey to the fridge.

"You want what?" he asked with an expression of shock, temporarily delaying the well-worn passage to his favourite piece of furniture: the fridge.

How could he be shocked? I wondered. The children had had enough of him too. Our few short years of bliss had ended, and as far as I could see, we were not going back to that beautiful place in the foreseeable future, if ever. He cared only about himself and had successfully eroded *my* self-belief, murdered my self-confidence to the point where I was suffering severe bouts of depression and felt myself spiralling down towards a nervous breakdown which Amelia had warned would happen. It was time to listen to the threads of "me" that were left. Someone else could work out his mental health issues. It was time to end the combat with my inner saboteur; we'd been fighting for years. I had to stop bluffing myself that Dion would change and that I was the catalyst that could help him make those changes.

The girls had listened to more aggressive verbal abuse and angry threats of physical violence than any child should ever hear. They'd seen their father so drunk he had no control over his faculties. It broke my heart. I needed to get them away from him. I didn't want them to hate and despise him. Miraculously, they still loved him, and I wanted to protect the purity of his children's unconditional love. I envied it because I understood it. He could be so easy to love, but sadly, the impact he'd already had would carry into adulthood and become part of their baggage and contribute to their emotional imperfections.

Dion seemed impervious to guilt. His love was a dangerous dependency. Love had a different meaning to Dion, even towards his children, and their love for their father was becoming more diluted. So, before it was all but gone, I felt it my duty to remove them from the unhealthy environment they'd been exposed to off and on. (More on, than off.)

Dion had never physically hurt the girls. He adored them in his own way; he seldom disciplined them – that was my job. Dion had no idea about boundaries and self-discipline and certainly couldn't teach his children about them. It was his indifference that was perhaps more eroding and hurtful, and they hated the way he treated me, apart from being terrified of him when his mood changed. Vivienne was not the bubbly child she used to be. Storm was a stronger character, but she'd had enough. There was simply no point in living this illusion anymore.

"Don't leave me, liefie," he said pathetically, having quickly processed what I'd said, understanding what it meant for him (a selfish knee-jerk reaction). Knowing I meant it, he whimpered, "Please."

Bittersweet emotion may have been tugging at him, but I'd long forgotten what it felt like to be overwhelmed by sympathy for him. His pleading just made me feel sick, angry and disappointed.

"Oh, come on, Dion, you've had so many chances. We've been over this path so many times it's now boring. It is 'over'. Get it into your head now it isn't blurred by your imaginary life support system: alcoholic bliss."

"Please, my skat," he begged again, which only made me feel more contempt.

"How many times have you promised to stop all your bullshit? I give you a chance, try and help, and you abuse that too. And how often have you dumped the blame on the children and me? We don't deserve it."

He looked at me with a sad expression I didn't want to acknowledge as genuine. I went on now that I had his undivided, sober attention.

"The amount of money you have wasted on booze is staggering. It could have paid off the plot. I can't remember when you last made any meaningful financial contribution to anything other than the bottle store and the pubs."

I could feel ugly resentment starting to ooze out of my mouth, and I stopped it going any further. I wasn't in the mood to regurgitate all the crap, knowing it would just trigger a nasty reaction. Besides, I could see he'd gone into shutdown. What I was saying was not penetrating. The curtain of harsh truth was now drawn.

"Give me another chance. Please, liefie?" he begged again, putting on his best quivering voice.

In the past, he'd not even had the good grace to break a sweat when screwing me over, leaving me to foot the bills, protect our children from their psychological woes because of his despicable behaviour and I still had to keep working. There was no denying I felt a huge loss and a pang of genuine sadness, but there was a sense of relief that blended well with my decision.

The following day, I filed for divorce. The papers were served a week later, and despite what I'd told myself, I was devastated. I couldn't ditch the feeling that I'd failed him in some way, which my mother and William found absurd and said so.

No more jokes, no more piano lessons, no more singing, no more of the man who could be a darling. It was all a distant memory. I couldn't fight the monsters that consumed him any longer. My work kept my mind busy, and Derek's kind words of encouragement helped soothe the rocky road; he and my colleagues got me through the painfully tricky weeks that followed.

"The storm will pass, Elizabeth, it always does. Then the skies of your life will clear, and you will look up and see only sunshine."

These were the handwritten words in a "congratulations" card colleagues had got for me. Profound words indeed, and reading them over and over, I realised how much they'd all been a part of the tragedy. How fortunate I was to have a boss that grounded me. Relief was what I was feeling now. Guilt was no longer annoying me, sitting on my shoulder shouting at me, "You should do, you should have." At last, I felt a surge of renewed hope. The birthing of an overwhelming gratitude for my internal strength, born of past difficulties I'd learnt and grown from. The road ahead would be tough on my own, but it would be worth it.

It felt amazing to be standing firm in the world, on my own.

I couldn't contain the excitement that was bursting in Storm and Vivienne since telling them we were spending the December holidays with Ouma. We packed our bags a day earlier than the official end of term, piled Splodge and our bags into the car and headed for Brandfort. Mom's house was filled with their laughter; those wondrous, uninhibited sounds neither of us had heard for a long time. A few days with Mom to begin the holidays, then we shipped ourselves across to be with William and the family on the farm for a week.

I hardly saw the girls during that week. They discovered the mysteries of nature again under the watchful eyes of tens of loving staff following them everywhere; they were never alone, but I was. I spent that week soaking up the timelessness of nature I missed so much, allowing its pure energy to earth me, rejuvenating what had become a rather battered soul.

As hard as I tried, no amount of persuasion could get Mom to come with us, sadly. The attack had shattered every strand that had made up her life and love of the farm. The trauma was too great. Nothing could fill the void since being forced to leave her beloved land, whose earth she carried in her heart and soul,

200

but there was no way she could summon the courage to go back, though we all knew it was what she needed to do.

After a refreshing week on the farm, we livened up her life again as the girls got stuck into making Christmas decorations from tree seed pods, grasses and other natural things we'd gathered from the farm and used them to decorate Mom's house, just as I'd done as a child. There was silver, gold and red spray paint all over clothes, but they were old and we binned them when we had finished.

Dion didn't bother to call the girls on Christmas Day, nor did he send any gifts, and though I appreciated Christmas was not about gifts, the girls didn't. Mom was our Christmas cheer as we were hers until Vivienne shattered the cheery mood while they ripped the paper off their presents Mom had placed beneath the tree.

"Papa playing the piano with us, and… and singing with us. Oh, and… oh yes, 'member… how we used to tease Papa with a mouse," she squeaked with mirth, then she whispered, "I miss Papa, and he's forgotten 'bout us, Mama."

Mom and I looked at each other, our hearts dissolving like soap left in hot water. I struggled not to allow tears to form that stung the back of my eyes.

Storm stepped in, rescuing us from response. As quickly as the sad moment was upon us, it had gone again, as the two of them launched into reciting stories of chasing after Dion while holding a precious, albeit terrified, little field mouse that they'd found in the vegetable garden, in the palms of their hands. Petrified of rodents of any sort, Dion took off to loud guffaws from the girls and as more stories came tumbling out, their voices got louder and sillier as they imitated him. Then, collapsing in a heap on the floor, laughing hysterically, the sadness we had felt was lost in the moment. Only children can lighten a mood so quickly.

The holidays passed and soon it was back to the routine of daily life. Only this time it was all different; we were living with Mom in Brandfort. Getting to work from Mom's to Bloemfontein was awkward and expensive until I located a lift club. The girls were now at school in Brandfort and between Mom and Miriam, they took care of that responsibility for me.

On the day of the divorce hearing, I took my car and nervously headed to the courts. It was the end of January and still Dion had not contacted the children. I felt edgy and uncertain about meeting him in the courts, but the verdict was that Dion was to remain living on the plot. The courts awarded fifty percent ownership of it to me. That ignited crimson fury in Dion. He was further ordered to pay alimony for the girls, school fees and he was to add them to his medical insurance scheme immediately. I'd won a battle, but not the war. Visitation rights would only be granted once it was proven he was no longer dependent upon alcohol and *not* until then.

I was overjoyed. In fact, I was so happy I felt like having a few drinks myself! It felt so good to see him squirm with the realisation that responsibility was being imposed upon him by the law and not me.

But it wasn't long after the divorce hearing that I learnt more of the horrors that lurked below the surface of a psychopath, sociopath, narcissist, and I was forced to pay Dr Gouws a visit. After leaving his consulting rooms, armed with his advice, I headed down to the police station and placed a restraining order against Dion. The duty constable handed me over to some other disinterested law enforcement officer who wasn't particularly empathetic or helpful, but I got it done and vented my frustrations with Mom that evening after the kids had gone to bed.

"They have no idea the perils of being closely associated with a man like Dion, or is it because most black men here treat their wives with such disdain anyway, they can't understand why us white people demand more respect? I'm gatvol." (Had enough in Afrikaans.)

It was at times like these I hated Dion du Toit and it burnt in my soul.

"Did the police suggest other ways that you could be protected?" Mom asked.

"They don't give a shit, Ma, if the truth be told. They informed me that what Dion is doing is not a criminal offence. He is free to drive up and down the street shouting abuse at me. It's so embarrassing I want to die, but it's not a crime. The worst is there's no alternate route to take to the office. The cops tell me he must become a public nuisance before they can step in and act. Just proves that we women don't matter in this man's world. I can't see how the restraining order offers me any protection. I'm just following advice from Dr Gouws. I don't want him to think I am ignoring his advice because if I do, it may bounce back and hit me.

"It's a waiting game. We know that. I am to wait for him to hang himself, so to speak, for there is no doubt he will break the law, it's just a matter of time, then the police will step in." I sighed feeling beaten again. "In my mind, he's already broken the law by causing endless traffic jams during morning rush hour. It's chaos, Ma, but I'm going to follow instructions and see what happens."

Mom swallowed her last mouthful of coffee, patted her lips with a tissue and sighed. She wasn't convinced the advice was going to support me, and I could see she was concerned for my safety.

"The traffic gets blocked for at least ten minutes while he yells obscenities at me. It starts from the point I'm dropped off. Yes, he discovered that too, and it goes on all the way to the office."

"I'm worried, Elizabeth. Let me see if Jannie de Kok will get involved. Bloem is out of his jurisdiction, but you never know," Mom suggested.

Jannie was the station commander in Brandfort. He had actively tracked down Mom's attacker after the event. He also had a soft spot for my mother. I'd always hoped it might come to something, but it didn't. He'd said she could call on him if she ever needed help.

"Thank you, Mom. I need someone of authority to step in. What's amazing is all the other drivers sit on their horns, hooting at him to move on and he ignores them. I'm sure he gets perverse satisfaction by pissing off everyone. Embarrassing me is his first goal, especially as he knows I am helpless to change the situation. What is another worry is his drinking buddies are half the police force!"

"No one will ever work out the thoughts that go through that man's mind, my dear. That's proven," Mom said, graciously voicing her guarded opinion.

The following day was another straw that broke the camel's back. I felt no guilt, no love, no sympathy, only a deep loathing for him that was so intense I changed direction and marched to the central police station instead of my office, and there I raised hell. The policeman on duty was enjoying the moment, watching me lose my temper. The urge to slap the patronising look right off of his face was teetering on the brink of becoming a reality and my palms tingled. I managed to control myself, even though he was blatantly goading and offending me. I let rip verbally instead.

"I took out a fucking restraining order against the bastard. You do not know how dangerous this man can be," I yelled.

"Yes, Mrs du Toit, we do understand," came the automated and uninterested response.

"No, you don't," I yelled louder. "If you did, you would have done something to stop him, like being at the scene to witness what happens to the morning traffic during rush hour, let alone what I have to endure."

"Mrs du Toit, shouting at me is the same as your husband shouting at you. It does not constitute a crime even though it is unpleasant." He'd momentarily disarmed me, but I wasn't backing down.

"Don't try that on me," I spat with anger and resentment, but I knew I was getting nowhere. "The man is a certified psychopath. If anything happens to me, the blood will be on your hands. I'm going to go to a higher authority."

I turned and left him to ponder my words, but in truth I had nothing else to say.

As I expected, Dion was waiting for me the next day, and just as before, he drove alongside me at walking speed, baiting me, yelling to anyone who could hear, the ghastliest accusations and disgusting comments, and it took every ounce of resolve to ignore him and keep walking.

"Missing my dick inside you?" he shouted out of the car window as loud as he possibly could.

I felt my face turn crimson, which was followed by more revolting questions for all to hear.

"How many penises have you had since mine?"

It was rude and relentless, and I headed down towards the police station again, but a man in the queue of cars felt like I did. He jerked up his handbrake, flung open his car door and ran to Dion's car. He reached in, grabbed Dion by the throat and lifted him off of his seat while yelling at him, their faces inches apart.

"Listen here, fuckhead. I'm warning you, leave that poor woman alone." He dropped the grip he'd had on Dion's shirt front as if he was discarding a piece of trash and returned to his car, by which time the queue of cars behind him extended for miles back, causing a serious traffic jam.

"Prick!" he shouted as sirens suddenly interrupted the air around us, and four police cars arrived on the scene at last.

The degree of congestion was considerable and irritated commuters now leant out of their car windows and were shouting, horns were hooting, and it became a cacophony of vehicle sounds mingled with angry shouts from drivers late for work; now the traffic police had their work cut out.

I smiled as I watched them take in the seriousness of what I'd described the day before. Eventually, they cleared the backlog of traffic and took Dion down to the charge office. I watched the charade; it was more fun than going to work this time, and for once, I had the last laugh. The morning harassment stopped, but Dion's stalking didn't. I had to find a cottage to rent and move us from Mom's house. I couldn't put my mother through any more of the nonsense.

I found a small, quaint, thatched cottage with two big bedrooms, two bathrooms and an open plan living area in Bloemfontein. The girls and I moved and the girls went back to their old schools. It was perfect. Splodge thought so too. A high wall on two sides enclosed a small but pleasant garden. It was secure, private and quite adequate for the three of us. That was, until late one April night.

Dion came flying through my bedroom window, showering the entire room with a hail of glass shards, waking me rapidly. I sat bolt upright, confused and terrified and became fully awake in an instant. There he stood, at the foot of my bed, still dressed in his suit with his tie half undone and he was frighteningly drunk.

"Where is he?" he screamed, frenzied by a dangerous mix of jealousy and alcohol.

"Where is who, Dion? And what the hell do you think you're doing?"

From the soft light of the lamp in my room, I could see he was in one of his dangerous moods, and no amount of reasoning was going to help.

Will I ever get away from this man? How the hell did he find us?

"Theerr bastard youse sleeping whiff." His words rolled out of his mouth with dribbles of alcohol-infused saliva while he scanned every inch of my bedroom suspiciously. It hadn't registered to him that he'd woken me from a deep sleep, and I was alone in my bed the moment he crashed through the window.

"You've gone mad, Dion," I bellowed. "Go and look for yourself. Look through the house. Let the girls see you searching for the mystery man in your mind that is supposed to be living here, then maybe, just maybe, you will realise what idiotic games your mind plays, and you might see for yourself what an arsehole you are." I pulled the bedclothes up under my chin and flicked the glass shards off the bedcover.

The crashing sounds of breaking glass in the dead of night had woken the girls and they rushed to my room, barefoot. I yelled, stopping them just inside the door. They were not to come further in, they were to go back to their room and get their slippers on. The two of them took one look at their drunken father and slunk away. Storm, in her wisdom, quickly ran to the phone to call the police, but before she dialled, all hell broke loose as the neighbour burst through the front door and into a sobbing, terrified Vivienne whom Storm was now trying to pacify.

"The police are on their way," dear old Mr Venter, my wonderful landlord and neighbour, announced. "What's going on here? I heard a shout and breaking glass."

An embarrassed Storm didn't know what to say. Dion was still standing at my bedroom door, but he'd heard Mr Venter saying the police were on their way. I heard Dion laugh, an evil laugh that scratched its way up his throat as it escaped into the room and sent those familiar shivers down my spine.

"They're my drinking buddies." He leered towards Mr Venter with ugly intent.

"Don't you dare," I yelled at Dion when I saw what he intended to do to the old man.

Suddenly, the cops swooped in and cuffed Dion. It was one moment I wished I'd captured on camera. It was reassuring to know that not all the police were his friends.

"Fuck you," Dion shouted, but the two policemen ignored his drunken curses while they handcuffed him.

His two devastated daughters stood by and watched, with grim fascination, their father's removal from our cottage and as he was marched out, they burst into tears. So traumatised were they by the events of the night, I kept them home from school and booked a day off myself. I arranged for a new pane of glass to be fitted to my bedroom window and then began the arduous task of trying to get my bedroom carpet free of glass bits. It took me ages to clean.

Dr Gouws was the next person on my list to call, and he made preliminary arrangements to have Dion committed.

Then I called the police station and, to my horror, learnt Dion was no longer in custody. "Who the hell authorised that?"

"I don't know, ma'am," came the reply.

So, he did have more "buddies" in the police than I'd thought.

"You'll live to regret this, trust me," I snapped at the policeman on the other end and slammed the phone down.

Dion never did get committed.

We had a few months of peaceful reprieve, but guardedly waited for the harassment to begin again, as I knew it would.

This time, it started with telephone calls in the middle of the night and all that came through the receiver was heavy breathing, then the phone went dead. I knew it was him. This went on for weeks, always around one o'clock in the morning, purposefully disturbing my sleep patterns, and often the two girls would wake to the ringing sounds of the phone too.

Grouchy and exhausted, the three of us concentrated on getting through the days. I'd advised the headmistress of the circumstances and their teachers were understanding, but a drop in their work and falling asleep in class was hard on them both. As children can be positively cruel to each other, the teasing started because they couldn't concentrate and kept falling asleep in class. As if the phone calls in the dead of night weren't enough for us to endure, he began depositing dead animals at our front door. Storm found the first one: a dead crow.

At first, she innocently asked, "Mom, how would a bird manage to die, right at our front door?"

209

"I have no idea, my darling. Weird, isn't it?" I answered while the hair on my arms stood up.

That crow hadn't decided our front door was a good place to end its life. It had been placed there purposefully. A few days later, a dead tabby cat lay at the front door, one that had been dead for a few days and rigor mortis had set in. Its lips had stiffened, curling up and exposing its teeth in a macabre smile and unfortunately, once again, it was Storm who opened the door. This time she knew who'd left the animal at our front door and she screamed, a scream that expressed all her fears, her anger, the terror and revulsion she was feeling.

I pulled Vivienne away from the door and covered her eyes and ears, resulting in another day out of school for both girls. I called the headmistress and wondered whether I should call the police, then decided not to. Still shaking with anger, I called my brother. To put an end to this, I had to get William involved. None of us could tolerate, or be subjected to, any more harassment, and I knew, the only person in the world Dion was afraid of was my brother. The hardest part was asking Storm and Vivienne to participate. I didn't want them to feel they had to be dishonest or disrespectful to their father, so I carefully and truthfully explained what my intentions were.

They agreed to help, much to my relief, for I was not going to allow Dion to go on humiliating and terrorising us.

William arrived at my cottage an hour before the pre-arranged children's collection time; Dion was supposedly having the girls for the day. It seemed feasible, for they hadn't seen him socially for months. They hadn't wanted to go and still didn't, but Dion didn't know that.

Bang on time, Dion knocked on the door. William was ready for him and flung the door open with such force I thought it would fall off of its hinges and he sunk his fist into Dion's chest.

That first punch knocked him backwards, the next blow rearranged his nose and dentures as he squirmed on the floor clutching his broken, bleeding face, begging William not to hurt him anymore, but William had seen enough of how Dion had hurt us, and nothing was going to stop him. He pulverised Dion then hauled him to his feet like a useless puppet, dragged him to his car, opened the door and hurled him head first across the front seats where his beaten body lay limp – his hearing was still intact.

"No more calls late in the night. No more dead birds and cats deposited at their front door. No more harassment. Let this be your last warning, Dion du Toit. Behave yourself or you will never see Elizabeth or your children again. Do you hear me, you useless fucking drunk?"

Dion didn't answer but shifted his torso, then William walked back into the house.

"Has Papa gone now?" Storm asked.

"Not yet, Storm. Oom William has given Papa something to think about. He will probably leave shortly."

Storm nodded, innocently confused but accepting of what she'd been told.

"Did he promise not to bother us again?" Storm needed a bit more reassurance.

"Yes, he did, and I hope this time Papa keeps his promise."

Storm nodded again; wisdom shone through that innocent look of hesitant acceptance. She wasn't sure her father would ever stay away.

Vivienne was sitting on the edge of the sofa in stunned silence, suffering her silent trauma as I squeezed her hand gently and suggested Coco Pops for breakfast and a homemade milkshake.

William called me to one side and whispered, "If Dion's car is still there in half an hour, call an ambulance."

I nodded, but my eyes widened.

William returned to the farm, knowing as I did, the beating served to give me time to act. Dion wouldn't change.

Slowly, carefully, Dion pulled himself up, then holding onto the steering wheel, manoeuvring himself into the driving position, he slowly disappeared down the road.

Thankfully, the girls didn't witness the beating; they never knew their beloved uncle William had even touched their papa, they thought he'd just warned him. I left it at that. When William got home, he called on Jannie de Kok for some advice on what to do next if the harassment continued. If Dion laid a charge of assault with intent, how were we to respond?

"Shit, William, he could have you for attempted murder."

"Ha, let him try, then I will fucking kill the doos (idiot), it would be worth it."

Jannie roared with laughter, knowing how William felt about Dion.

No charges were ever laid against William.

The next time Dion saw the girls was four months after William had pulverised him. He was collecting them from school and taking them to the movies. Hours later they still weren't home. I called the police who, for once, flew into action, and when they found them, both the girls were in a terrible state.

When Storm saw me, she cried hysterically and wrapped her arms around my waist.

"Mama, Papa locked us in the car and drove scarily fast, telling us he'd kill us all if Viv and me didn't agree to force you to go back and live with him."

Vivienne was holding onto her sister. I stood there. Their little bodies wracked with sobs; they were both deeply distressed. I went into a cold, protective, maternal rage.

"Oh my God, what the hell will he think up next?" I growled.

Thankfully, the police had got to them before disaster did.

Dion was arrested and jailed.

The following day, Dr Gouws called me after visiting Dion in jail, and what he suggested appalled me.

"I can't possibly do that. You have got to be joking, doctor. You need to come up with a better suggestion, I'm afraid," I said with finality.

"Mrs du Toit, you must understand, the longer you are apart, the more dangerous he is going to get and that's guaranteed. He will feel nothing for taking your life, then his daughters' and then himself. It's a possession thing. He will do anything to prove he cannot live without you and if it means killing you all, believe me, he will do it. You are in grave danger, my dear."

"Then have the bastard committed. Get him out of the way. He's not just a danger to us, but society. You promised that last time."

"Mrs du Toit, I understand, and yes, we can do that, but it's a complicated process that will take time. What you need to grasp is this: he will come out of rehab and then you will be in greater danger than you are now, and that I can guarantee."

"So, what is the use of rehab then?"

"If we commit him, it is unlikely he would be in for more than six months. He understands the system intimately and knows how to work it to his advantage. You, of all people, should know that. You are his 'possession'. He is obsessed with you, dangerously so. I can guarantee he's not taking his medication, though he swore he was, but as we both know, he is a particularly good liar. He admitted to drinking heavily again, so even if he was taking his medication, the alcohol would obliterate any good the drugs might have done him."

I cringed as the doctor's words sank in. I couldn't answer and I couldn't agree; I didn't know what to do. An uncomfortable silence settled between us, then I remembered.

"In the divorce court, he was warned that he would not see his children until he was dry. That is contempt of court. Surely, we can stop him from seeing them again?" I asked, clinging to whatever I could.

"He knows the law, Mrs du Toit. It's how these people operate. Eventually, he will commit a serious crime and that's what we want to prevent."

I understood his underlying message. I couldn't bear the thought of living with Dion again, let alone being anywhere near him.

"I have arranged for him to come in and see me. He will be brought here cuffed and in a police car. They are keeping him in jail for a few days to give him time to think about the consequences of his recent actions. He might realise that not all the cops here are crooked and support what he does."

Sobs rose out of nowhere suddenly; I couldn't control them, but I managed to stammer, "I can't do this, Dr Gouws, I just can't."

"Give yourself time to process it all, Mrs du Toit. You have a few days. When I meet with him, I will tell him that we have spoken. I'm prescribing different medication and will offer him two choices: get back on his medication and give up drinking to get you back or be committed to an asylum for two years. Are you happy with that?" he asked, but no words could leave my mouth, my ability to speak had gone.

Then he said, "Just a thought, would you consider meeting with him here after his first appointment?"

"How will that help, doctor? In front of you, he's charming and sweet. He will promise to do anything for the girls and me, you've just said that. I've said it before, and I'll repeat, it's what you and everyone else don't see that scares the shit out of me, to put it bluntly."

"It's worth a try, Mrs du Toit. I'll leave it with you."

I discussed the conversation I had with Dr Gouws with William. He suggested that, under the circumstances, I should meet with the doctor and Dion and make my decision after that meeting. I mulled it all over and called Dr Gouws and agreed to meet with him and Dion.

Chapter Twenty-One

Twenty-four hours of sleeplessness, tossing and turning, fighting with myself, sweaty breakouts, and shivers and sobs had filled my night. Somehow, I had to prevent Dion from coming back into our lives, no matter the circumstance. I skipped over the nitty-gritty, but asked the girls how they felt about having their papa living with us as a family again. Neither gave me an answer; neither needed to. Their expressions were enough. Torn between what the girls had conveyed with their expressions and what William and the doctor had said, I didn't know what to do next.

I sat at my desk in a daze, staring blindly out the door, trying to process the events and information I'd been forced to address. I ran through the suggested details from Dr Gouws with Derek; he was at a loss as to what to advise me to do, but said that saving my life, and the life of the two girls, was where I needed to focus. I nodded, but where was I to start? Would Dion actually do that?

"My wonderful mother always said to me, 'When life is not going your way, you must try to see the funny side of it.' Well, I'm sure when she said that she didn't know another human being like Dion existed. I cannot find anything funny about any of this crap."

"You have my sympathy, my dear. And a shoulder to cry on, but, as far as I'm concerned, that man should spend the rest of his life in an asylum. No one in their right mind could possibly find anything funny about what Dion has done to you and the girls. He's a head case." Derek was about to go on when the telephone rang.

I leapt at the sound and realised how edgy and vulnerable I felt.

"Hello," I said with a shaky voice.

It was Dr Gouws; he'd spoken to Dion. "Dion is happy for you to join the conversation. The appointment is tomorrow morning at nine."

I felt queasy.

"I will be there, doctor."

I put the phone down. Crushed and defeated. Those awful sensations had become the way of my life. Was I cursed? If only I had answers other than terminating his life. The rest of the day passed in a blur. I couldn't focus. I couldn't concentrate. Everything was a jumble in my mind.

The following morning, I arrived at the doctor's rooms fifteen minutes early and was sitting reading a magazine in the waiting room when Dion sauntered in.

"Hello!" he said with a triumphant smile.

I nodded. He sat down beside me and smiled again. I so desperately wanted to wipe the smirk from his face.

An hour of what I can only describe as an "interrogation" took place in Dr Gouws' office. I expressed my opinion without reserve, my fears and uncertainties, and though I sensed Dion's annoyance by my blatant honesty, outwardly, he was calm.

I was not going back to live with Dion, not now. He had to prove himself first, then I may consider it because the girls had suggested that if Papa went back to how he was at the plot, they'd agree to be a family again. That spoke volumes. If we all had to go to court for Dion to hear his children saying that, that's what I was happy to do.

"Maybe give Papa one last try, Mama," Storm had said after I had explained parts of the meeting she was able to grasp.

Had it been my decision only, I would have never considered it.

Dion agreed to everything, of course. He agreed to taking his meds, being monitored, no more drinking, not a drop, permanently. He'd already been put on new medication. If he consumed even as much as a teaspoon of alcohol, it would make him so ill he would be hospitalised. He'd agreed to six months of close monitoring.

I knew he could do six months, he'd done it before for three years without monitoring, but then what?

That evening, the girls and I curled up on the couch together. I explained, skimming over some details of what Dr Gouws had suggested, and they both agreed Papa had to prove himself first.

"I will tell him, Mama. But is Papa able to change?" Storm said thoughtfully, showing a wisdom far beyond her years.

As she said it, I wished Dr Gouws could have heard the truth spoken from a child's view of her father's behaviour. Storm read her father like a book, and they too were suffering the uncertainties of living with their unstable father again.

"We can only hope so, my precious. Let's see what happens over the next few months."

Vivienne had remained silent all evening, refusing to talk. That worried me. I knew she found it difficult expressing what she was feeling, but for now it was easier for her to close up and manage her difficulties in silence. It was not a healthy response and in that moment I wasn't sure what to do about it, other than taking her to a child psychologist.

Mom was disgusted that Dr Gouws had even suggested a reunion of any sort, and William was outraged. However, that didn't diminish the fact they were concerned for our safety. William agreed with Dr Gouws that Dion could end all of our lives. With that knowledge, they remained my rock, supporting me through the most awkward and trying decision of my life: to stay single with the kids and risk our lives or go back and pray that this time, under Dr Gouws' guidance, Dion would be cured.

Six months later, we were back as a family, living on the plot once more. I was naturally more guarded than the two girls; their little thoughts were more focussed on being let loose with the space they'd once enjoyed. It was far more fun than worrying about what their father might do.

Shortly after the move back, Derek retired. I was heartbroken, and though he'd been talking about it for ages, I wasn't ready to release his camaraderie. He had been such an important part of my life, but it got me thinking. It was an obvious time to make a change to my career. I called the other rock in my life, Amelia. She agreed there wasn't much else she could do, to be fair, but she was always there as a shoulder to cry on, even though it was always over the phone. A few days later, I gave in my notice and decided to take a month off before looking at what to do next.

I'd been home for two weeks, being blissfully lazy and enjoying some vital quality time with the girls, when Dion took some leave too.

Life together was raw and touchy. We didn't avoid each other, but it was going to be a massive effort to rebuild a foundation of shattered respect and trust. The love was gone. What remained as the cement to the relationship was the girls. I'd promised them I would do whatever it took to make sure they were safe.

Two weeks together on the plot was awkward. It took several more months to gradually become more comfortable in each other's company. Dion began to open up a little more and I became less cranky. Even the two girls slowly released the protective wall they had built around them.

Dion found vulnerability difficult, but he was working on it. He began to share snippets of deep inner secrets, which provided me with more of a glimpse into what had moulded him from the tragedy of his childhood. He admitted to the relationship his father had with Selina. It finally came out. He admitted his father was nasty. A man who had done terrible things to his wife and to him and his brother, even being locked in a wardrobe together for two days as a punishment. When he let them out, they were seriously dehydrated and hospitalised. There were other awful stories he found hard to tell.

It was complicated, but it left me with no doubt, in his peculiar way, he loved his two beautiful girls, and he adored me and he was following Dr Gouws' guidelines religiously. He was taking his medication, which eased the tension and stress considerably. I was still guarded and a bit sceptical, but under the circumstances, we were making progress and the monitoring was helping. At the onset of this trial period, I had laid a few clearly defined boundaries and gave Dion a new affectionate name: "Gogga". A word with multiple descriptions in Afrikaans, but in this instance, I used it affectionately to describe Dion's somewhat devious character.

We had all agreed that only kind, loving and positive words were to become a part of our daily conversation. The transformation seemed to be working. The girls were doing well at school again, and with faith in their father's change, their self-confidence was restored.

Storm had a powerful singing voice, inherited from her father. With Dion's careful coaching, it was developing beautifully. Coaching his daughter was the highlight of his days. As it always had, music settled him better than any drug, including alcohol. He was proud of Storm, as I was. Her voice showed a lovely, sensitive, gentile side to her character when she got lost in the sounds and the tones as she practised. The only negative to this situation was Vivienne became very jealous of the attention her father was giving Storm and I could see a deep-rooted rebellion beginning to form. I needed to spend more time with her.

None of Dion's past misdemeanours had affected him; he'd brushed them off and found it enormously difficult to understand why I was still so cautious after the time that had passed. I had to remind him I'd only been home for a few months. I was ready to start looking for a new job. I was beginning to feel too isolated on the plot. At least, for now, Dion was employed.

Amelia called me often after our move. She was concerned about our safety. She refused to visit the plot, and when she was transferred back to Bloemfontein, we'd meet in town as we always had. During the first week of my search for a new job, Dion tarnished the status quo by asking me to marry him again.

I declined with each persistent request, though it didn't deter his resolve in attempting to convince me it was what we should do. He went on patiently begging until finally, nearing the end of our third year back together, with the children older and more secure, I felt it was safe to say he'd proved himself. I gave in, convinced our rollercoaster life was finally over. Dr Gouws was happy that Dion was over his need to turn to alcohol when times got difficult. He was considerably more emotionally stable too.

We married again at the Home Affairs offices without a wedding party. Derek agreed to be with us as a witness. William and Mom refused our invitation.

The girls excitedly witnessed the proceedings, happy we were marrying again, although they were disappointed that our "wedding" didn't have the typical trappings and was over in fifteen minutes. It was a beautiful sunny day and our moods were as bright and happy. With the formalities complete, we walked out of the offices holding hands. I was feeling optimistic and the two girls happily bounced their way down the steps ahead of us.

Standing on the last step, Dion stopped and turned to me, his sexy, beautiful dimple set deep in his chin, the twinkle in his mysterious brown eyes shining like the sun, just as they had been on our first wedding day many years before. Holding both my hands, he captured my gaze; it was a special moment, until he said, very quietly, "Now you belong to me again."

I froze. That fearful chill from before ran down my spine, as it had so many times. The monster was back as he bent forwards and kissed my hand. The kiss of death? Happy smiles, which moments before had spread across my face, evaporated in the warm sunshine, withering away like a flower in the desert.

Chapter Twenty-Two

It was hard to believe the scoundrels were back – the whole lot – with carte blanche to do as they pleased, now I'd signed my life away. I was their legal possession once more. They owned me, each one of those complicated personalities that lurked behind that handsome face. I'd never known another human like him – the change happened in an instant – and where was Dr Gouws when I needed him to witness it? There, on the steps, in front of my eyes, I watched him morph once more from a loving, sober companion of three years into a venomous ogre. It was this distinctive switch that beggared belief. It was what I'd tried so hard to explain to Dr Gouws and everyone else who'd dealt with him for all these years. No one could understand it, not even me.

I kept up pretences for the sake of the girls and then, to my utter horror, discovered I was pregnant. I didn't let anyone know, including Dion, until one evening when he was particularly smarmy and intolerable.

"Cut the crap, Gogga. I don't need the window dressing. Why did Phillip call you?" I asked.

The two brothers were not close. Dion had damaged their relationship years back, but I sensed there was something unsavoury being born.

"Well…" He paused, trying to work out what was the best way to lie to me now he was aware I knew him better than he knew himself. Spread out across the couch in much the same way Splodge typically lay, owning the space as only he could, but without oozing the same sincerity that the cat did, he said, "Phillip suggested we sell up here, move back to Bethlehem and buy the Elna sewing machine franchise."

I stared at him in disbelief.

"I hope you said no. What do you know about sewing machines anyway?" I asked while dipping a rusk into my coffee.

He purposefully didn't answer.

"Sell up here and buy a sewing machine agency with the money from our home? Are you out of your tiny little mind?"

As I asked the question, the girls burst into the lounge before Dion could find an appropriate answer. Their soaking wet hair flying everywhere, their bodies wrapped in bath towels, they stopped, noticing a rise in my voice and a change to the tone. Their playfulness was gone in an instant. They looked at each other, then back at me, decided all was good and continued the chase, shrieking with laughter. Their happy sounds tugged at me. How long was it going to last now?

Dion went on trying to convince me that his brother's idea was a good one, between interruptions of hysterical laughter from Storm and Vivienne, until Dion couldn't take their merriment a moment longer and reprimanded them. In seconds, the room was quiet, the spell of the "happy mood" broken, and they disappeared hastily to their bedroom. I followed, reassuring them Papa wasn't angry and then went back to the sitting room. They knew I was covering up for their father.

"Then what, Dion? Back to renting a house? Not a chance…" I sighed and curled my legs up underneath me, with the weight of the world on my shoulders once more. "Who is going to run the business anyway, Dion?"

"We'll run it together, build it up, sell it and buy another house in two years." Dion smiled confidently. "Besides, you won't be working, and it will give you something to focus on."

I couldn't fault that, but reality told a different story.

"That's not the point, Dion. Why put the girls through this? It means a change of schools, disrupting their lives again, removing them from their friends at a crucial time, and I don't want to move from here. It's a healthy environment for the girls to grow up in, and we own it."

Dion was becoming agitated with my fierce resistance. He didn't mention the idea again for a few days, but I also knew that when Dion went silent, it spelt danger; he was planning something devious. I was right. When he got home, he announced he was buying the shop. I erupted, barely able to articulate my words.

"Does… the safety… security and welfare of … your family ever enter your mind… when… when you make decisions?" I stammered breathlessly. "You never discussed this with me, Dion. Is your brother more important now?" I asked, anger-infused spittle accidently flew from my mouth. "I'll buy you out, the girls and I will stay put, and our next child will have the pleasure of growing up with space around him like every little boy should."

Dion's eyes narrowed. Perhaps I should have told him earlier. Delaying it those few days may have been the wrong decision, but what was ever the right one with this man? I watched the colour drain from his face, turning his complexion from a healthy one to a pale, sickly grey. For the first time in a long time, my statement left him without an instant retort. He eventually responded.

"What? Are you... are you pregnant?"

"Yes, five months along and it's a boy, from what they can see."

"Why didn't you tell me before?"

"Perhaps I should have, Dion, but you've been so wrapped up in your own life again you scarcely notice we exist, let alone my changing shape, with or without clothes on. And now you want to disrupt our lives again. I can live without you, Dion, you know that, with two children or three. You go on and run your little shop with your brother. I want no part of it. I shall be calling Dr Gouws in the morning."

He sat for a moment, shaking his head, looking at his feet. I couldn't read his response to me calling Dr Gouws again.

"Why didn't you tell me you were pregnant?" He was obviously quite perturbed by the news.

"Because you don't give a shit about us, Dion, no matter what you tell the world, and that is why I never told you. We're just a make-believe anchor for you, and in your calculating way, you hold us to it. There is only one person that matters in your life, and that's you. Cast your mind back to the trouble I had with contraceptives and recall the doctor telling us that because I'd been on the last contraceptive for so long, I'd be sterile. Early on in this pregnancy, I didn't think anything of the missed periods."

"You and the family *will* move with me, Elizabeth." He'd not taken in a word of what I'd just said.

"Not a chance. This was your decision. You go ahead without us."

A very slight flicker of concern showed on his face; my threats weren't idle ones, and he knew that. He also knew it wouldn't bother me if he never met his son. That, I hoped, was my trump card.

"I will run the shop successfully, Elizabeth, I promise." He tried to redeem himself. "You know I can't live without you."

"Talk crap. If you really can't live without me then why make such rash decisions on your own? So now you're going to have to learn to live without us again, Dion."

"Don't you think I am fucking capable of running the shop successfully?" he asked, angrily.

"Quite frankly, no, I don't. And your promises... well, I'm sorry, I've learnt they mean nothing to you, so don't bother making any. Your history is in sales (and I wanted to say, steeped in lies), not retail. Running your own business requires commitment and responsibly, neither of which you are capable of."

That struck a sensitive chord. He walked out of the house, slammed the front door defiantly and left. Though I had no idea where he was going, I had a nasty hunch.

The next day, he called to say he'd signed the deal; he'd sold the plot.

The bank loan I'd secretly applied for was approved twenty-four hours too late. He'd caught me in his net again.

Chapter Twenty-Three

Storm and Vivienne were devastated and sobbed for days. Not even the announcement of a growing baby brother lightened their mood. Mine was as bleak. I wasn't looking forward to the rest of the pregnancy; he'd doused any excitement there may have been found there too. How I had wanted our little boy to grow up with the freedom his sisters had experienced for six years of their lives. It was where little boys should grow up, but Dion snookered me again. The yin and yang of my life couldn't find a harmonious link.

The thought of leaving our wonderful plot, the place I'd turned from a dry, dusty shell to an oasis paradise, broke my heart. The children were secure and happy, and after pouring so much money, work and love into it, the property meant the world to me. The mere thought of having to say goodbye to it when the school term ended was unbearable heartache for the three of us. Much to Dion's disgust, paying me my half of the property and his part of the franchise left him with very little spare cash. Phillip was a silent partner and insisted he remain in his secure job, living in his own house in Bloemfontein.

On 9 December, we made our way, with shattered hearts, to Bethlehem. Kneeling, with their tummies pressed against the backrest, the girls looked back and quietly sobbed as I drove slowly down the road, and with every metre we covered, my heart was being slowly ripped out of my chest as we gradually left the property we adored for good.

The girls waved sadly to Miriam, who stood watching us go, crying into her apron that she'd lifted to her eyes until, eventually, she was out of sight. How I wished Dion had been there to witness the heartache he had caused us – except it wouldn't have moved him like it did us.

"Mama, why can't Miriam come too?" Vivienne sniffled as she turned away from the back window and sat down, her arms folded across her chest as she pouted.

"Why did Papa do this?" Storm asked angrily at the same time; her bottom lip was quivering as she sniffed.

That morning, before leaving, the girls had walked every inch of the property in tears, storing memories and hugging Miriam, begging her to come with us, just as they had pleaded with me to stay on the plot. Their lives were falling apart around them; their beloved home had been sold, and they were helpless to change anything.

As we drove on, emotional exhaustion took its hold on all of us. I turned on the radio, hoping the music would help lift the mood.

"Please go back, Mama, please," Vivienne sobbed and tugged at my arm in a desperate attempt to stop this happening. Losing Miriam and their treasured home was just too agonising.

"We can't, my girl. Papa sold the plot."

Vivienne sat down again while unhindered tears streamed down her cheeks. As the grief pulled at her, she took deep, shuddering breaths. All I could do was hope she'd eventually fall asleep.

I'd secretly made a promise to Miriam that I would call her when we settled, but I didn't want to tell the girls in case her return never materialised. Just as Vivienne's shuddering sobs were subsiding, Storm announced, "I hate Papa."

"So do I," Vivienne whispered, before fatigue took over and she fell asleep.

We arrived in Bethlehem a few hours later, emotionally depleted.

To appease me, or so he thought, Dion had rented a comfortable home in a pleasant suburb on the side of a hill overlooking the town. The town lay sprawled out below us, and the views of the rugged mountains beyond helped lift dampened spirits.

We had our evening meals on the veranda and watched the molten ball of spectacular African sun setting as it melted into the horizon, leaving a delightful palette of vibrant colours in the sky, but not even that put a spark back in the girls. They remained sombre and miserable. All they wanted was to be back in the home they loved. Dion had just shrugged.

A few days later he attended the compulsory franchise orientation training in Johannesburg. The course was six weeks. This was to ensure the standards laid out were maintained. With him away, I ran the shop in his absence. To my surprise, it was busier than I'd expected, which was a welcome relief, and I began to feel fractionally more positive that it could offer us a decent income.

Perhaps we *could* buy another house in two years.

When Dion got back from Johannesburg, he took over again; I was too far into my pregnancy to go on working all day. He also needed to find an assistant for the repair division and employed a man called Bernard, a ruffian alcoholic with a most unpleasant manner whom I didn't approve of, but he had years of experience in sewing machine repairs.

Our little Pieter made his appearance during the evening of 28 February 1984. He was a big boy, and I struggled, but the struggles and pain were soon forgotten when I had him in my arms. Dion was ecstatic. He had a son. The girls were charmed by their baby brother, smothering him with love and cuddles as often as they could, fighting over who got to him first, who changed him and helped at bath time. Despite the fun with their baby brother, the girls were still moody and unhappy; the time was right to contact Miriam. She didn't have another job and shrieked down the phone, promising to be with us in a week.

I didn't tell the girls of Miriam's impending arrival. It broke my heart seeing them so quiet and depressed, but within a few minutes, Miriam would change that. They scraped their chairs out and plonked themselves down at the dining table and hardly spoke before lunch.

"Close your eyes. Let's say grace," I ordered.

"Aw, Mom, do we have to?" Vivienne moaned.

"Yes, we do. We have to give thanks for our food."

With their eyes tightly closed, Miriam crept out of hiding and stood beside Storm. I stretched grace out to last fractionally longer, and when they opened their eyes, pandemonium broke out as the two girls exploded with delight, bouncing off their chairs, knocking into each other in their haste to wrap their arms around Miriam's ample waist, joy on their little faces once more. Miriam was happy to be back with us and meet our delightful little Pieter. The timing of her return could not have been more perfect – Dion was back on the bottle. I would need her more than ever.

"I do not believe it, Dion. You've just thrown away our home, the one the girls and I loved, now you're throwing away any chance of buying another, and you're running the risk of losing your children and me again. Does that make you feel good?"

"Oh, don't bloody start. Whine, whine, whine. It's all you ever do. I'm also fucking sick of it, you know. I suppose you're going to find me a psychologist in this town too and try and have me committed," he spat with stinging sarcasm.

The bastard! His reaction was confirmation that, no matter what I did, he was *never* going to change. It was time for me to gather my wits and cut the cord. Forever. Dr Gouws and all his advice weren't worth the monumental effort and sacrifices the children and I had made.

I found a job and Miriam stepped in as surrogate mother once more. A role she played with excellence. She cleaned the shop three times a week, keeping an eye on what Dion was up to, while I filled the position of relief housemother at the Mother Teresa Orphanage. I took the job because I could take Pieter to work with me. The salary wasn't what I was used to, but it was better than nothing. I still had my portion from the plot in savings. I hadn't been at the orphanage long when they offered me the live-in position as housemother of the group of boys I taught and looked after during the day. The post included a quaint cottage, and I was sorely tempted to take it on my own.

Moving to the cottage meant saving the rent on the other house, so I accepted, telling Dion the money saved on rent was to be injected back into stocks for the shop. Miriam rented a room close to the orphanage and in the morning, she worked there, and in the afternoon, she worked for us.

Ten wonderful orphaned teenage boys, their ages ranging from thirteen to seventeen, lived in comfortable, homely surroundings in a large house adjacent to the cottage. The older boys slept two to a bedroom and the younger ones were three in a bedroom. There were three bathrooms, a spacious open plan lounge and dining room, which led out onto an expansive veranda looking onto manicured gardens. A beautifully equipped kitchen wasn't used by the boys, as meals were prepared in a central kitchen, but I decided to teach them all to cook. It was a lovely, homely environment for the boys, all of whom had experienced tragedy in their short lives, but despite that, they were polite and respectful to the girls and made settling in next to them worry-free.

They were good lads who soaked up my teachings, proving to be hungry to learn boy stuff, like changing light bulbs, attaching plugs to electrical cords, changing car tyres, mending bicycle punctures, and using a screwdriver and hammer effectively amongst the other necessary activities boys of their age like to learn and hadn't been taught.

Once they'd perfected some simple boy skills, we moved onto knitting, sewing buttons onto clothing, fixing clothing with tears or where seams had come adrift; all important little necessities they grasped quickly and enthusiastically. They enjoyed their knitting so much I managed to persuade the local haberdashery store to donate wool and knitting needles, and we set up an in-house competition to see who could knit the best scarf in the shortest time. I'd got monetary prizes for the best three scarves. The boys enthusiastically knitted their hearts out. They all wanted to be winners of the money.

Then I started the cookery classes, but in time, all the attention I paid to the boys triggered the nasty, jealous ogre to emerge in Dion. He'd have sudden outbursts of ludicrous resentment towards them. They considered me their adopted mother for no one else had ever offered them this level of care and guidance, but Dion viewed it all with his own brand of twisted thoughts, and the tension began to rub off on us all, especially when he insisted they stop calling me "Mama". They became very protective over me, so in an urgent effort to include him, I suggested he get involved too. There were lots of lovely children keen to learn to play our piano and teaching those that were keen to play would keep him out of the pub. The boys responded with enthusiasm, and soon girls and boys from the other houses lined up for lessons and our house became known as the happiest place to be in the orphanage.

A few months later, Miriam called me to one side, telling me I needed to check the shop.

"It is not good," was all she said.

Curious, I popped down during one lunch hour and was horrified by what greeted me. The shelves were bare of stock and neglected – a business in trouble – and though I was disgusted, I didn't have the energy to care anymore. There was only one solution and that was to get out and for good this time, making sure it was a successful escape.

School holidays started the following week. I bundled the kids into my car, and we spent a few days with Mom. She'd recently had a hip replacement and the least we could do was help her for a few days. She also hadn't seen us for quite some time. Our stay was cut short when, on the fifth day, I was summoned to return to the orphanage and report to the headmistress' office immediately. I wondered why it was so urgent and prayed nothing had happened to one of my special boys or any of the other orphaned children in the home. I dropped the girls at the cottage and rushed across to the offices.

Standing in the headmistress' office was reminiscent of my own school days, and I smiled at the memory of how terrified we used to be when summoned to the headmaster's office, even if no "crime" of naughtiness or disobedience was the reason.

Mrs Mostert, the head of the orphanage, was a lovely, warm, compassionate woman, but she didn't have a look of warmth about her now. A tense, rather unpleasant, atmosphere dominated the room, and I wondered what could have happened in five days that was so bad.

"Elizabeth…" she began, then looked at me and hesitated, magnifying the uncomfortable atmosphere. "I am sorry to inform you…" She took a deep breath. "I have to ask you to resign."

What? I was shocked rigid. Was I hearing her correctly?

"This is very difficult for me, but… um… your husband…"

I froze.

"He was caught sexually molesting one of the girls."

I stood, feeling the internal tremors begin to shake my entire body.

"What? Oh God, no, no. Who?" I stammered.

"The first night you were away, he was excessively drunk, behaving in a particularly unacceptable manner, which he repeated the following night, and he was asked to leave the property if he could not behave while you were away."

She could have been talking about a child, I thought.

Shaking my head in shame, I didn't know what to say as I fought a nasty mix of emotions. I couldn't speak.

"I am so sorry, Elizabeth. You're the best housemother we've ever had. We're all devastated."

Nothing could have prepared me for this news. My cheeks were hot with rage and all I wanted to do was castrate the bastard. He didn't deserve to live, in my opinion. Mrs Mostert went on. I almost wished she hadn't, as her words ripped into my heart.

"I'm so sorry," she said again, the warmth in her voice returned and touched me deeply. "You have led by example and given the boys more than duty required. We are eternally grateful for that, as I know they are. They will miss you terribly."

I bit down on my bottom lip to prevent myself from sobbing as the grizzly reality rapidly sunk in.

"Oh my God." I covered my face with my hands, pushing back the tears. "Who was the girl?" I asked in a whisper, at the same time, dreading the answer.

"Moira," Mrs Mostert said sympathetically.

"Dear Lord, no, not Moira. Oh God, I should have known better," I sobbed. "How could he have even considered it? Will there be a court case?"

Mrs Mostert nodded. "She was the girl he was teaching to play the piano, wasn't she?"

"Yes, I feel sick, for it was my suggestion. I hope they lock the son of a bitch up for good and throw away the key. Where is he now?"

"In that shop, I would imagine. My dear, do not blame yourself."

"I can't help it, Mrs Mostert." To think the father of my children had committed this evil deed was beyond redemption. How was I going to explain this to the girls? Did I even dare? Storm was not much younger than Moira. My heart was thumping in my chest.

"How is Moira coping?" I felt an urgent need to go to her, comfort her, hold her. Nausea moved into the pit of my stomach as I thought of her. A young, beautiful, orphaned girl – her innocence being so callously violated in the most insensitive of ways could not be forgiven. I had to make sure of that.

"She was in a terrible state and only found the courage to tell us yesterday. It was rape. Though she said he sweetly coaxed her into exploring her sexuality."

I moaned aloud; I knew just how convincing Dion could be.

"Poor, poor Moira," I whispered, shaking my head, looking into space, my gut in knots.

A young girl like Moira would not have known how to cope or say no to his coaxing; agreeing to his persuasions would have been her only way out. I also knew he would have twisted it to make her feel it had been her decision. She'd carry the guilt and the scars; an emotion he carelessly discarded.

"I know how hard this is for you, Elizabeth. Immediate resignation or divorce are your only two options. He is forbidden access to the property. I'm so sorry."

"Yes, of course. I understand," I answered, wanting to run from the world to a place where no feeling existed. Defeated, disgusted, humiliated, angry; I didn't want to feel anymore. If it wasn't for the children, I would have ended my life.

Another divorce was pending, and this time, I would ensure the swine was jailed, but right now, my thoughts were on how to protect my beloved children from the embarrassment and cruelty their school mates would surely dish out as soon as this humiliating information found its way around the town.

The sordid scandal spread like wildfire, as I knew it would. Everywhere I went people whispered or avoided eye contact and conversation; that was the natural human part. The sickening struggle was trying to help the girls deal with the cruelty.

The disgraceful pig somehow snivelled out of the court case. He paid a handsome pile of cash to some unscrupulous police officer, and the evidence disappeared.

Was there no end to this man's wicked ways? Just when I thought it couldn't get worse! I never did learn who that someone was in the police force, though I tried. I tried for Moira's sake, I tried for my children's sake, but with the evidence destroyed, I was hamstrung.

Chapter Twenty-Four

None of us quite knew how to respond to the situation in which we found ourselves. It took the urgent search for a new home and my mother's reassurance that she'd be with us soon. The whirlpool of hardships was trying its best to suck me under. The children were what I had to stay strong for. I longed for the day when I could face the world again without being confronted by the prying, questioning eyes of others. But life has its ways of giving strength to draw on in times like these. When I thought there was no hope, change popped in from the most unexpected place; a simple tatty old piece of furniture changed the course of my life.

I'd found a house to rent and Mom moved to Bethlehem to help the children and I regroup from the recent humiliation. She was the lifeline who kept me from coming apart at the seams. One evening we were sitting on the tatty old lounge suite, commenting on the state of it, while sipping our coffee. I couldn't do anything about it other than chuck a pretty throw over it.

Then Mom piped up. "Why don't you recover it, Elizabeth?"

"Mom!" I exclaimed, laughing. "Don't be absurd. I barely have enough money to feed us, and I have never done upholstery before."

"I'll give you the money. We'll take it apart, one chair at a time, and do this last," she said, patting the cushion of the couch she was sitting on.

The simplicity and logic of her statement resonated somehow; I could sew and was pretty good at it, so why not? I had enough money in my savings account. After the rental and electricity deposits, the first month's rent, school fees, which were in arrears, and Miriam's salary were paid, I had enough saved to last us six months without having to borrow from Mom. In a fixed deposit account, I had 5,000 Rand, but that I could not touch for another year.

"We can cut the pattern from the pieces we undo, sew the new pieces together and see what happens," she chirped.

I wasn't sure what to do with the emotion of the moment. The timing of her inspiration could not have been more perfect.

"Ma, you are wonderful. What would I do without you?" The words sounded oddly shallow as they left my lips, but I was deeply inspired and meant it.

"It's what mothers do. Look what you have put up with for your children. I think you overlook that, my child."

She was right. Up to now, I'd navigated my life for everyone else. Now it was her magic steering me in a new direction.

Over the weeks following the Moira rape, I refused Dion access to the kids, wanting nothing more to do with him, ever. Then the law turned against me. I was not permitted to deny him access to the children: "he'd committed no crime". *All the evidence against him had been destroyed.* He seemed to get away with the most despicable behaviour at every turn; surely one day, he'd have pay for it?

Thankfully, and I say this in the kindest possible way, the girls were so disgusted and ashamed of what their father had done to Moira, *they* refused to see him. The law was forced to consider that.

After Mom's innovative suggestion, I lay in bed, emotionally and physically spent, staring up at the ceiling, trying to summon the freedom to feel charged with excitement, but it wasn't happening. I was too scared to be optimistic. That was my last thought before drifting off to sleep. A flutter of excitement was trying to nudge past the confusion. The challenge of recovering the lounge suite was what I needed and it turned out beautifully.

"Well, my talented daughter," Mom said, looking on proudly at what we'd achieved in a few weeks, "Why don't you start your own upholstery business?"

I burst out laughing, but the tatty old piece of furniture sprouted a brand-new life.

Chapter Twenty-Five

No more job hunting for me! *I* was the boss. *I* would write my salary cheques. These and other exciting thoughts were whipping through my mind. I had to recalculate my savings and had to borrow a small amount from Mom to launch my upholstery business. I understood the risk, but I was determined to make it work.

I named my business La Provence Interiors, sounding considerably more upmarket than the humble beginnings that it was. I placed the first small advert in the classified section of our local newspaper and sent it on its way with a sprinkling of colourful prayers. The response was more than I could ever have dreamt possible. It was the most liberating, expansive feeling that filled me with hope and a sense of purpose.

Job lot 001 in my invoice book: Re-cover loose cushions for a cane lounge suite. This was my despatch note to freedom, and from that first job, my business grew.

Dion had not been in town since the Moira incident. The coward had bolted; no one could have been happier than Moira and me. Our visits were frequent and fulfilling, and we developed an incredible bond, fortified by tragedy, but we pieced the bits of our lives back together to a place where we both could rise tall, claiming our feminine power once more. She and Storm had grown to be great friends even though Moira was older.

Towards the end of the second year, La Provence Interiors was doing so well that Mom decided to sell her house in Brandfort. Between us, we bought a rambling property, which had once been a doctor's consulting rooms and had it converted into business offices, our workspace and our home.

I had to keep pinching myself, reminding myself this was real; this was *my* fantastic thriving little business.

Though Dion may not have been in town, the nasty Bernard was a thorn in my side. He reported to Dion our every move, seen only through Bernard's inebriated eyes, of course. I could only assume the twisted lies and ghastly untruths he would have fed back to his like-minded friend, Dion, who was now, apparently, living in Johannesburg.

I needed help and I interviewed several ladies who claimed to be seamstresses and finally whittled them down to one delightfully funny, rather shy, coloured lady, Mariah. She had considerable experience on domestic sewing machines, but was terrified by the power and speed of the industrial machines. I overlooked that as she had everything else I was looking for in an employee.

"Eish, missus." She laughed when she first started. "Like airplane, too quick." She beamed.

She soon got used to its power and after only a few days, skilfully guided metres of fabrics under the footer guide, becoming the asset I knew she would be. Not only did she bring her sewing skills to the business, but barrel loads of delightful humour, so typical of people of colour from the Cape.

Mom opted to spend her time helping Pieter with his schoolwork. She was the girls' support system too, and cooked up some tantalising meals for us all for lunch and dinner. Into her seventies now, her gammy foot was arthritic, even more misshaped and painful. Her knees were weakening, but her hip replacement had been successful. She never complained, but I knew how much effort it took to take on what she had. I was soon totting up a handful of happy years in business on my own.

It seemed impossible as the years had gone so fast. Storm had grown into a beautiful, self-assured young lady who was in her last year at senior school and happily took many of the household chores away from Mom. Vivienne, on the other hand, was growing into a hormone-dominated handful, with many inherited paternal traits, and she deeply resented the close relationship Storm and I had. If her current attitude was the gauge for the next two years of her schooling, we were headed for a nasty nightmare that would undoubtedly disrupt my life.

Sooner than expected, she proved me right by ruining a peaceful evening by letting out a blood-curdling scream at the front door. Scrambling hurriedly out of bed, I grabbed my gown and ran to see what was happening. Viv had gone to the movies with friends. A devastating sight was waiting for her and, like before, the ghosts of the past came rushing back for us both. I had a horrible premonition that Dion was back in town and up to his dirty old tricks again.

Distraught and sobbing, garbled words toppled out of her mouth, mixed with sadness and alcohol, making them indecipherable, then I saw him: my most precious companion of so many years. Darling Splodge lay dead at her feet. I dropped to my knees; my heart tightened in my chest as I reached for him. He'd lived so many lives with us, he'd seen me through the darkest days of my life, and I felt a disturbing emptiness as I stroked his cold, stiff body.

Picking him up, I carried him through the house to the back veranda, where I found an empty box and lay his body down inside it, covering it with a towel. If Splodge had passed over due to old age, why at the front door?

To be sure Dion didn't have a hand in ending my precious cat's long life, the vet assured me he'd died of old age. Only then did I allow myself the freedom to release the grief I was holding on to. The house was empty without Splodge. A week later we went to the SPCA and came home with two delightfully fluffy kittens. Pieter named his Harry and Vivienne called hers Daisy. Daisy got more attention from Pieter and I; boys took precedence in Vivienne's life. As they grew from kittens to cats, so La Provence grew from a fledgling company to the largest interior decorating company in the town. For the first time in years, I was making a comfortable living.

Dion rarely phoned to speak to his children and he contributed nothing towards their expenses. He hardly knew his son, which broke my heart for Pieter's sake, though he assured me he didn't yearn for any paternal influence to enhance his youth.

Storm was finishing school soon, then joining the Metropolitan Police. She wanted to join the drug squad after her initial training. She believed she could make a difference to the lives of children ruined by drugs, or those who'd fallen off the wagon because of being raised by addicts. She had first-hand experience of living with an addict. Vivienne, we didn't know, but her belligerent determination to be as difficult as she could be was blatantly clear. Trying to have a civil conversation with her was as rare as water in the desert, and her behaviour became more and more insufferable for us all. Pieter, on the other hand, was a sensible and balanced child and wanted nothing to do with Vivienne, but he adored Storm. This caused different ructions – where was the manual for parents on raising opposites within a household?

"What's the matter, sis?" Storm asked with genuine concern as Viv came to breakfast sobbing.

She plonked herself down next to me and rested her head on my shoulder. We all sat quietly waiting; Storm looked across at me with raised eyebrows, and Pieter looked bored.

"Ma, I'm pregnant."

My brain felt like a battalion of busy ants had suddenly invaded it, causing a tactical muddle of indecision. Storm's mouth opened – nothing came out. Pieter said nothing, he was watching my reaction.

"I'm going to leave school and get married," Vivienne announced and her "crocodile tears" dried up.

"Don't be ridiculous, Vivienne. We need to sit together and work all this out sensibly."

"You heard me, Ma." Her chin jutted defiantly. She was too like her father.

"Vivienne!" I snapped. "That is the craziest thing that has come out of your mouth recently. Go and wash your face, and we'll talk this through when you come back."

Pouting, she pulled her pyjama top down to cover herself and sauntered out the room. Storm was still staring at me as Pieter got up and shouted from the kitchen.

"Slut."

Vivienne erupted.

"I'm not a fucking slut," she screamed at her brother.

"That's quite enough swearing from you, young lady," I reprimanded Vivienne, then Pieter fired her up again.

"She's not a lady, Ma."

"That's quite enough from both of you!" I shouted back. "We need to work this out as a family."

"She doesn't want to be a part of this family, Ma, don't waste your time," Storm joined in.

"Whoa, stop, stop, stop, all of you. What is done is done. There is no turning back now. Vivienne has to accept the responsibility of what she has done."

Storm got up and left, leaving Vivienne and I alone.

"Don't ask me to have an abortion, cos I won't," Vivienne snapped before I had said a word.

"You know that's against my principles, Vivienne," I said gently. "We do, however, need to talk. I'd like to know who the father is, what does he do, and does he know?"

Vivienne stared at me; her lips had formed into her theatrically rebellious pout again. "His name is Andre Venter, he's twenty-two years old, and he's training to be a diesel mechanic. He wants to marry me, and he's happy I'm pregnant."

"Well, that's a good start, but… um, I'm very disappointed in you for falling pregnant before leaving school. So very young to shoulder such responsibility. You know you will have to give up drinking and partying, young lady. You have two months left of this school year, which you will finish whether you like it or not," I said with finality.

"Okay," Vivienne said, sighing her best irritating sigh, emphasising how unhappy she was about finishing school, but fully aware she'd got off lightly. "I'll finish this year for you, Ma, but then we're going to live in Durban."

There was no point in trying to stop her.

"Oh, I see! How long have you been planning all this, Vivienne?"

"Not long." She smiled triumphantly.

My mind was spinning. My youngest daughter fleeing the nest, pregnant at seventeen and gone in just three months. Storm would be gone too. I'd heard about the empty nest syndrome; now I was feeling the threat of it closing in, but at least I still had Pieter and my mom.

"Before you go anywhere, I want to meet Andre and his parents."

"You will meet Andre this afternoon. I'm spending the night with him and will be back tomorrow evening. You won't meet his parents. They live in Durban," Vivienne informed me with about as much disrespect as she could muster.

I let it go, but I thought sadly, *Insolent and arrogant, just like her father. Not a thought for anyone else's feelings, no remorse, no apology, no shame.*

Andre seemed to be a pleasant young man and obviously adored Vivienne. Storm was happy her sister was leaving home, but she was angry at her for hurting me. Pieter spent the night with a friend. He didn't want to see his sister or meet her husband-to-be. He needed space and time to deal with what his sister had done.

Vivienne left at the end of November. She didn't bother letting her father know any of the details. I waited, wondering how long it would take Bernard to report the details to Dion. It took longer than I expected. Dion called after Christmas. He offered no words of encouragement and good wishes to his eldest daughter, who was starting her career in January – one of the biggest milestones of a young person's life.

"Vivienne is long gone, settled in Durban and expecting in April. She sounds happy and secure," I said.

He was furious he had not been told.

"You have yourself to blame. Neither of them want anything to do with you. I honestly don't blame them. If you'd bothered to call regularly, you'd have known. Didn't Bernard tell you?"

He ignored that dig. "Can I speak to Pieter?"

"He's not here. He's with a friend playing hockey."

"Playing hockey?" He sounded surprised.

"Yes, Dion, and what a disgrace you are as a father. You've broken their hearts, embarrassed them, you've not been there for them when it mattered, so don't push yourself on them now." I put the phone down.

It always happened in threes for whatever odd reason, but three years had passed and he'd not provided for his children, had rarely spoken to them, and now he expected to weave himself back into their hearts after the careless, cruel scars he'd left behind.

There was no point in saying it to him. There was always someone else to blame and he always protected himself from the corrosive effects of shame.

Chapter Twenty-Six

"Mom, is it wrong to sit and wish Vivienne wasn't my sister and Dion wasn't my father?" Pieter asked, looking burdened by guilt.

"No, my precious, it isn't wrong. Under the circumstances, I think it's natural. Sisters often irritate their brothers. We won't discuss your father, but feel no guilt, my boy. One day, you may find it in you to forgive him, or maybe not. Time will tell."

"There's no way I can forgive him, Ma. You protected and cared for us, and this is what they do to you."

I wondered where Pieter was going to take this conversation.

"I don't know how to handle my anger. That's why I escape to my room and bury my thoughts in my computer. It's the only way I can suppress my fury," he said apologetically.

I'd bought him a second-hand IBM 286 Hercules, of which he was immensely proud. He changed the subject.

"I've just installed CGA Gold from a DOS program. Hey, Ma, I love computers."

I smiled at his enthusiasm. Was the conversation on his sister and father going to continue?

"Hey, Ma, I have a new golfing game. It's hysterical. It's such a massive program and runs so slowly. When the golfer lifts the club to hit the ball, it's all in slow-mo. It cracks me up. Then the birds and crickets in the background have to pause so the

250

animated man can complete the swing to hit the ball, then the birds start to chirp again."

We laughed together. I decided it was time to get him involved in my computer. It had Lotus 123 on it. He was ecstatic.

"I can write my very own programs now, Ma. It's so cool." He beamed. He never broached the subject of his father, so I left it.

"I'm proud of you, my boy. These self-taught skills will be a huge asset to you one day."

Pieter was playing a new golf game, Mom was on the other couch dozing, and I was watching her. She was struggling, her eyes were closed, though I knew she was listening to the background noises coming from the golf game Pieter was playing. I could see how fast she was withering into old age, and it scared me. I couldn't bear the thought of her not being around. Pieter joined us in the lounge a little later.

"How's Jan doing, Pieter?" I asked.

"He's a good friend. He's had a hard life too, that's probably why we get on so well. He's like a brother to me."

"He certainly is, and you're both so good at hockey and indoor cricket. How's he with computers?"

Pieter burst out laughing.

"Can hardly switch one on." Pieter looked sad suddenly. "Mom, do you miss Storm as much as I do?"

"Even more than you do."

"I can see how your face changes when Storm is home, Ma. You love her so much, don't you?"

"Yes, I do, but I love you all. I don't always like what Vivienne does, but I still love her, like I love you." I wrapped my arms around my computer whiz kid.

The following morning, 7 April 1998, Andre called to say Vivienne had given birth to a beautiful baby girl, my first grandchild, and despite the circumstances, I was overjoyed.

"Congratulations to you both. Give my precious Vivienne a big hug. We'll chat when she's home. Have you let Dion know?"

"No, and I have no intention of doing so either. I'm sorry."

The next encounter we had with Dion was another unhappy one. We'd not seen him for a long time and one evening, he unexpectedly walked through the back door and into the kitchen, grabbing a knife on his way through. By the time we saw him, he was heading my way.

"Don't you dare touch her," Pieter yelled, but being fifteen, I was sure he wasn't going to be able to stop his rampaging, knife-wielding father without getting himself hurt.

Time stood still as I watched Dion poised to stab me. Pieter was moving towards us as I blocked Dion and grabbed his arm, the point of the knife millimetres from my face.

Fortunately, Storm was home that weekend. She heard the commotion and moved in on her father as swiftly and silently as a leopard. She launched, protecting Pieter by pushing him out of the way and pulled her father off of me, but it was too late. The knife had sliced through the top of my eyelid, splitting the skin up into my forehead. Blood gushed out of the wound like an open tap and ran down my face in rivers of red that descended to the floor.

Pieter stayed crouched down with me while Storm dealt with her father, pushing him back up against the wall using tactics she'd been taught in the police.

I whispered to Pieter, "Phone the police, my boy, then the hospital."

The struggle between father and daughter continued.

"We've got to get Mama to hospital," Pieter shouted above the racket.

I heard Storm screaming at her father, "I hate you, I hate you, get out."

Sounds and actions all faded into a singular noise as my shirt front became drenched with blood. Pieter had called the hospital and tossed a tea towel at me before joining his grandmother. She was on the phone to the police. Dion heard her and fled like a stray dog caught digging in a dustbin. By the time the police got to the house, Dion was gone.

Fingerprints were taken and the knife placed in a plastic bag as evidence. Storm whisked me off to hospital leaving Mom and Pieter to clean up the kitchen that now resembled a war zone. Thankfully, there was no damage to my eyeball – eleven stitches held the gaping wound together across my forehead.

When I got home, Pieter said angrily, "All I wanted to do was grab that knife and thrust it into Papa, end his life, so he would never hassle us again."

Chapter Twenty-Seven

The doctor had done a beautiful job stitching my eyelid, but the scar would be another constant reminder that evil in human form was never far away.

Pieter suffered deep emotional turmoil. Their roots embedded in anger and the helplessness of youth. Storm offered to help him through it. She'd soothed other youngsters whose parents were abusive. It was all part of her job now. Between her magical therapy and his computers, they did work it out.

Dr Gouws' words rattled in my head once more: "No matter where you are, Dion will never leave you alone."

William and I discussed the possibility of Mom returning to live on the farm. She would be safe. It took an awful lot of persuasion, but she eventually saw the sense in it. She was too frail to deal with any more drama.

Packing up her belongings and saying goodbye to my mother was one of the hardest things I'd done. The day Mom left, I organised for the house and office to be burglar-proofed. I also had external cameras mounted, so if Dion did return, I'd have evidence of him breaking in, or trying to break me which ever came first.

I sobbed as Mom was driven away, but she would be safe with William.

The police came back and suggested I lay an attempted murder charge. I refused to do that; he'd make a fool of me again with his unscrupulous friends. I didn't want to give him the opportunity to boast he was untouchable.

"Are you quite sure, Mrs du Toit? It could happen again."

"I know, and it will happen again." I shrugged, but did not want to tell him I'd had cameras installed. I was never sure who in the police was friend or foe. With cameras, I'd have evidence that he couldn't escape.

The cop was nodding his head and writing on his pad and I could see he was thinking I was mad. "There's still time to change your mind. If you do, call me. I'm not on his side." He gave me his direct line number.

"Thank you," I said. That took me by surprise. I felt relieved that not all the policemen in town were friends of Dion's.

"Mom, why didn't you lay charges? You need to teach Papa a lesson," Pieter urged.

"How many times have I tried before? He's won again because we've had to send Ouma away, but one day, it will catch him."

I hugged Pieter, feeling fatigued and old beyond my years. I'd lost every battle, but I wasn't going to lose the war on Dion du Toit. For some inexplicable reason, Dion always made me feel like I'd failed him somehow.

Some weeks after Mom left, an old-established carpeting company happened to come on the market. I snapped it up. Though it put me back in debt, it added value to my business. La Provence Interiors was now a one-stop interior decorating company.

I needed someone to run it for me and Andre came to mind. He and Vivienne had just been made redundant, within weeks of each other. They were struggling to find employment.

My head told me it could work; my gut was telling me something different. They were my children. I went with my head.

Andre accepted happily. He managed the job well, but it was after working hours that they exhausted me. He and Vivienne spent most evenings out, drinking with Dion. He'd moved back to Bethlehem. Apart from being their nanny, I found myself paying for everything too. It was time to bring their freeloading to an end and set the boundaries.

"Andre, I can't take on the burden of financially supporting you and your family. Living here didn't mean I pay your way too. It's time to pay for your boarding. And Viv needs to get off her arse and find a job to pay for a nanny or you must find another place to live."

I had grimly watched Vivienne follow the same cycle of financial abuse as her father. When she came begging for more financial support, I refused to help.

Carrying barrel loads of bitter resentment, they moved out, and on that day, the sun set on my darling mother. My "forever" rock ascended to join my father in a happier place, reunited again after all these years. I was distraught.

I went home. The farm, to me, was always home. Storm and Pieter followed a few days later and we attended Mom's funeral together. She was laid to rest in a specially prepared sanctuary at the bottom of the garden, deep within the earth that had given her life's purpose, the land she loved so dearly. I stayed a few more days, visiting her grave often. There I would thank her for all she'd taught me. Alone and quiet, I released the pain of losing her. Whispered conversations helped heal me. I was going to miss her.

Andre disappeared for a week without letting anyone know where he'd gone. When he returned, he bragged about all the cash he'd earned that week. I was flabbergasted by the sums of money he came home with, but annoyed by his lack of commitment to my business, I suggested he look for another job.

Coincidence, the fact of two things happening at the same time by chance in a surprising way, was the explanation, but what happened next was no coincidence.

Dion called suggesting he would take over where Andre had left off.

"That's not a good idea, Dion. It wasn't that long ago you tried to kill me. You can hardly think I would want to employ you."

"I never tried to kill you, Elizabeth. When Storm and Pieter grabbed me, the knife slipped."

Meting out the blame as always.

"Our opinions differ on that. Goodbye, Dion."

"Listen, liefie, wait, wait, wait. I don't have a job, and I would like to help you out."

"Firstly, I am *not* your liefie. Secondly, I have told you, I will not employ you."

"Please, Elizabeth. I'd also like to see more of Pieter."

"Why now? You abandoned him and he feels it. I'm not sure he wants to see more of you. Goodbye."

"When will you let me know, Elizabeth?" he said quickly.

"I just have. Keep looking," I snapped.

"Why can't you give me a chance? I'll get you lots of business."

"I've given you too many chances. You failed each one. Goodbye." I put the phone down before he could go on antagonising me.

That evening, I mentioned Dion's absurd telephone call to Pieter.

"You owe him nothing, Mom, remember that. I don't want to see him. All he's trying to do is make you feel guilty again. Don't fall for it this time. The bastard should work for you for free. He owes you so much, Mama."

Some home truths to mull over.

"What are the odds of not employing him? That could trigger his vindictive streak, then who knows what he will do to us next? Maybe he will try to kill you again, Mama."

I began the tedious task of interviewing. I employed an educated, well-spoken African man who'd worked for the previous owners of the carpet business. He came with a glowing reference and was delightfully humble. Joseph took over what Andre had abandoned.

Sitting at my desk, I decided I needed a holiday. A week in a health retreat. I dreamt about submerging myself into a steamy hot Jacuzzi, bubbling with spring water and staying in it until my skin crinkled and all my stress was bubbled away.

Sadly, Joseph wasn't suitable. He needed guidance and I didn't have time for that. The interviewing process began again and with it, a series of events that were to change my life.

The day I said goodbye to Joseph, Vivienne called to say she was pregnant again. Andre had been made redundant for the second time, but I was not to worry, he was going overseas on one of his *trips,* but could they move back with me?

Storm was my light, the warmth, the rainfall, the gentle breezes, and the sunshine in my life. Now I needed her. Vivienne was my night, dark, with the occasional twinkling star, her moods like the lunar phases. What should I do?

Pieter kept himself absorbed with his computers, his friends and his sport. Jan, his dearest friend, was living with us after losing his parents in a tragic car accident. Viv, Andre, Annie and the one on the way moving in with us would be a disaster.

This kind of chaos was the story of my life, then Vivienne added another dimension to the already existing chaos. She begged me to employ her father. I stoically fought against her and said I would sell the carpet division.

Vivienne blew, fuelled by vengeance; she was brutal. She accused me of cutting off her father, blaming *me* for his behaviour, spitting out her fury like a viper and her final injection of poison was a vicious reminder that her father couldn't live without me.

"Your success has gone to your head," she spat venomously.

I called Dion the following day and gave him the job. Anything for peace at home. Why had I let Vivienne back in? Because the fight had gone out of me.

Chapter Twenty-Eight

"Morning, Elizabeth. Excuse me for barging in on you, but I think you should see this."

Carol, my bookkeeper, handed me a bundle of papers before sitting down opposite me. Carol had been with me a year after I started La Provence Interiors. I trusted her implicitly. She was as sharp as a ray of early morning sunshine, and always there. When she called my attention to something, I listened.

"What's the problem?" I asked as I stretched back in my chair and took a deep breath. I was so tired.

"You look exhausted, my friend. But I think this is going to make you feel worse. There's a problem in the carpeting section."

No sooner had the words left her mouth, my stomach lurched. Words I'd feared I may hear. I covered my ears momentarily. Did I have to listen?

"Explain," I said as I moved my hands from my ears.

"I found a discrepancy that rang alarm bells, especially as it was associated with carpeting and your ex. If I'd had all the facts to hand, I would have brought it to your attention last week. Dion has spent his three-month probationary period cunningly ripping this company off. I can only imagine he came in with this plan."

"What's he been doing?" I grimaced, cursing myself for trying to appease Vivienne by employing Dion before allowing her to come home. Storm had warned me.

"He's been syphoning money off. Now it's serious. I'm sorry, Elizabeth. I could kick myself for not picking it up earlier. I also didn't want to ask too many questions in case you'd authorised some of it."

"When it comes to Dion, I authorise nothing to do with money. So, how's he been doing it?"

Carol began to explain. It was almost too hard to listen to.

"A false receipt book, the cunning swine," I breathed out.

"He's been buying all the materials for numerous cash jobs on your supplier accounts and, of course, no one questioned him," Carol explained.

"How much has he taken?"

"About 59,000 Rand," I heard her say.

That had been spent in our local bottle stores.

Anger wasn't what I was feeling; it was far worse. Murderous, yes. The same intense feelings I had all those years ago when I drove to the farm in Lime Acres. Though I'd promised myself never to allow those sensations to overcome my rationale again, they were back.

So, this is how he's going to crucify me finally, is it? I had to resign myself to the fact he'd now won the war too.

"Oh my God, Carol. I never learn with that swine," I admitted. "I gave in to keep the peace at home with Viv, and being so fucking tired, I couldn't fight her anymore."

"I'm so sorry, Elizabeth. Don't be hard on yourself. I should have been more vigilant, knowing his history. I didn't have enough proof, and to begin with, I wasn't looking."

"It's not your fault, Carol. The most important thing now is to find a way out of this mess."

"Do you want a coffee?" she called out as she left.

"Yes, please."

I never said no to coffee, but caffeine wasn't the answer I was looking for. Lumbered with debt, the children draining me and my business now financially ruined, it was time to have some questions answered, not just from Dion, but Vivienne and Andre too. I arranged for Dion to get to my office urgently.

"Sit." I scowled, pointing at the chair opposite my desk, when he appeared.

Carol closed the door and took her seat.

"What the fuck? What's up?" he asked.

"What the fuck have you done with all my money from the carpet business? You have an awful lot of explaining to do. As of this moment, you are fired."

If I'd had my pistol, I would have used it.

"What do you mean?" he asked, putting on the "innocent victim" look, glancing from me to Carol and back to me.

"How many jobs have you pocketed the cash for in the last four months?"

"None. Why?"

"Of course not! How stupid of me," I said sarcastically and threw my arms in the air. "Dion, Carol isn't stupid, but I have been. I shouldn't have listened to Vivienne plead for this job on your behalf. Carol has the proof of what you've been doing. Your act of vengeance is actually fraud, Dion. You are to leave immediately without remuneration. Get out and never step foot in these offices, or my house, again."

He got up and, stopping at the door, the devil personified grinned at me, then he left.

"My God, Elizabeth, what did I just witness?" Carol had never seen the other Dion. She was ghostly white.

I collapsed onto the sofa in my office and sobbed until there were no more tears left. The following day, I needed to advise our account holders.

"Carol, can you make appointments for me to see the directors of each of these companies?" I handed her the list I'd made. "We need to keep these sweet. They are vital. The others we can write to and arrange extended terms. Most of them we won't use again when I have sold the business."

"Yes, sure, Elizabeth."

"How many jobs need to be finished?"

"I'll check and let you know. Teams went out with Johannas today. He's on it."

She turned and left me to wallow in the turmoil Dion's lies had caused.

By 2001, I couldn't go on, nor could my business. I was on the verge of physical collapse and financially I was sunk. I found myself lying to creditors, something I'd never done nor would have ever considered outside of this mayhem.

My sister was furious with me. Vivienne was livid I'd fired her father. Storm was tearful and desperately worried about me. Pieter wanted nothing to do with his father; he was focussed on his computing. William suggested it might be better for us all if he stayed away.

Night was the worst time. When the last rays of sunshine dropped behind the horizon and the horrors of darkness swept in, it brought with it panicky sweats, leaving me sticky with fear. Creditors were hounding me like flies. I was making empty promises to keep them off of my back. I had every intention of paying off my debt; I just had to find a plan to do it quickly.

A knock on the lounge door interrupted my thoughts. It was Andre.

"Ma, may I come in? I have a suggestion I would like to share."

There was no harm in listening.

"Sure. I hope it's a good one. Where's Viv?"

"With her father. Listen, I have a contact in Johannesburg. I know you won't like what I have to say, but hear me out. They pay tens of thousands of Rand for certain jobs. Those weeks I was away and came home with money, remember?"

He smiled looking a little embarrassed – would I forget those awful weeks?

"Well, I thought I would do one more and give you the money. You've helped us so much. I know it was a huge strain on you having us live here. I also know the clashes you and Viv had over employing Dion and look what he's done. I feel I owe it to you to help."

Andre was a good man, but the suggestion had an ominous tone to it. If anything happened to Andre, Vivienne would blame me.

"I don't want you doing anything illegal. You have a wife and children to care for, before helping me."

"No, Ma, it's cool. I'll do another job."

"Don't do anything stupid and get into trouble," I warned. "The family has been through enough without inviting more."

"It's no trouble, Ma," he lied. "There are a few risks, but it's good money."

Something didn't feel right. I felt uneasy and couldn't sleep that night. I needed more information. We got together again the following day, and he explained.

"Nee, Andre, you are not to do that. It's not right."

"I knew you wouldn't approve, Ma, but it'll get you out of die ding (slang for being in a tight spot). I will happily do it for you. It's the least I can do. I've contacted the Nigerians. I collect the package in Paris, fly to Japan, deliver it, then fly back. All expenses paid and 40,000 Rand is yours."

"Nothing is that simple, Andre. What's in the package?"

"They never say. I heard via someone working with them, it's uncut diamonds. I know it's not ethical, but I'm prepared to do it one last time."

After Andre left, I sat at my desk calculating the exact amount I needed to pay off my debt. I kept asking myself whether it was worth Andre taking such a risk. I wished then I was a clairvoyant and could see into the future. I discussed the "job" again with Andre, and just as we were about to finish up, Storm called.

"Mama, can you look after Rika over the weekend?"

"Yes, of course, my angel," I responded without hesitation and glanced at Andre. I indicated with my thumb that I was satisfied with what he'd told me.

Storm and Robert were moving. Babysitting would be a perfect opportunity to think on my own.

After breakfast on Saturday morning, I popped into our local shop, grabbed something for us all for lunch and was looking forward to a day of peace and relative quiet. I was feeling a little easier. Andre had given me a glimmer of hope.

I didn't tell Storm what Andre was planning. That made me uncomfortable. I'd never kept anything from Storm. I did some research and read that people got hung for smuggling drugs. I wondered if being caught smuggling uncut diamonds was as dangerous. Andre had done it before. I assumed the last two trips he did must have been drug packages. Had he said he would be moving drugs this time, I would not have agreed to let him go, especially after hearing from Storm what she had seen and dealt with in the drug squad. The only consolation, diamonds wouldn't hurt any children and would give one child, her brother, a chance for a future he dreamt of: a university education in IT.

I shook my head to clear my thoughts. Rika, my precious granddaughter, had slept most of the day while I read. It was well after sundown before Storm and Robert finished carting boxes and breezed in carrying a few hot cheesy pizzas; the smell brought a rush of saliva to my mouth, reminding me I hadn't eaten all day. I left Storm's house somewhere around ten that evening, ready for a restful night's sleep. When I opened my front door, I walked into mayhem.

Drunk neighbours, lying on the floor or across my chairs, looked up at me with pathetic vacant stares that only drunks can deliver. I was livid; how could Andre do this to me? I threw them all out. Those half-sober sheepishly sidled past me and there on the floor, a tangled mess of drunken humanity, was Dion. Where was Pieter? I called out to him, but he didn't answer. I hoped he was asleep. I ordered Andre to wake Vivienne, who lay slumped inelegantly across the sofa, and get her to bed, warning them they had to clean my house in the morning. I threw the neighbours out and slammed the door.

"This is it. I've had a gutful, Andre. How dare you do this in my home."

I looked around my lounge, not sure whether to scream or bawl my eyes out, then I heard Dion retching and in moments, he was spewing vomit all over my lounge carpet.

"Get him out of here, Andre," I roared, noticing Dion had wet himself too, which repulsed and disgusted me. "When you get back from Japan, you will have to look for another place to live. I cannot deal with this shit anymore."

Disappointed and angry with Andre, at life, with everything, all I wanted to do was run away and hide; disappear to a place where not a solitary human resided. I needed the space of a deserted island more than ever.

I knocked on Pieter's door, but there was no response. Leaving the disgusting chaos behind me, I closed my bedroom door and sobbed gut-wrenching sobs that left me exhausted. Maybe someday I would be released from the hell I was living. I climbed into bed, closed my eyes and tried to find answers.

"Oh, God, why are you doing this to me? Why do you never hear my prayers and you never answer them either?" I asked, my voice laced with bitterness. "Do you even exist?"

I felt so disillusioned and betrayed. I couldn't work out where I'd gone wrong, if I'd gone wrong at all. I had asked for His wisdom and guidance every night. He'd surely seen how hard I'd tried. He knew my conscience better than I did, and now I couldn't help feeling He was a figment of my imagination. It wasn't long before I found myself begging Him again to listen to me.

Maybe I should go to Japan.

Trouble was, I wanted to be sitting at a place called God's Window high up in the mountains above Pilgrim's Rest in Mpumalanga, gazing out across the vast expanse of unspoilt Africa. Breathing in unpolluted air and relaxing while listening to the cicadas screaming, wild herbal scents permeating my nostrils, and bird calls soothing my frazzled nerves. Maybe, if I was seated on the edge of the mountain named after Him, He'd hear my desperate pleas – I needed wise guidance more than ever before.

I woke on Sunday morning still thinking about God's Window, but more pressing was the thought that maybe I should be going to Japan. I should be doing this "mission" to get myself out of financial trouble. Either way, a week's break in Mpumalanga or a week in Japan, I couldn't hang around much longer, or I'd be driven to do something I'd regret. I needed to get away from Dion urgently before I snapped. If I didn't, there may be no holding me back; this time I would pull the trigger. I could see no other way of getting the evil out of my life for good. If I went, I'd have money to resuscitate my business, I would have had a week's rest, and my business would be up and running again. Andre and Vivienne would be living elsewhere, I'd be mostly free of debt, Pieter could get through the end of his school career without the stress he'd been exposed to recently and go to university in early February; life would be tolerable again.

Chapter Twenty-Nine

I needed to meet with Andre before he left. I didn't want Viv to know of the meeting. Since the Saturday night debacle, he and Viv had moved in with friends, giving me space while things settled. I'd arranged to meet Andre at the Wimpy. I ordered a large coffee for myself and, as it arrived, Andre walked in.

"Before we talk of anything, Ma, I want to apologise again for Saturday night. I'm ashamed of how it went down." He had the decency to look embarrassed.

"Yes, I was not impressed and very disappointed. Let's not talk about it. I appreciate your apology and for moving out. Pieter and I needed some space."

"Sorry, Ma. So, what's on your mind?"

"This mission you're going on shortly. I've been thinking, why don't I do it?"

Andre looked shocked. "No, Ma, that's not a clever idea."

"Why not? I thought you said it was relatively easy." I raised my eyebrows, looking enquiringly at him.

He sat in stunned silence for a moment and then hastily ordered coffee.

"Ma, it's quite a dangerous mission. I don't want you doing it."

"I'm aware of that, Andre, but the officials would hardly suspect a grandmother, would they? Find out from your contacts what they think. It's my debt, not yours." I thought about that for a moment. "Well, it's not my debt, it's that bastard's debt, but he's too useless to do this mission, isn't he? Though he should be the one finding the solutions."

"I agree, Ma, but we cannot depend on Pa. I'll call them, but I'm quite sure they won't agree. Rather let me do this."

"Let me know when you've spoken to them. I'm not happy about you doing it. You have a wife and children to consider, and God forbid, I'd rather die than have Vivienne blame me for the rest of my life if anything happened to you."

By the expression on Andre's face, he hadn't thought of that consequence. We finished our coffee, and he promised to call me later.

I spent the rest of the day thinking of the pitfalls. The dos outweighed the don'ts or was my list born of innocence? I knew nothing of this underworld that Andre understood. I'd never even flown out of the country before. How would I manage flying halfway around the world? When Andre called, I felt nervous suddenly.

"Can I pop around to the house, Ma?"

"Yes, of course. Have you heard from your contacts?"

"Yes. See you in ten minutes."

I put the phone down and waited.

"I'm not at all happy about this, Ma," he said as he walked through the door.

Pieter was in his room studying, so we had some time to finish the conversation without him knowing Andre was even in the house.

"They said you could do it, but *I'm* not sure you should." He rubbed his brow.

"I insist. You must be with your wife and children."

"No, Ma. I can't let you do it. I know how they operate."

"I know you do, Andre, but I've made up my mind. However, there is one thing I need to know first. Are you certain it's diamonds and not drugs? Once that's confirmed, I'll do it, and you can prepare me for the trip, what I should and shouldn't do."

"Okay, Ma, if you insist. I'll work with Carol the week you're away. Is that a deal?"

"Okay, and you vow to me that neither Storm nor Pieter will know about this. And Dion goes nowhere near my business. As far as they'll be aware, I'm going on holiday. Going to sit at God's Window."

"Guaranteed."

"This is something Dion should be doing. It's his debt."

"Ma! You know him better than that."

We laughed together; I wasn't sure why I'd even said that.

"He couldn't do it. Dion can't take instructions and carry them out. You don't want to know what they do to people who let them down."

That was a warning.

"I know, and that thought doesn't make me feel secure. Tell me how it all works."

"Ma, don't you want me to find out what will be in the package first?"

"Yes, I do, but there's no harm in telling me what to expect. I may not do it in the end."

Andre and I spent an hour going over the pros and cons; I felt ashamed and tarnished, and I hadn't even left, but it seemed to be the only solution. I didn't really have the money to spend a week on holiday. I did have a little in savings still, but it was all I had.

Then, the appalling thought of lying to Storm and Pieter about where I was going for a week filled me with a terrible sense of betrayal. But nothing was as bad as my need to exterminate my ex-husband. Both decisions terrified me, but I had to get away.

I waited with anticipation for the next instruction from Andre. *I've managed fear before*, I thought, more boldly than I felt.

"Ma, we need to go to Johannesburg tomorrow to organise a British passport for you."

I swallowed hard. *A British passport?* What was wrong with my South African one? Then I remembered I would need a visa on a South African passport. My stomach filled with butterflies in chaotic flight, like my mind. My legs felt weak. It was all happening – paving the way to financial recovery with hard truths and unpleasant lies, but off we went.

My new British passport was ready in a week; I felt sickened.

Only a week away, I kept reminding myself, while the whispers fluttering through my head were saying, *Don't do it, Elizabeth.*

It was my only salvation. I had to do it.

Storm was excited for me. If she knew the truth, she would stop me.

"Ma, I'm so envious! You'll have a wonderful time relaxing, doing nothing other than resting, reading and walking in that divine fresh mountain air. It'll do you so much good. You deserve it. I wish I was coming with you."

I felt faint. How could I lie to Storm?

Time ticked on. It was getting closer to my departure date. The gnawing fear and crippling sense of shame never left me, but I had to free myself of this debt.

I would be flying to Paris. After one night in Paris, I'd then take the flight to Japan, deliver the package – a box contaminated by lies all wrapped up in desperation – then fly home. Just a week to sort out my life and pay my debt. Andre had primed me; it was a waiting game. I was to keep calm and follow instructions. He'd done it, so could I. The thought of seeing Paris and a glimpse of Japan filled me with a detached sense of excitement. On weighing up my options, this decision was better than being tried for murder and locked away in a South African jail.

The day was upon us. Everything was organised, except me. I said tearful farewells to Storm and Pieter, who laughed at me for crying.

"Enjoy it, Ma! It's only a week, and no one deserves it more." Storm chuckled into my ear as she hugged me.

I didn't want to let her go. I held Pieter close to me, kissed him goodbye, then Andre whisked me off under the pretence that I couldn't miss my bus from Johannesburg to Pilgrim's Rest.

"You can do this, Ma, just breathe deeply. Once you're on your way, you'll be fine," Andre said.

"Of course, just drive," I snapped. "What I hate the most about this is lying to Storm and Pieter. It makes me ill."

"They will understand, Ma."

Margaret Barnes (my new name) was on her way to Paris. The week before, in the privacy of my bedroom, I had practised being Margaret. I'd pinned my hair back like she did, I wore glasses like she did. I had to have "Margaret" firmly entrenched in my mind.

"Remind me, what is Margaret supposed to do once she gets to Paris?" I asked Andre as we got closer to Johannesburg International Airport.

"They will tell you, Ma. Just follow their instructions precisely and you'll be fine. Remember what I told you. It's like being in the army. It's a 'hurry up and wait' game."

"Oh, Andre, I feel sick. Can you stop?" I asked urgently.

Saliva was rushing into my mouth as Andre pulled off of the road. I flung the car door open as it came to a stop and vomited, hanging my head in shame out the car. Andre passed me a bundle of tissues. My nose burnt from the bile.

"Right, let's go," I said and had a few sips of water.

"Ma…"

"Don't talk, just drive."

I needed to deal with the last minutes of this journey in silence. I was to collect my ticket with further instructions from the Nigerians who were meeting us at the airport; at least for the early part of this loathsome decision, Andre was with me. Then suddenly, Andre was pulling into the first-floor parking, and my stomach lurched again.

"First stop is the loo, Andre."

He nodded patiently, remembering how it was the first time he did this journey.

Sitting on the toilet, I felt trapped; I wanted to stop it all.

"Am I mad?" I whispered to myself, covering my face with my hands while I waited till the trickle of urine ended.

The airport was noisy; people rushing here, rushing there, some crying, some rejoicing. I felt numb.

I was about to board a plane for the first time in my life. At fifty-two years of age, with a false passport and very little money,

I was flying to a city I had only ever seen in the movies, filled with the knowledge I was embarking on a particularly unsavoury mission, guided by people with no conscience, with guilt written all over my face.

"Have faith," I whispered into my chest.

I joined Andre who was standing with the Nigerian organisers. Two tall men, dressed similarly, one wearing black jeans and a red sleeveless T-shirt showing off massive, toned biceps and a well-developed body. Not a physique one would voluntarily want to mess with. The other was also well built and wore blue jeans and a white T-shirt, also with cut-off sleeves, his expression more fearful than the other's build. I instinctively knew they were trouble. They were the types that, with just one glance, you intuitively knew were dangerous. The man wearing the red shirt handed me an envelope with foreign currency in it, the plane ticket and my new British passport. My hair was pinned back like Margaret's photograph, my glasses were in place, though I wasn't wearing them in the passport photo. He opened the passport to check, looked at me and nodded his approval. I opened the envelope and counted the money and looked at him questioningly.

"How am I going to live on this for six days in a foreign country?"

His expression was dismissive. "You will be contacted when you land at Charles de Gaulle. Follow instructions, as we have explained. You won't go hungry."

"What if no one meets me in Paris?"

"Margaret, you must just listen. If you are not met, they will call you on the phone and tell you what to do. Do not panic."

"Do not panic? I'm terrified," I muttered.

"You will be fine, Ma," Andre said as he put a reassuring hand on my shoulder.

It was time to check in, say goodbye to Andre, then "wait" to board.

Wait, a verb. Stay where one is. I was numbed with fear. Wait: to hold back, stop, cease. I'd felt the sensations in the ladies' toilet. All and more.

Wait, a noun. A period of waiting, an interlude. I was suddenly quite stunned by my grasp of English. Then when that disappeared, all I wanted was to get on the plane, get the ordeal over and done with, get back home and go on with my business.

Andre hugged me, wished me luck, shook hands with the two men and disappeared. My mind was reeling, my feet were rooted to the spot. I was too terrified to move. I felt absurdly alone and abandoned. My mouth dried out in an instant and the butterflies in my tummy took off in frenzied flight around my stomach, leaving me nauseous. I was out of my depth. I'd never done anything purposefully illegal before – this was huge, and the enormity of my decision hit me hard.

I moved off slowly; my feet leaden from the burden of apprehension. I headed towards the check-in desk, smiling nervously at the lady who was beckoning for my passport and telling me to put my suitcase on the conveyor for weighing. Then, with a smile, she handed me the boarding pass, saying, "Enjoy your flight."

"Thank you," I answered and followed the signs to Terminal A, passed through security and by then I was desperate for something to drink.

I sat down at a window table and glanced at my watch. Only an hour and a half to wait before boarding at Gate 28. I sipped alternately between hot chocolate and water, then wandered around the duty-free shops, bought a book and headed down to the boarding gate.

Soon, I was standing at the entrance to a massive jet airliner for the first time in my life, wishing the reasons I was there were different. The smiling stewardess indicated where I would find my seat, and I followed the others down the narrow aisle. I had a window seat, which helped take my mind off of the reason for this flight. I secured my safety belt and nervously read the safety instructions listed in the in-flight magazine.

It was 30 March 2002. The aircraft doors closed, everyone was seated. I felt the plane begin to move and held onto the arm of the seat. The gentleman sitting next to me smiled sympathetically.

"Is this your first time flying?" he asked.

"Yes, and I'm terrified."

My body was visibly shaking as we taxied onto the runway in preparation for take-off. Then the engines shuddered and whined; I wanted to die. I closed my eyes, gripped the arm rests and stopped breathing as the plane gathered speed. The engines whined louder, then I felt myself being pushed back into my seat. The sensation made me gasp for the breath I'd been holding onto. While oxygen and adrenaline surged through my veins, the magnificent flying machine lifted gracefully into the air.

I was on my way to Paris.

Chapter Thirty

Europe

Eleven hours later, I arrived in Paris and disembarked. I followed the crowd off of the plane, through immigration and joined the hum of people in the "hall des arrivées" and had a good look around before finding a seat to begin the proverbial "waiting". I kept a vigilant eye out for a tall black man dressed in a dark suit, as described. Another Nigerian, I assumed.

The hum of people arriving, leaving and greeting loved ones would have been far more exciting to watch if my brain wasn't playing tricks on me. Suddenly, all the black men I saw were dressed in dark suits, they were mostly all tall, aloof and unfriendly. My mind was racing, wondering how they would identify me, and what if *they* didn't contact me, amongst a jumble of other terrifying thoughts.

After sitting for half an hour, I got up and wandered around in weary awe of my surroundings. Coming in from Africa, the first time off of the continent, I'd never seen so many white people in one place in my life. I managed a little laugh. Fifteen minutes later, I sat down with a bottle of water and checked my phone for messages or missed call alerts – there were neither. The momentary laugh at myself hadn't eased my tension. The floodgates of irrational thoughts opened. I had to remind myself of the Nigerian's words in Johannesburg: "They will contact you, just wait." That "wait" word again. I remembered what Andre had told me about the army: "Hurry up and wait."

As the minutes rolled into hours, waiting became more and more challenging. I couldn't even focus on the women's magazine I'd bought to pass the time. My heart was racing; I desperately wanted to go home.

"Why the hell did I agree to do this?" I murmured under my breath as another hour ticked by.

An icy fear gripped me. I was tired, panic-stricken, alone in a strange land with nowhere to go.

It was light now; a new Paris day was dawning. Margaret needed to take control and decide what to do. I was too tired to think clearly; all I wanted to do was sleep, but the new day was nearly upon us. I dragged myself to the information desk and asked where I would find a cheap hotel and how I would get there. A well-spoken information clerk efficiently booked me into a cheap hotel and kindly drew out instructions on getting to the hotel after I'd explained I'd never been to Paris. My travels weren't over; I had to take the underground train to get to the hotel.

The underground? I'd never been on a train in my life either, let alone an underground one. Trains were not the mode of travel many white South Africans used, and there was no such thing as an underground one. Collecting my thoughts, I followed the signs that lead to the underground station and managed to find my way to the hotel and checked in.

Walking up the steps to the entrance of the hotel, I was surprised at how grubby the facade was, having a preconceived notion that everything in Paris would be glitzy and glamorous. The threadbare carpet in the foyer was as tired as I felt, but it was a cheap place to stay until they called.

Having the key to a room on the second floor, I dumped my suitcase and asked where I could have breakfast before I fainted; I was starving.

I was guided to a pleasant little bistro not far from the hotel, and as I got to the door, the smell of good coffee and hot bread made my mouth water. Sinking my teeth into a freshly buttered croissant was heaven. The scrambled eggs were good; the coffee filled me up with a good dose of caffeine, then I wanted a cigarette. With a full tummy and coffee, a cigarette was essential to complete the meal. I hadn't brought many packets with me. I couldn't hold out any longer. I paid, walked outside, and lit up; it was the second cigarette I'd had since leaving Johannesburg. I pulled every bit of the smoke deep into my lungs to calm me, and as I exhaled the first puff, my phone rang. Grappling for the phone in my pocket, I noticed it was Storm calling. I let it ring and she hung up. I could not have answered that call. The appalling stirrings of deplorable guilt surfaced again. I'd lied to my most treasured daughter. I took another long draw on the cigarette.

I had asked the family not to call while I was supposedly relaxing at God's Window in one of the most beautiful parts of South Africa, many thousands of miles from where I was now. But I couldn't help wondering why Storm should try calling me. I guessed if it was urgent, she'd call back a bit later.

I'd just got back to my room, nestled my head on the pillow when the phone rang again. I jumped up thinking it was Storm. This time I would answer, but I saw on the screen it wasn't her.

"Hello," I said hesitantly.

"Get on a train to Brussels," a deep male voice said. "You will be met in Brussels in the morning." The phone went dead.

Oh great, how the fuck do I get to Brussels? No time was given, no details, nothing! What kind of instructions were these? Andre had said they could be very blunt, leave you wondering what to do, but somehow it worked.

I didn't have the faintest idea where I was in Paris and now I had to get to Brussels! Why Brussels?

I sat on the edge of the bed, alert again; it didn't last long. I lay back and fell into a deep sleep, waking after seven the following morning. With all my wits about me after sixteen hours of sleep, I began to question why I was being sent to Brussels and not on to Japan. This diversion had not been mentioned before I left Johannesburg. Something didn't feel right, but for now, I needed to shower, pack up and find out how to get to Brussels.

The receptionist kindly explained and three-quarters of an hour later, I was seated on a train, on my way to Brussels. I desperately needed a cigarette to calm my nerves, but no smoking was permitted.

During the journey, a different voice shouted down the phone at me. "You're doing well, lady."

Yes, I thought so too! I didn't dare verbalise that.

"When you get to Brussels, lady, you will be met. Now listen carefully," he warned.

"I'm listening," I replied sharply, "And I hope there will be someone to meet me, not like at the airport."

He ignored me.

"A tall well-built black man will meet you. He will be wearing a red shirt with black trousers." The phone went dead, as before.

I was furious. This was ridiculous. Andre never told me it was a cat and mouse guessing game I would play around Europe.

Damn them. I breathed out loudly, and the lady sitting across from me frowned. I smiled back, politely. She returned the smile.

Having the most frustrating people to deal with and the lack of adequate instructions annoyed me. It wouldn't have been so bad if I knew where I was going and what I was doing. My shoulders were on fire, my neck was as stiff as a rod, my mood sharp and fear was on the prowl down the avenues of my mind; I needed nicotine. Urgently.

I arrived in Brussels, starving, shaky and disorientated. My stomach felt disconnected from my mouth. I'd spied a small cafe as we came in and I went directly to it, grabbed a sandwich and sank another cup of coffee, defiantly thinking, *If they can't find me, they can phone me.* I'd get the hang of this soon enough.

Living off rubbish like sandwiches and snacky type meals since I'd left Johannesburg was also making me feel ill. With the tight budget I was on, I didn't have much choice. The sandwich I'd just eaten tasted like no other; it was the freshest one I'd had so far. Chicken mayonnaise on wholewheat bread, dripping with the best mayonnaise I'd ever tasted and loaded with tomato and lettuce. After the second one was consumed, which hadn't taken me long (historically, I was a very slow eater), I collapsed on a bench and lit a cigarette. Inhaling deeply, my eyes closed in the ecstasy of filtered nicotine giving me a lift. I leant my head back and exhaled, blowing smoke circles above my head. I felt someone tap my shoulder and my eyes flew open. It was a uniformed man carrying a baton – it wasn't the baton that terrified me, but looking straight into the face of a man in uniform. He said something to me, and I looked at him dumbly, indicating with my hands that I had not understood him.

He said in perfect English, "No smoking in public, ma'am."

I squashed the tip of the cigarette and dropped it back in the packet; something I would never have done at home, but these weren't normal circumstances.

The next man that tapped me on the shoulder asked if I was Margaret. For a second, I was about to give him a piece of my mind, then remembered, *I* was Margaret.

"Yes," I said, "That's me."

Holding my shoulder so he didn't lose me in the crowds of people racing around the station, he marched me out of the impressive station building, then reached for my hand, which I ripped away disapprovingly.

"I'll keep up. You don't need to hold my hand," I snapped indignantly. I wasn't a child and I didn't want a strange man holding my hand.

Soon we were walking down a rabbit warren of quiet back-streets and entered the lobby of Hotel van Jeanne, another low-budget, ancient-looking dump of a hotel. This one was smaller than the hotel in Paris, and in worse condition. The nameless man in red and black paid the bill for my room, two meals and refunded me what I'd spent on the last hotel and my meals and added another meagre allowance for food.

"Wait here," he instructed, then quickly disappeared before I could ask him for more precise instructions.

One syllable instructions from nameless faces in foreign places! Grrrr. It was most disconcerting, thoroughly intimidating, and annoyed me. I wondered how Andre had coped with it.

I guess men handle it all differently, I thought. The whole purpose of me doing it was I looked and behaved like a little innocent, rather reserved, grandmother. It was the image I needed to portray. Andre, on the other hand, was about as big and muscular as the men I had to take instructions from. He had that burly South African rugby player look: take no shit, man!

I was shown to my room by a surly, rotund woman, who motioned I should follow her up a dark, dingy staircase to the first-floor landing. She only just fitted between the wooden banister rails as she heaved her large frame up each step, catching her apron frills between her bulk and the rails, puffing like a steam train, cursing all the way up until we came out on the landing. I thought she was going to expire from the exertion.

"All... the... rooms lead off... this landing... madam," she said breathlessly, gasping for air. "You... are... room 13," she added, pointing to the door and handing me the key.

"Oh no, not number 13!" I moaned superstitiously.

Under these circumstances, I didn't need bad luck; I'd had enough of that in my life. Four steps to my right and there I stood in front of room 13, feeling very apprehensive, and inserted the key. The room was tiny, just enough space for a narrow single bed, a small space to hang clothes, two coat hangers and two small shelves. A single glass door led onto a small balcony and was the only source of natural light. At least this one had an en suite.

As I was stepping out of my jeans, preparing for a much-needed shower, the phone rang.

I answered, waiting for the next one syllable instruction. The voice instructed me to remain at the hotel until they called again. I felt my shoulders relax a bit; I had some time to myself. I took a shower, washed some clothes in the basin and hung them up to dry, draping them over wherever I found space. I was too tired to bother with supper and too depressed to feel hungry.

Later that night, the noise in the room above woke me. It took me a few moments to establish where I was, then try to work out the noise. Ah, I got it. I struggled to block the sounds and stop myself from chuckling wickedly, wondering if the couple above knew I could hear all their orgasmic groans, sexy little shrieks, and even louder cries of ecstasy. Sniggering gently, I pulled the dusty pink duvet over my head. Eventually, the sounds of erotica died away, and I fell asleep again.

The following morning, I packed up my things and headed downstairs to the dining room for a leisurely cooked breakfast. It was my first hot meal in three days. I savoured every mouthful. Back in my room, feeling satiated and comfortable, I pulled out the book I'd bought at the airport in Johannesburg and started reading, but the picture on the cover of a windmill standing alone on a farm in the barren Karoo reminded me far too much of home. I began to sob. The burden of this mission was getting to me; a deep sense of guilt, fear and homesickness snatched at my chest. I put the book down and allowed rivers of salty tears to pour from my eyes. How blessed I had been to have grown up on a farm in Africa, surrounded by wide open spaces, beautiful clean air, solitude, and peace, unlike here. A constant cacophony of busy, over-populated, polluted city life, and I wondered how many people here had ever experienced the silence of the African bush, or even silence!

With swollen eyes, I ventured out onto the streets. I couldn't read; it was hopeless even trying. I wandered around close to the hotel, peering into shop windows, fascinated by how different it all was. A little side street beckoned to me. I curiously ventured down it and I found a quaint cafe tucked in at the end of the street. I snuck into a seat right at the back and ordered a salad, a glass of water and a cup of coffee. My heart ached for home, my children and conversation in my mother tongue.

Back in the room, I mentally ran through the instructions so far. Everything was different. I wondered why, but I knew it wasn't for me to question. I was itching to get the job done and get home. I was beginning to think I should have sent Andre – he knew what to do. I had not heard from anyone all day, and that night I lay awake with the burden of this decision weighing heavily upon me. I was about to drift off to sleep when the phone rang, as it always seemed to do, but this time it was one o'clock in the morning. I answered, feeling quite spikey and annoyed by the disturbance. Braced and ready for the next veiled instruction, I withered. It was Dion.

"Jesus Christ, Elizabeth, where are you?" His words all ran into one jumbled question from the interference of humming and crackling sounds on the line.

I listened, then killed the call and switched off the phone. He was the one person I did not want to talk to. It was because of him I was here in this mess. Sleep came in waves between terrorising thoughts.

In the morning, just after switching the phone back on, the Nigerians called. I was to stay where I was and they would see me later that evening. Another day's delay, which added to my tension and anxiety and gave me more time to think. I didn't want to think, I needed to get the hell out of Europe, on to Japan and home. I had dinner and put it on a tab for the men to pay when they collected me.

A loud knock on the door startled me. I opened it hesitantly – two strangers stood at the door, men I'd not seen before. I was about to slam the door shut when one of them spoke.

"Take the train to Amsterdam tomorrow. Leave here at 6 a.m. There will be someone to meet you there."

"Why do I have to go to Amsterdam? I was told to collect a case in Paris and go on to Japan. Why am I being lied to and kept in suspense like this?"

Neither of them answered. Instead, I was handed a bundle of money, and they left without providing an answer.

A young man was there at the station to meet me. He informed me we were to make the journey to Amsterdam together. Relieved by the news that I'd have company on the next leg, my tummy began to make noises that it needed filling again. I was starving. Breakfast was another bloody sandwich, but this time, I bought an apple and a banana, which I ate on the train.

Our train arrived early. This escort was a little more talkative – I wouldn't learn his name, but he was friendly and polite, quite different from the others. Chatting openly about how often he'd escorted South Africans, he said he would show me around the station when we got there.

Bizarre, I thought. Train stations in South Africa were buildings you didn't want to hang around in too long.

Once we'd got off of the train, he started the tour. This was no ordinary train station. Well, for me it wasn't! High above me were impressive arched roofs, and around me grew healthy manicured gardens: a perfect spectacle, a delightful mingling of nature and chaos. Then we went outside. I'd never seen architecture like it in my life. I couldn't take my eyes away from the beautiful, iconic Renaissance facade the building boasted, temporarily lifting my spirits and taking away terrifying thoughts of what lay ahead. It was simply stunning. Railway stations in my mind were dirty, scruffy places that no architect would want to put their name to! I wished I'd had a camera.

My new companion was very kind to me, but I found it awkward trying to strike up a conversation with a person with no name.

"This really is beautiful. Thank you for showing me. Do you mind if I call you Jack?"

"Nope," he answered cheerfully.

I had no idea where I had suddenly pulled out the name of Jack, but it worked. The conversation seemed to flow more smoothly after that. Jack told me a bit about his life and how difficult it was as a Nigerian living in Holland. He missed his family. He explained how unhappy he was doing the job, but he made good money. It supported his family and his parents, who were poor rural folk. They scraped out a living, only if the rainy season was kind to them. They grew maize and vegetables and sold eggs and chickens. His mother made a special flat bread, which she sold too.

I couldn't help feeling sorry for him, even though he irritated me by insisting he buy me small gifts, which I declined.

Eventually, Jack got the call he'd been waiting for, and we hurried off to find a taxi, which took us to a grubby suburban sprawl in a seedy, dirty part of Amsterdam. Rows upon rows of red brick terraced houses stood shoulder to shoulder; they were unkept and the architecture ugly. As the taxi wove through the dingy streets of what I'd heard was a stunning city, I wished again that the circumstances were different so I could see the tourist spots, the beautiful parts. I caught a few brief glimpses of the famous canal system as we crisscrossed over old arched bridges built in the same red brick as the terraced houses. As impressive as the bridges were, living in row upon row of houses all attached to each other was utterly alien to me. I was glad I was only going to be here for one day in this rundown part, where the pavements were dirty and decorated with ugly dustbins that stood along both sides of the narrow streets. Even the trees looked tatty and tired; no wonder Jack wanted to get home. Home to open spaces and fresh air. Then the sickening realisation of why we'd come to Amsterdam suddenly dawned on me – we were in the drug capital of the world. I wanted to vomit, to get rid of the lies that polluted my innards. For a moment, I naively hoped that what I'd just thought was not going to materialise; it still could be diamonds. I had left without Andre confirming it, blinded by my debt.

"What the hell are we doing here, Jack?" I asked, feeling the quiver in my lower jaw.

By the expression on my face, I guessed he was aware of what had just passed through my mind. He smiled casually.

"Collecting the suitcase that you will be delivering to Japan."

"I think this whole trip has just been continuous lies, Jack. I wasn't told any of this in Johannesburg."

"Ask no questions, they tell no lies." He waved his index finger at me.

The taxi dropped us outside one of the grubby-looking terraced houses where we met with another "no name" Nigerian. Looking at their living conditions, who they were and the underworld they operated in, I wondered how it was possible they got into these European countries to live and work, *and* manage to send money back to their families without being questioned by the authorities, but as Jack had warned: "Ask no questions."

Waves of shame gripped me like menopausal sweats.

Had Andre lied to me? Were diamonds a smokescreen to appease me?

I'd not paid attention to the street name or the number of the house, all I could think of was what lowly, dishonourable and filthy levels I'd stooped to in my desperate state of mind. Was that what bankruptcy did to a person?

Sitting inside an empty lounge on a tatty old chair, looking down at a threadbare green carpet that looked like a badly mown lawn and knowing what I was waiting for mortified me. The thought made me fidget. Would I ever get over this disgraceful act? At the time, I thought I was acting in the best interest of my family and my business. Had I known the truth of how this mule thing really worked, I would *never* have agreed, but I reminded myself it was too late. It was futile trying to fight with the noise in my head and the hundreds of voices screaming at me. There would be time for recrimination once I got home. Two more days left. I could do this. I had to do this.

"Did you bring the suitcase?" Jack asked the new man.

"No suitcase yet," he answered, shrugged and quickly disappeared without another word.

There we sat in a cold, heartless place, the stench of unscrupulous dealings crept into the crevices of my soul, dirtying every living part of me.

We sat in silence. Jack lay down, seemingly oblivious to the world around him, and slept. I watched him and envied the way he could switch off and sleep in the most uncomfortable of surroundings and under such circumstances. I wondered then if people like Jack felt the same vulnerability and fear I was experiencing. Perhaps not. He seemed totally at ease and accepting of the situation, even though he'd expressed how much he missed his cultural norms and his family. We were both in it for similar reasons: to support family. He'd explained that if he didn't do this, his family could die of starvation. If I didn't do this, I'd have murdered my ex-husband! But as in Jack's case, family were the primary reason. For me, without a business, I couldn't afford to send Pieter to university. No matter how small or brief my part in smuggling goods around the world, it *was* unforgivable. Self-loathing was often over-whelming.

Finally, the other man returned, pulling a small black suitcase up the steps and shoved it towards me.

"For you."

Hearing voices, Jack stirred and jumped to his feet as if he'd never been asleep and urged me to hurry.

"Take it, take it, time to leave," he insisted.

Uncharacteristically irritable, he grabbed my sleeve and dragged me roughly out of the house and off we went at a pace, backtracking some of the way we'd come in the taxi, then we took a shortcut back to the station. My feet were killing me when we got to the station. Moments later, we were on the train back to Brussels.

"You get off, go back to the hotel and wait."

"This is fucking ridiculous, Jack." I'd had enough of the bullshit.

He never answered, looking at me with a strange enquiring expression.

"Why are you looking at me like that, Jack?"

"What are you doing this for? You don't look like the kinda person who should be doing this job."

I'd had those thoughts too, more than once.

He handed me a tightly wrapped bundle of euros and nodded. He understood. Ask no questions, tell no lies!

I got back to the hotel, dragging the dirty black suitcase and my little red one, hauled them up the narrow stairway, unlocked my room and collapsed onto the bed. I was exhausted, tearful and filled with bitter regret.

I counted the notes Jack had given me, dialled room service and ordered a hot meal. Twenty minutes later, there was a knock at my door and the smell of roast beef and gravy was the best thing I'd smelt since leaving home. The plate was loaded with the vegetables I craved: carrots, broccoli and potato wedges.

As I put my knife and fork together on the empty plate, I looked at the ominous black case with its malevolent aura – it was staring at me, beckoning me to open it. An hour later, it got the better of me. Gripping the zipper tag, I peeled back the lid and gagged. A dirty old T-shirt and a pair of men's jeans lay at the top. A whiff of stale, dirty male body odour drifted up my nose and I had to swallow rapidly to prevent my dinner coming up. Bracing my jaw and swallowing hard, I stood for a minute with my eyes squeezed tightly shut. Eventually, I turned back and lifted the clothing. Two brown paper packages bound with endless string, shrouded in suspicion, lay on the bottom of the case. Were these drugs or were these diamonds? It wasn't for me to question what was in the packages, all I had to do was get them to Japan, hand the suitcase over, collect my plane ticket and fly home. Job done, except...

Halfway around Europe, just for this? Why didn't someone bring it to Paris for me? None of it made much sense. I believed I had been misled from the start. But, no matter what, I had agreed to do it.

Later that night, tossing and turning in bed, all I could think about was getting out of it. Now I had the packages the implications of ducking were ominous. I had enough money in my savings to book into a cheap hotel somewhere else, lie low for a few days, giving my sister time to get me a ticket home. These thoughts took on a reality, but then logical ones warned me of the consequences, and what could happen to Andre and me. I decided it wasn't worth contemplating. These guys were ruthless. I knew there was no way out; I had to go through with it.

The room stank now I'd opened the case. It was stuffy enough without the overbearing stench that hung in the room. It only served to reinforce the menacing feeling that tormented me when a knock on the door startled me.

"Who is it?" I called out.

It was Jack, so I opened the door a fraction and noticed Jack was not alone. The stranger with him spoke quietly.

"Tomorrow, we buy plane ticket to Japan," he said. "One man meets you at ticket office. You get money, buy ticket and bring back to this man." He pointed to Jack, then he handed me a little more money for the hotel bill and my food.

The following morning, I boarded the train to Charles de Galle once more. Weakened by a fitful night, my intestines knotted up rebelliously and I couldn't concentrate. I was a nervous wreck. I was desperate to get the hell out of Europe as fast as I could. Just two days left, but the worst was still ahead of me.

Jack was there to meet me as promised and handed me the money for the plane ticket, which I purchased.

"You will be met at the airport by a tall black man dressed in blue jeans, a denim shirt, wearing a cap with a football emblem on it." He smiled, then added, "The World Cup is being held in Japan."

What did I know about the football club emblems? Everyone would be wearing football regalia if the World Cup was on.

Timing was everything now. I had to get off of the train and run like a woman possessed, get through passport control and onto the plane with no time to spare.

"They didn't give me much time, did they?"

Jack just shook his head and said farewell. "Good luck. Eyes wide," he said and left.

A power failure halfway to Charles de Gaulle brought the train to an abrupt halt, leaving me more of a jabbering nervous wreck. All the other passengers were in an uproar. All I could hear was the rapid beat of my heart in my chest.

I *had* to be on that flight. Five long minutes later, the power came back on, and we were on our way again. (My extreme panic was brought on by the fact that a powerful failure in South Africa lasts considerably longer than five minutes!) Then I learnt, through incessant jabbering on the coach, there were some essential footballers on board the train; the flight to Japan was waiting, but everything had to be done quickly. We were ushered through, our luggage checked in, and we raced to the boarding gate and ran onto the waiting plane in record time.

Once I was seated, I wondered how the ominous black case had got through the airport X-ray machines. Ask no questions...

Flight attendants quickly got everyone into their appropriate seats, the aircraft doors closed, seatbelts were fastened, and we were in the air in minutes. The intercom announcement warned of tight security at Narita Airport in Japan. Korea–Japan World Cup Soccer… expect delays at the airport, we were advised.

In less than a week, I'd been halfway around the world to collect two brown paper packages. We disembarked and, by this time, my bad shoulder was throbbing riotously and hurt like hell. It was almost too painful to move, but I was one step closer to home.

Chapter Thirty-One

Japan

I stood nervously at immigration check-in. I did my best to appear relaxed. An unsmiling Japanese immigration officer's face and lifeless jet black eyes were staring at me, beckoning for my passport. I stepped forwards, smiled and handed it to him. I watched as he fingered through pages of my fake British passport. He looked at the photograph and looked up at me, then he looked back to the passport photograph with a doubting stare, then looked up at me again. The second time he frowned which prompted my gut to tighten. A sensation so powerful, I struggled to maintain that "relaxed, smiling look". He glared at me just long enough for me to understand I could be in trouble.

"Do you have any other form of identification?" he asked politely.

This time I flashed a bigger smile at him and shook my head.

"No, sir," I said politely, praying my lips would not quiver.

He put my passport down on the counter in front of him and picked up a magnifying glass.

My body went rigid. I thought I was going to faint.

Desperately trying to stop myself from fidgeting or licking my lips or fiddling with my fingers or doing anything else that may give me away, I fixed my focus on watching him. He ran the magnifying glass over my photograph – ironically, it was the

296

only part of the passport that was authentic. Then, as I feared, he carefully checked the rest of the document. The photograph had been taken with me wearing my hair pinned back. Today it wasn't pinned back and when he looked up at me again, I quickly pulled my hair away from my face. All I got in return was a cynical glare.

"Please wait here," he said.

I knew in an instant what may happen to me if they suspected I was a fraud. I had to abandon the black case.

Leave it pressed up against the counter or in the toilet, I thought, but to leave it up against the counter, the passenger behind me would surely alert me to it; I needed the toilet.

There was no name tag on the suitcase to link me to it.

I was panic-stricken. I was rapidly running out of options. I had to think quickly, but the official was back before I could do anything.

"Come with me please," he said politely. He led me to a glass cubicle and motioned for me to take a seat on the wooden bench.

"May I use the toilet please?" I asked politely.

He nodded, pointing to the toilet signs, but ordered me to leave my suitcases where they were. There was no fooling this immigration officer; he'd seen it all before. I was foiled again. With crushing dread, I realised that unless I could somehow talk my way out of this situation and convince them the suitcase wasn't mine, I would be arrested.

I found the toilets. I chose the western style one and collapsed onto the seat. Nothing was working. I couldn't release a drop. I sat for a few moments longer and willed myself to empty my bladder, then everything released. In my innocence, I'd not given *being caught* that much thought. Probably because Andre had done this twice and got through. I believed I would too. The Nigerians and Andre had skirted over the possibilities of arrest in our interview. We agreed that it was unlikely that customs would suspect an older woman being a "mule". I realised now that was idiotic naivety! As I stood up, I began to shake violently and struggled to pull up the zipper on my jeans. That primal fear was clicking in. It was so real I could smell it – a sickly sweet, metallic smell.

I returned to the cubicle and sat down on the bench. My bladder, and everything else, empty. My tummy felt more able to deal with what was to come next. Then three Japanese policemen marched into the glass cubicle. I didn't dare look at them. Staring ahead of me, I remained as outwardly motionless as I could, then one of the officers said something I didn't understand. The one who'd spoken motioned that I should follow him. I could hardly breathe as I was escorted into a small office and ordered to sit down. Survival makes every sense alarmingly crisp; even the din in the airport intensified as waves of panic and terror swept through me.

The interrogation began.

They asked where I was from and what my name was. I told them I was from Britain and gave them my false name. A name that I'd engraved to memory. I was her; she was me. Then they asked for my passport number, and I recited that too, realising then I may have walked into the trap. How many people bother to remember their passport number so readily, unless...

Then they asked for my residential address in Britain.

I glanced at them, not knowing what to say while attempting to prevent the insufferable fear I was feeling from showing on my face. The three men looked at each other, then looked back at me. Their expressions mirrored my thoughts. Time stood still; the silence was tormenting.

"Sorry, ma'am, but this is not you," one of them said, pointing at my passport photograph, shaking his head.

It genuinely was me, but I knew they were not referring only to the image, more the fake passport.

"That is me, sir," I said. (Amazing how one's tone changes when one *is* telling the truth.)

They ignored me.

"What's in your suitcases?" one of the other police officers asked.

"I have only one suitcase, sir," I responded.

"I see there are two with you." He was taunting me and enjoying it.

My insides shifted uncomfortably.

"Only the red suitcase belongs to me, sir," I responded as politely as I could under the circumstances, then I explained how I came to have two suitcases.

"My train was delayed in Paris, sir. In a rush to get on the waiting plane, one of the men who was on the train with me, and booked on the same flight, asked me to take his hand luggage through for him."

I noticed one of the officer's shift his feet. He appeared to be listening intently for he knew of the delay. I prayed he was considering that I was telling the truth.

"The airport staff forced us to hurry, sir. They said we were to get on board quickly. So…" I breathed out to control my voice. "I agreed to carry it through for him for he had two other cases. I had every intention of giving it back to him, but then the immigration official told me to follow him to this glass cubicle before

I had the opportunity to hand it back. The owner is probably still waiting, sir."

I looked boldly into the eyes of the policeman. He turned and nodded to the other. I didn't dare drop my shoulders or change my position even though the tension was excruciating.

"May we look inside that suitcase, ma'am?"

"Yes, of course. I don't care what you do with it. Perhaps it would be polite to return it to the gentleman it belongs to," I said as calmly as I was able while I watched the officer open the case.

He too whirled away as the putrid smell of stale male body odour assaulted his nasal passages. I prayed that might get me off. I watched him dig through the men's clothing with a grimacing expression while holding his breath. He lifted the layers of filthy clothing, then found what he was looking for. Lifting the two bound paper packages out of the case, he handed them to his co-worker.

"Are you aware of what is inside those packages, ma'am?" he asked with an icy tone.

"Of course not, sir. I've already told you that's not my suitcase," I said sharply and shifted my body weight insolently. I genuinely didn't know what was in the packages. If I had, I wouldn't have been there.

He began opening the packages in front of me.

"What is this?" he asked.

"I don't know. I've never seen anything like that in my life." And once again, I genuinely hadn't! But that didn't save me.

"It's about five kilograms of marijuana." He lifted the packages up and down as if to confirm their weight.

One of the other police officers took some away for testing.

"What? No wonder that bastard wanted me to take his case," I snarled, trying to ignore the nasty sinking feeling in the pit of my stomach. "Sir, I have been framed."

He ignored me, but he had just confirmed my thoughts in Amsterdam. I felt crushed and betrayed by my son-in-law. I was sure he would have known the packages held drugs. Viv must have known too. How was I ever going to forgive myself for this? Storm would never forgive me, how could she?

Switching my thoughts back quickly to the present, remaining steadfast in my determination to convince these two officers I knew nothing of this, I vaguely heard the officers talking: one believed me, the other two didn't.

"I told you, sir, I have been framed. That is *not* my suitcase," I emphasised. "There has been a big mistake. Check my red case to satisfy yourselves, then let me be on my way."

"You are a liar," came the scornful response from the man who didn't believe me.

I was losing ground, and I knew it, but I stuck to my story and raised my voice.

"Sir, you are making a false accusation, which I consider demeaning." I could sense all I was doing was irritating him further.

He took one step closer to me and prodded his finger into my shoulder, which, just my luck, bounced off of the rolled-up tissue I had tucked under my bra strap. That triggered a whole new line of questioning.

"What are you hiding in there?"

Incredibly, I remained composed and stared angrily at him for touching me, which I understood was not permitted. I should have caused chaos for him for doing that, but I didn't.

"It's a roll of tissue, sir." I pulled it out and shook it defiantly in front of him just as the results came back positive for drugs.

"What else is on you?" he demanded.

"Excuse me, sir. You are being rude. I have nothing on me. I own my handbag and my red suitcase, nothing else. I'm here to meet my aunt and watch the football," I lied, and gave him the address of the hotel I'd been booked into.

They hadn't pressed again for my residential address in Britain, and I prayed they wouldn't. The only city that came to mind was London, and I couldn't think of a proper street name in English. Fear had terminated my ability to think clearly in English and as a result I began to stutter. Thankfully, a mixture of anger, resentment and adrenaline came to my aid and miraculously, I spoke quite good English.

The nasty officer was like a fox terrier. He was determined to break me and bury me with others he had caught for drug smuggling. I was shocked when he asked permission to have me X-rayed. I didn't refuse. I didn't need to. I was keen to prove the son of a bitch wrong.

"Yes, you may X-ray me," I said, keeping my eyes focussed on his as I answered, for I'd agreed without hesitation.

Then I heard the officer who believed me speaking in Japanese to the nasty one. It was dangerous to assume under such circumstances, but he thought I was telling the truth. My hopes were in vain as I watched angry gesticulating between them, and he was ordered to leave. He came back about five minutes later and shook his head, saying something briefly to the mean officer, who smiled. I was bewildered and wondered what was going on; whatever it was, it didn't appear to be in my favour. I was left alone in the office while they collected the X-ray results. They seemed to take forever, but there was no point in making a run for it, so I sat and waited.

The two nasty officers finally returned and, pointing to my suitcase, he said something to his companion who unzipped the lid and flipped it open. He began making an inventory on an official pad of everything inside, what I was wearing and what was in my handbag, then I knew. I'd been caught. I refused to hand over my phone when they asked for it; it was my lifeline to my children.

"Why are you doing this, sir? You have no proof that I have committed a crime."

He didn't answer, but his face suggested I shouldn't anger him further.

"Let me ask again," he said forcefully. "Give me your phone."

"Why, sir?" A hot sweat began to melt my icy resolve. My pulse was racing.

We stared at each other. I tried to keep a steely look of anger sending daggers into his, but acting and lying were not my strong points.

"You are guilty of drug smuggling into Japan with a false passport. You are under arrest. Now hand over your telephone."

I wanted to die in that moment.

"Who are your contacts?" he asked.

"Who? I don't understand."

"The people that got you to do this act."

My lips stuck together, my mouth had dried out, and I couldn't answer. I sat motionless and silent until he prompted again with the same question.

"I'm sorry, I don't understand. What act?" I managed to say, smoothing my tongue over my lips.

He was getting more annoyed, but kept his composure and asked a third time.

"Who are they?"

"I don't know who you are talking about!" I snapped at him, refusing to let go of this tiny thread of hope, but he was relentless, and I finally broke down.

It was over, everything was over, and I fainted.

When I came to, I was lying on the floor looking up into the face of a petite, uniformed Japanese lady.

Even though I could detect no emotion in her eyes, her voice had a gentle timbre to it, and she asked kindly, "Are you all right, ma'am?"

I nodded, disappointed I was still alive. Then tears began to pour down my cheeks.

She packed everything I owned back into my suitcase and when she'd finished, she marched me out of the office in handcuffs and took me down to the holding cells within the belly of the airport buildings. Every muscle in my limbs quivered wildly. My temples threatened to explode. She ushered me into a small room where we were met by another lady officer who searched me physically, violating every crevice a woman's body has. Stripped naked, she asked me to bend forwards. With a gloved hand, she inspected deep into my anus and then my vagina. I let out a guttural animal sound, which had risen from deep within me; the sound of naked fear and terrifying humiliation, which then gave way to uncontrollable sobs.

Something in that moment died within me.

From somewhere, I heard a different voice. It sounded far away. The voice was saying I could expect an eight-year jail sentence. Committing suicide was a very appealing fate. I stood, naked and vulnerable. One woman checked my ears, inside my nostrils and inside my mouth. The other removed the underwire from my bra. When they gave back the bra, they handed me a pair of old trousers with an elasticated waist and a pull-on shirt with a V-neck and collar. Any clothing with buttons and zippers was not worn in the holding cells. Shoes weren't allowed either. Socks were permitted, and I was handed a second-hand pair and marched down to the cells.

I looked and felt like a dirty, worthless tramp. An experience far more humiliating than losing my business.

All I had left in life were memories. Some I treasured, many haunted me. Everything I owned had been confiscated, including my life. Not even my toothbrush, toothpaste and personal toiletries were permitted to go with me. All I wanted to hear were Storm and Pieter's reassuring voices. Just once more, but there was no way of contacting them or anyone else in the family.

Chapter Thirty-Two

Pieter

"Look what you've done." I ran towards Papa, screaming hysterically, waving the local newspaper under his nose. "You've killed my mother."

Revenge was pressing and suddenly, without a moment's thought, my right fist connected with his jaw. The drink he was holding flew across the carpet.

"It's you who should be dead. You're a nothing, and now you've taken Mama down too."

I stepped back, tears of anger and devastation poured down my cheeks. Though I was shaken by what I'd just done to my father, I had no respect for him; that had gone long ago. He was no role model and never had been, merely a biological attachment, and even that I wished he wasn't.

I learnt of my mother's fate in the worst way possible being an impressionable, vulnerable teenager. The news of her arrest came to me in the jeering chants and nasty whispers from cruel fellow scholars. Most of them savoured the gossip and revelled in watching my pain.

Back in my room with the door locked, feeling inconsolable anger, I couldn't fathom how Mom could have done what she did. It was so unlike her. The more I analysed the situation, the more deep-seated the hatred for my father became. I knew

Mom would have been doing whatever she did for me, so that we could get away from him. Those truths made me feel worse. Concentrating on studying for a science test in the morning was impossible. There were so many conflicting thoughts in my head. I had to find somewhere else to live. Someone to help me through my last year of school. But who? I couldn't go on living with my father; I didn't trust myself to be near him. Now I understood, with greater clarity, why Mama had a desire to end his life on many occasions. It was his fault Mama was in jail, and I'd never forgive him. Ever.

Then I heard a light knocking on my door. Storm's tearful voice was calling my name. I opened the door and we fell into each other's arms, sobbing bitterly. I closed the door, locking it to keep Papa out.

"Why did Mama lie to us, sissie?" I sobbed.

"She wouldn't have meant to hurt us. She went to do this for us. Andre told me he was going to do the job, but she insisted on taking his place. She felt he should stay and look after Viv and the children. She kept saying it was her responsibility to get out of the mess she was in."

"Why didn't that useless drunken father of ours do it then? He got Mama into that mess in the first place."

I couldn't stop crying. The visions of my precious mother in a prison cell, terrified, alone and very far away, while Papa sat in his comfortable armchair, drinking, were unbearable.

Storm tried hard to soothe my brokenness. Eventually, I calmed down. She'd been sobbing too; we both had swollen eyes and puffy faces.

"How are we going to get Mama home, sis?"

"I don't know. We have no contact with her. The consulate contacted me today. They will send her a little money and, apparently, she will be able to write soon."

"Oh, sissie, why? Why did Andre and Viv let her go?"

"It's too late to think about that, boetie. We have to be strong now and support each other."

Storm left my room an hour later, and I cried myself to sleep.

In the morning, I raced through a bowl of muesli then hurried off to school to write my science test. I hardly remember writing it, and I could barely hold my pen, but somehow, I got through it. Luckily, it was the last test before the final exams which were in a couple of months.

The days after Mom's arrest passed in a blur. My future suddenly seemed very dark. I only had a few months left of high school, then what? College wasn't something I could look forward to any longer. My hopes, my dreams, everything, dashed. Taken from me by a self-centred addict. That night, I knelt beside my bed, as I had done as a child, and prayed someone would take me away. A few days later, my prayers were answered.

Uncle Ernest and his business partner, Uncle Niels, came to my rescue. I moved in with Uncle Ernest and his family for the remainder of my school year. It was a huge relief to be away from Papa.

I missed Mama terribly.

Leaving home caused another huge row with Papa.

A friend helped me move out one night when Papa was passed out drunk on the couch. We thought he was too drunk to notice what we were doing. I'd handed Frikkie my computer and ran back upstairs to grab my suitcases, but Papa was waiting for me when I came down the stairs, blocking my exit. He was no match for me, but this time I screamed at him to move out of my way. He took no notice, encouraging me to hit him again. Instead of hitting him, I pushed past him, knocking him out of my way and put the cases in Frikkie's car boot and went back for the last few things in my room. I wasn't going to be intimidated by a drunk with no conscience. Father or no father.

As I walked into the house, Papa locked the front door behind me and followed me up the stairs. I grabbed the last satchel off of my bed and turned to face him. I wanted to do the decent thing and reason with him, but he lurched towards me aggressively and tried to hit me. I ducked to avoid his flying fist, and the next thing I remember, I was stepping over him at the bottom of the stairs. Taking my set of keys out of my pocket, I unlocked the front door and left home forever.

Chapter Thirty-Three

Japan

Adrenaline was pumping rapidly through my veins. Ahead of me were the temporary holding cells at Narita. The sight of them made me want to retch, spew out the shame, the pain, the lies and humiliation that were poisoning me. I violently pulled back against the two ladies who were holding me like a child refusing to go to school, I sat down, my heels firmly pressed against the cement flooring which created the desired friction. I was not going to go into one of those cages. I was not a stray dog, but a human.

The vision of what lay ahead was far beyond my grasp. Another guttural sob sounded from the pit of my stomach as I fought the two ladies. They took little notice of me. They waited beside me while I put my head between my knees trying to gather my thoughts, then they pulled me up off of the floor. I stood still, shivering and weak, and my legs were trembling. I was petrified all urethral sphincters would let go, leaving me wet and more humiliated, but my legs gave way instead. I collapsed in a crumpled heap on the cold cement floor once more.

"Just breathe," the lady warders said kindly, trying to assure me I would be fine.

My mind was numbed. My body paralysed by fear. How could I be fine? I couldn't move; nothing moved as my eyes stayed fixed on what was ahead of us. Patiently, they coaxed me into believing I would survive this ordeal. I took a few deep oxygenating breaths and rose to face my fate.

The wire mesh cages were getting closer with each step we took. I wanted to yell out again that I couldn't go into them, but instead, I whispered pathetically about how sorry I was.

There was no response from the two ladies. No one gives a shit how sorry you are or how badly you needed money. In their eyes, all you are is a lowly criminal.

Before they put me into the cells, I was shown where the lockers and cupboards were. The bedding store cupboard remained locked and was only opened at night for prisoners to collect their bedding. My closet had in it a spare set of second-hand clothing, similar to what I was wearing, then they guided me to the cell block.

It was eerily quiet in the hall. Everyone captured, quietly mourning their fate. I was expecting it to reek of stale urine, halitosis and dejection, but surprisingly, the place was immaculate, except for the stench of crime, and I smelt like that filth.

Futons, the Japanese "beds", were what we slept on. They sounded rather fancy, but when I saw them, they were far from what I'd seen in furniture stores.

At a prescribed time, we collected our futon set, which consisted of a sparsely padded mattress, a quilt and a pillow. The pillow was a strange cushion filled with masses of tiny little plastic pipes to give it some semblance of buoyancy.

On entering the cell, I was handed a cushion to sit on, a crumpled old square made of tired foam that had seen the bums of many prisoners before me. It wasn't going to provide much comfort.

The cell block filled the more significant space in the middle of the hall. The block was grouped into multiple cells, separated by sheets of clear Perspex. This ensured the low lives within could be viewed from anywhere in the hall by the roving police. There was nowhere to cower. Nowhere to hide from the shame and guilt I was feeling.

The floor covering was made from interwoven grass matting the Japanese called "tatami"; it helped to hold back the cold, but nothing could hold back the cold I was feeling inside. A layer of this woven matting was about three inches thick. Had it not been so old and tatty, it probably would have worked well.

Clutching my cushion, I slunk into the cell. If I'd had a tail, it would have been firmly between my legs with my spine curved upwards in submissive fear like a stray dog. Entering with me was a deep penetrating self-loathing, along with other fearful feelings that rapidly filled the crevices of my mind and soul. I didn't want to be alive.

I put the cushion on the floor, away from the other prisoners, and sat on it. I propped my back against the Perspex wall and wrapped my arms around my knees, pulling them up to my chest protectively. The sweet musky odour, the initial fear response, had settled and dried on my skin and drifted up to my nose, ensuring the memory of the interrogation became firmly etched in my mind.

My new "home" for God alone knows how many days was three metres by four metres. There were six of us crammed i nto that small space for three days. In the corner of the cell was a western style toilet, which my eyes fixed on, registering with horror that its Perspex surrounds were only blacked out to waist height.

"I can't do this," I wailed, and the other inmates looked at me with blank stares. This was not a place where sympathy was found.

How was I to do my ablutions? I didn't even do that in front of the people closest to me. I surrendered to oblivion, removed from this horror for only a moment and came around hearing the police officer saying to someone that the holding cells were busier than usual. I was forced to face the truth of my new world once more. I looked about me somewhat dazed, then someone else mentioned the World Cup was to blame for so many smugglers (mules) being caught. Airport security had been on high alert, as I'd experienced.

A crushing emptiness filled me. I stayed on the floor and curled into the foetal position on the matting, putting my head on the square cushion and tucking my hands between my thighs, trying to shut out this grim reality.

"Oh, Storm, what have I done?" I whispered into my chest. I was still trembling from inside out, feeling raw and vulnerable. Then it was time for supper.

Seated cross-legged on my futon, I watched with numbed single-mindedness the "dinner" that was slid into the cell through a small opening at the base of the door. On the plate was some rice and a strange, unappetising pinkish slop, which I was supposed to negotiate with a pair of chopsticks. I starred at it and suppressed a groan. I couldn't eat. When the plates were collected, a small styrene cup of hot green water, that had an awful pungent smell, and a mug of cold water were pushed through. I drank the water, then took a sip of the hot green water and spat it back in the cup – I'd never tasted anything more disgusting.

I moved my futon back against the Perspex walling and propped myself against it once more. I closed my eyes, trying to breathe rhythmically and ignore the aches in my body. I went on rocking gently backwards and forwards throughout the night, asking for water every time a police officer passed the cells. Hunger pangs had gone with everything else I was dealing with, but I was severely dehydrated.

The cell was as silent as a desert at midnight, and just as cold. I constantly shivered, both from the cold air that surrounded me and my raw shameful thoughts. In the early hours of the morning, a million little voices were screaming accusations and questions at me. None of which I could answer. None of them would have been satisfactory had I found an answer.

Nothing was going to change my predicament.

The only sounds were the intermittent sounds of police officers checking on us, like black cats scuttering through empty streets in search of rats that may have escaped. I hadn't sought an escape route yet.

During the night, probably nearer the early morning hours for my watch had been removed, I signalled to one of the officers and pleaded for water in a much bigger cup. My mind was foggy with exhaustion, and my vision was blurred. I desperately needed to rehydrate. I knew I had to put the embarrassment of peeing or defaecating in public behind me somehow, but I had to drink or I would end up seriously ill. Water, in copious amounts, was what I needed to get my kidneys functioning again, as I watched my feet swell to double their size and my lower limbs grow puffy.

"Two cups please," I asked, showing a sign with my fingers.

The police officer shook her head, indicating just one. I shook my head, urgently gesticulating that I needed two large ones, and she nodded. I thought I saw a glimmer of a smile. She came back with one large cup, which I downed while she stood outside the cell, waiting for the empty mug. Then I asked for one more, which she obliged. I drank the second one more slowly.

The life-restoring liquid flowed into me and an hour later, my system began to function. Clarity of thought returned, but a burning sensation in my bottom shot hot spikes of pain down my legs and a tingling sensation in my feet. I had to get up and move, but there was so little room. I stood up and rubbed as vigorously as I could manage until the pain eased, then I needed a pee. There was nothing I could do but succumb to a bladder that was now about to burst. I sat on the seatless cold porcelain, closed my eyes and let go. Oh, the relief. I'd done it. Most of the prisoners were still sleeping but peeing with my eyes closed felt less exposing. Now my focus had moved from my bladder and the hardships of sitting exposed on the toilet, other thoughts tormented me like a runaway bushfire, burning the passages of my mind, scattering ashes of disgrace and erasing memories of happiness. Then horrific scenes I'd seen in movies of ladies' prisons played around in what was left of my mind.

Suicide felt like a comfortable, almost exciting, option.

This living hell continued all day and into the following night. I kept wondering when I could make a call to South Africa.

The sequence of events is not particularly clear, but I stopped rocking on my haunches. I had to as they were bleeding and too painful to continue rocking. They were almost too painful to sit on for any length of time. I'd not intentionally hurt myself, but what I'd done by marking my cushion with blood was frowned upon and would not serve me well.

315

Finally, at lunchtime on the third day, they told me I could make one internal call only.

"One internal call? That doesn't help me. I don't know anyone in Japan," I sobbed. "I need to call South Africa."

International calls were not permitted.

As the days passed, the other prisoners were transferred or released, and I was the only prisoner left in the holding cells. I was sure there had to be something wrong. I was expecting to be in the holding cells for five or six days. The silence was eerie, and I beckoned to the lady police officer whom I sensed was more sympathetic than some of the others and asked her what was going on.

"You can write a letter," she responded quickly in English.

"I have no paper, no pen, no money. How can I write a letter?" I wailed helplessly in response.

She shrugged and walked away.

That afternoon, a young Filipino girl was admitted to the cell. She spoke a little English and Japanese. That night we communicated quietly between officers' rounds, and I felt a glimmer of hope. She explained she'd asked the officer to arrange for a lawyer to see me the following day. Touched by her thoughtfulness, I gave her a quick thumbs-up, blew her a kiss, then lay back on my futon.

The lawyer arrived, but he neither spoke nor understood much English. However, between us, we got a letter drafted to Storm, giving her the address of the holding cells and the detention centre where I was to be moved to in a few days.

I spoke as often as I could with my new friend. She wouldn't be in the holding cells long; she'd been in before and understood the system. While we were out in the exercise area, she provided me with information on what lay ahead. She also taught me the importance of drinking green tea, and I slowly got used to its taste.

"It will nourish and rehydrate you," she told me.

Sip by delicate sip, I ingested it, and it did hydrate me. I began to embrace its known healing properties.

The following afternoon, my Filipino friend was moved and once again, I was the only prisoner in the holding cells.

Overcome with despair and loneliness, I began rocking on my cushion again. All I could think about was how much I longed to brush my teeth and have a shower. The only reassuring knowledge was the family would soon know where I was, though they would have been told by Andre what had happened and they'd have my contact address.

In the silence of the empty cells on day five, I wondered how my fellow countryman, Nelson Mandela, had dealt with twenty-seven years of this kind of hell. I couldn't bear the thought of another hour of capture. I speculated on what his initial thoughts must have been when he was caught near the main Johannesburg–Durban railway line in the heart of the Natal Midlands and was arrested. He would have kept his strong demeanour, I was sure of that; he had a political purpose, and I assumed his only thoughts would have been on freeing his people from the burden of apartheid. He never lost sight of that, and I knew that was what I had to do: focus on a purpose. I pondered on these thoughts for a long time and remembered that he'd said, documented somewhere, I could not recall where, "A saint is a sinner who keeps on trying." I had to keep those words in my mind forever.

The days passed in a blur of sadness and regret. On day eight, four prisoners came in.. On the same day, the lawyer came back to see me.

Depression became a part of my daily life as it became clear an eight-year prison sentence was what I would have to face. Eight years? I couldn't be in jail for eight years. I wept for hours. Once again, the thought of dying was preferable.

Chapter Thirty-Four

I had waited ten long days, the Japanese Consulate informed the South African Embassy that they were holding me. Someone from the embassy was to visit me. Two days later, they arrived and provided 1,000 Yen for me to buy the articles I needed. I thought it wise to request an Afrikaans translator for the court proceedings, which I did. I learnt later that the request would delay my release from the holding cells. I also learnt that before I could be transferred anywhere, the South African authorities had to verify who I was.

There was no other way to describe what I'd got myself into, other than a fucking awful mess.

Boredom became the catalyst. Boredom that made me whisper to my limbs and argue with my thoughts every minute of the day, even though I had a few books from the library that I could read to deviate my thoughts.

Finally, by day twelve, I had passed the stage of asking myself, why? It was time to dig deep, analyse internal factors that were to be crucial in my healing process and the development of what made me a human being and accept that the universal fear of poverty had destroyed all my common sense. I had to forgive myself. There were parts of me I began to look at through different eyes. I began to question who I was. How honest, how sincere, how generous, how vain, and so the list went on. I took the time in the silence of the confinement for introspection and put harsh criticism to one side. I took advantage of the quietness to find the path to deep spirituality and be gentler on myself, as tough as it was.

On day thirteen, a list of what I could buy from the internal shop was handed to me. I quickly learnt 1,000 Yen went nowhere. The lists prisoners were given served as a shopping record. Opposite each item was a little box. I coloured in the box, indicating the item I needed. I'd messed up my first "shopping list" by ticking the boxes; they had to be coloured in.

I coloured in the square for one writing pad, one pen, one bar of soap, one tube of toothpaste, one toothbrush and four stamps and envelopes. I couldn't afford shampoo, but I was able to take what others left behind; that was prison luxury.

On day six, I had my first shower. The sensations of washing my hair and showering for the first time in six days was ecstasy sent from above. The almost inexplicable sensation of being cleansed, inside and out, was amazing, but my mind still felt filthy, even though I had already showered twice since then.

I brushed my teeth for the first time on day fourteen, when I got the goods ordered on the shopping list. Taking a bath or a shower was an activity I'd taken for granted before, something many of us do. In prison, it became a treasured joy. A luxury I looked forward to twice a week, if I was lucky. If there were lady officers available to supervise the blissful, cleansing ritual I craved. What I did notice though, by showering only twice a week, my skin was beautifully nourished by its natural oils and I no longer needed copious amounts of lotions, which was quite a revelation and a saving. I missed the scents of my body lotions, but once one's body adjusts, it becomes quite odourless, unless I was taken out on regular exercise outings.

Having a notepad and pen made a huge difference to me. I stopped rocking mindlessly and began meditating. Writing relieved some of the boredom and I began a short grief-stricken letter to Storm. My pen hovered over the paper for a long time as I tried to work out what to say and how to say I was sorry. Saying sorry seemed so inconsequential and meaningless, but I knew of no other English words to express how I felt. I was not permitted to write in my mother tongue, for all letters were read before being sent. I wasn't ready to explain everything; it was all still a jumbled mess in my mind. I gradually processed the fact that I had gone from being a confident, focussed businesswoman to an emotionally anaesthetised convict, in a matter of weeks. It was not only unbearable to explore and put into words for me to understand, but to have to explain it all to Storm was unmanageable then. I first had to master my own tender emotions of guilt and shame.

When there was an available warden, they took me to the exercise area. This was a highlight for me. I made the most of every physical move I made, patiently and gently stretching muscles and tight tendons. Then I would do fast exercise to raise my heartbeat and oxygenate my mind and finish with the stretches again. The exercise became my drug, clearing away some of the negative depressing thoughts and replacing them with more positive ones.

By day fifteen, I knew Storm would have received the embassy letter, notifying her of my whereabouts. My handwritten letter was on its way and that was what I imagined she would have been desperately waiting to receive. Writing it had been agonising hardship. I was petrified she'd reject me, even hate me for betraying her. I only wrote one page and that one page was the hardest I'd ever written. Plus, I had to ask her to send me money. I prayed our relationship was strong enough for her to find forgiveness, and it was.

She sent me money and poured her heart out to me. It was almost too hard to read. Through tear-filled eyes, tears dropped onto the page, smearing the words she'd so carefully and thoughtfully written. I read it over and over again.

Pieter

I knew exactly why my mother had done what she did. She wanted to keep a promise she'd made to me. I recited Mama's pledge to me before she left.

"My darling son, I promise I will always keep the family together, no matter what it takes, and you, my boy, will have the education you deserve."

Now she was living the burden of the ultimate sacrifice she'd made. There was no doubt in my mind that when Mom agreed to take the package to Japan, she had no idea what she was carrying or the implications of being caught.

After all the years she had sustained endless abuse from my father, she remained a stable, grounded role model to the three of us. For her to give in to something like this was testament to what lengths she'd go to for her family. She did what she did, not to save her business for material gain, but because her honesty tugged at her. It was important to her that she appeased her creditors, people she was ethically beholden to. All apart from what she wanted to do for me. Social position or mega wealth didn't consume my mother. All she ever wanted was a comfortable, honestly earned income and to ensure I got a university education. For me, that was admirable. But it didn't remove the anger I felt towards Vivienne and Andre for letting her go. They had some hard times when they were both made redundant and they turned to Mom. They added to her financial burden, yet she rarely complained; she loved us all equally and would do anything for us.

Even before Mom left, I never asked for money. I delivered newspapers on my bicycle and earned my own money. It was hard graft for two years. Then I was offered a good job as a packer in a warehouse. It was owned by an ex-client of Mama's. Then, I took on some of their IT work. It wasn't long after that I was supervising the loading of trucks in the evening and was earning more money than I could spend.

I ached for my mama and prayed endlessly for her safety and an early release.

Japan

There was no restriction on the number of letters I could write while I was being held at Narita temporary cells. The problem was, I couldn't afford to buy the stamps required for letters to South Africa. Each letter I wrote I addressed to both Storm and Pieter to save on paper and the ink in my pen.

Storm's letter arrived with some money, enabling me to write a few more letters to them, individually this time. I wasn't ready to write to Vivienne and Andre without being accusing, so I left them off of my mailing list for a few more weeks.

Begging for money from my children made me feel bilious, but I was glad to have the extra pennies to spend on stamps. When letters arrived with the money inside, security police removed it, changed it, and added it to the small amount I had left of the 1,000 Yen. Prison officials managed everything; every cent I owned and my life.

The routine in the holding cells was tedious. Green tea was the first fluid to touch my lips in the morning, and though I felt its health benefits now, the smell still turned my guts. I'd drink it holding my breath. I seldom recognised what I ate, other than rice. Lunch was the same every day, and dinner was a slight variation on lunch. It took me a long time to perfect the art of shovelling sloppy rice into my mouth using chopsticks. The trick was to hold the bowl directly beneath my chin and scoop it in at speed. I was the slowest eater in the family, so this was no easy task; so much of it ended up running down my chin.

The first time I experienced the post-dinner mouth examination, done with a metal detector, I was appalled. This hideous examination was done to ensure we were not hiding anything in our mouths. It was horrific, but mandatory. Every morning, after I'd swallowed the green tea, I was marched to the cupboards to lock away the futon set. If there were others in with me, we all went as a group. In the evening, it was the same procedure and the same after dinner. I would lie down and cover myself with the quilt, pulling it up over my head and try to sleep. Lights were switched off at 9.30 p.m. Even though I was often the only prisoner, the exacting routine was never deviated from.

Three weeks had passed and I was still in the holding cells. While in this almost solitary confinement situation, I would spend time interrogating my thoughts, most of which were full of contradictions and hard to fathom. But during those hard and trying days, I made a pact with myself: I was going to be a model prisoner and be released on early parole.

Another of my more pressing battles was that I'd endured three weeks without a cigarette. Many of my early difficulties would have been slightly more tolerable had I been able to puff on a cigarette, and I craved the comfort of having one every day. Withdrawal symptoms were a war I couldn't win; the struggle for nicotine raged on, day after day. For years, a cigarette had been my constant and necessary companion. I was never a heavy smoker, but whenever I was going through troubled times, I'd light a cigarette and feel instantly calmed. I needed my daily nicotine dose more than any other time in my life. The physical need brought bubbles of perspiration to my top lip as the craving took its hold, off and on, during the day.

Eventually, I plucked up the courage to ask the exercise officer to bring me a cigarette. He made the flicker of a nod, and I lived in hope. The following day, one of the lady officers came to collect me for exercise. I found this odd for I was the only prisoner, and I'd been out on exercise routine the previous day. To have exercise two days in a row was unusual. She marched me to the exercise area and motioned that I should squat. While in this position, waiting for the officer who gave the exercises to arrive, my legs burnt like crazy. I eventually got used to the position. There was nowhere one could sit, but it stretched the hamstrings and was a common stance in Japan.

He arrived and bowed in traditional greeting to the lady officer, then he came to me and pulled a cigarette out of his top pocket. A smile must have stretched my whole face as he handed the lit cigarette to me. I could have jumped up and kissed him. Instead, as one does in Japan, I put my hands together and bowed in thanks. I wasted no time in taking a long pull on it, inhaling the smoke deep into my lungs. As I hadn't smoked for some time, the nicotine made me feel blissfully dizzy as it entered my body. It was the upliftment and tonic I needed to ease my stress and anxiety. My cigarette knew how I was feeling – I never had to explain my emotional state, it just knew. With each puff, a new energy I'd forgotten existed filled me. Then I began playing joyously with the exhaled smoke, blowing circles into the air and smiling for the second time in a month, gloriously lost in a world of my own for a minute or two. I was mesmerised by the simplicity of the smoke rings disappearing through the wire mesh that covered the exercise area and gradually vanishing into the universe. This ritual became the highlight of the days I was given a cigarette. Every puff was remarkably precious as I held on to the smoke, holding it inside me like a lover would, capturing its smell and the sensations it left in my lungs and my body. Each puff became a bizarre ceremony of blissful feelings amidst the terror of my grim future.

During the fourth week in the holding cells, some of the officers dared to spoil me a little more. On the odd occasion, I had as many as three cigarettes in a day and occasionally a cup of coffee or an ice cream cone. A visit to the library on my way back from the exercise area was another opportunity where I could hover in a relatively "normal" environment and select a book to keep me company. On one occasion, I found a *Fairlady* magazine from South Africa. I was so excited, but when I dived into its contents, it made me more homesick, so I refrained from ever looking at magazines again.

The weeks ran into months in the holding cells. I knew the officers felt sorry for me, hence the little luxuries they gave me. They took huge chances giving them to me. One of them told me they'd never had one prisoner spend so much time in the holding cells before.

On 25 September 2002, five long months after my arrest, I was transferred to Chiba, the detention cells, where I was to await trial.

Chapter Thirty-Five

Chiba Detention Centre

Chiba Detention Centre was exactly as my Filipino friend had described it. I wondered, with a stab of pain, what had happened to her. She must have been here often to have described it in such detail. I shall not forget her kindness, but I was going to miss my cigarettes and the generosity of the officers at the holding cells. The one plus in detention was there was a little more comfort offered and a fraction more variety to occupy one's dreary days.

There were two sections for women prisoners. One accommodated large groups of prisoners and the smaller division, which is where I was, housed only ten prisoners. As I entered, I was scrutinised again, this time by nine pairs of lifeless eyes, and a cold shiver ran down my spine as flashes of those awful movies I'd seen crossed my mind.

Things were different in detention. Prisoners who knew people on the outside or had friends and family in towns close by regularly asked them to bring in what they needed. I had no one, and no way of knowing when the next pennies would come from my children. My toothpaste, toothbrush and other personal belongings I held so dear were not transferred with me; they had been the things that kept me sane in this hell. Now I'd have to repurchase them, and I had hardly any money left. The response to my plea to the children would only realise any funds if they could spare it. With the transfer, I wouldn't hear from them for at least another three weeks.

I watched with envy those who opened their goodie bags, lovingly supplied by their families, and it wasn't long before they generously shared much of what was brought to them with me. Their kindness lifted me out of the swamp of emptiness that had overwhelmed me for months. Their incredible generosity changed my distorted view of the Japanese as cruel and ruthless people. These people were kind, respectful and considerate.

As much as I wanted, it was impossible to build any meaningful friendships; the language was a barrier and communication was not encouraged. I was expected to accept their gifts as part of what prisoners did for each other.

The things I needed most, like toiletries, weren't shared by the generous inmates.

In Chiba, as in the holding cells, a shopping list was provided. This one was more comprehensive, but with very little money left, I didn't have much choice. All I could afford to buy was another notebook, a red pen, one stamp for a letter to South Africa and a tube of toothpaste.

After a few weeks in detention, my financial plight became well known amongst my fellow prisoners. It became a topic of cheerful conversation. As soon as their goodie parcels arrived, they would inspect their gifts, decide what to part with then cheerfully say aloud, "Give to alien." And so, the pile of goodies they put to one side for me grew with each family visit. Their endless warmth and generosity always reduced me to tears and, in return, they always teased me playfully.

Boredom wasn't as bad in detention, but time was a constant enemy. We had to wash our clothes, which passed a little time, but this posed a different problem for me; we had to buy our washing powder. Outsiders were not permitted to provide that, so I washed my two sets of clothing with my precious bath soap. Occasionally, a small handful was discretely passed to me by a kindly inmate while I waited for money to purchase my own.

I received two long letters from Storm during the third week in detention. Her words broke my heart. The invisible words of the heartache and emptiness she was suffering pained me even more. My absence was tearing her apart, eroding her strength little by little, and there was nothing I could do to prevent it. It took a year before I found the appropriate words to describe to her my insufferable agony and how I felt about lying to her and what it had done to me. It was the reason I hadn't answered her telephone call on that first day in Paris.

I'd not heard a word from Vivienne and Andre in those first five months. I didn't expect to hear from Andre, but I prayed I would get a letter from Vivienne. We had our differences, but I loved her and missed her. Eventually, a letter from her arrived.

I'd had one accusing letter from my sister and one particularly sad, soul-searing letter from Pieter, telling me what Uncle Ernst had said, something neither of us will ever forget.

My kind, jy kan enige tyd my werk, maar dit is nie vir jou beskore nie. Jou ma wou gehad het jy moet verder gaan swot en ek sal jou ma se wense laat realiser. (My child, you can work for me anytime, but it is not for you. Your mother wanted you to go further and I will make your mother's wishes come true.)

After they learnt of my arrest, Uncle Ernst had held him in his arms and assured him that everything in his life would work out fine. Pieter explained in his letter how he was struggling to see how it would get better without me.

He wrote, "Mama, here is a man who is not even related to us, but cares so much. He is so kind and has so much compassion. I am still speechless that he took me under his wing and has given me so much, treating me like a son. Papa hasn't even asked after me, or how my exams are going. In his eyes, I may as well be dead."

I sobbed rivers of bitter tears that burnt as they ran down my cheeks. I read on.

"All that you have taught me, Mama, and now with what Uncle Ernst is doing for me, will live with me forever. I hate to say this, but what you have done is another lesson for me. I still love and respect you. I know why you did it, and I know it was against your will. Storm and I know that, and we pray for you. We love you and miss you."

I sobbed off and on for days after receiving that letter. I kept reading it until I was no longer reduced to tears by it, then the interpretation of it warmed me with his reassurance of love. Only then did I find the courage to put it away.

At night, thoughts of my mother often came to me. I often felt very connected to her, so much so, it felt she was in the cell with me, guiding me, whispering to me to do the right things, that there was always a lesson to learn from one's mistakes. I thanked God she was no longer alive. She would have been bitterly disappointed, but she would not have been accusing; she knew and understood my circumstances better than most.

There was another element to my guilt: not being able to thank the wonderful man who had taken Pieter under his wing.

Ernst had given him a chance to become someone and excel. He had made Pieter's life easier.

I couldn't send him to university, but Ernst sent him to college.

All photographs and letters sent to me were guarded carefully; they were my visual lifeline to my family. The little Filipino lady had warned me they took letters away once they had been read. I hid two small pictures on me, which amazingly they never found. I had one of Pieter and one of Storm. Every night, I held them flat against my stomach and imagined their energy and love feeding into me as I lay quietly meditating my future.

An unfortunate turn of events rocked the excellent reputation I was trying so hard to build – it was all over a toothbrush. Though I may have banged on about personal hygiene and its importance to me, it would never have crossed my mind to steal from an inmate, or anyone, for that matter.

The cells were checked for discrepancies every day. Checks took place while we were out on exercise routine. On this day, when the wardens were checking through my belongings, they found the toothbrush I was given. The problem was the name of the prisoner who'd given it to me was on the toothbrush; there was no one to verify my story was true. Rules were rules – rigid and strictly adhered to – and to my detriment, though innocence once more, I learnt another hard lesson and was severely punished.

The punishment was brutal. I was locked into solitary confinement, where I stayed for a long time. Presumed "theft" was a serious black mark against me. I tried to explain the legitimacy of how I came to own the toothbrush, but the warden, who didn't have a good command of English, refused to believe my genuine story. He was convinced I was a thief. Wardens always thought you were lying, and in some cases, you didn't even have to open your mouth. I had to accept that reality.

In solitary confinement, there is nothing – nothing at all but four white walls. I wondered how long I could hold on to my sanity. Was this where I would lose my mind? Was it going to be within these four white walls where I would mentally snap? Terror took on another new meaning. I didn't want to wallow in self-pity, I didn't want to live the "victim" mentality within these confines, but it grew like an infection. The road to insanity is a slow, quiet, cruel process that took me down some very rough tracks where treacherous sinkholes of manic depression sucked me in. Mealtimes were a minor distraction, and with each mouthful, I'd count how many times I could chew one mouthful until it dissolved. I'd sip on water and green tea, swirling the liquid around my mouth before swallowing, visualising and sensing its passage to my stomach. It was surreal and absurd, but I loved every sip as my mind wandered over steep, treacherous mountain paths, threatening my existence on earth, but I'd come down the other side and into the desert where I became lost and thirsty for hope.

On rare occasions, very rare occasions, the solitude in the single room was a welcome indulgence; it was quiet. Hope. An optimistic state of mind, they say, based on an expectation of positive outcomes in one's life. There was not much hope vibrating through my soul. As a verb, its definitions include: "expect with confidence" and "to cherish a desire with anticipation". How I wished those words could stick with feeling. Courage and the mentioned hopeful desires hung in my brain like the low-lying fog across the desert in the early morning, opaque and impossible to grasp. When it cleared, flashes of intense light beamed through, and I found a few positive thoughts, warmed by rays of purpose, and my senses sharpened. But most of the time, I numbly endured the three long, lonely weeks in that cold, emotionally chilling box and miraculously remained sane. I found the answers to many questions about my life and my purpose there. Panicked needs lead to unclear thinking. Depression leads to all sorts of ill-conceived plans, and the reality of an ill-conceived plan was this imprisonment. All I had thought about at the time was how to get my hands on "fast money". My intentions were good, but obtaining it was not.

I'd fallen into the trap, something I intuitively knew never worked. "Fast" money, no matter where it is sourced, always has its sacrifices; never did I think it would put me in jail though. But another reality check looked directly at me; one I'd so often questioned in my life. Money determines an outcome. Money even determines the experience of imprisonment too. We, as humans, cannot get away from the power it holds. When we raise our spiritual awareness and give way to trusting the universe, we experience positive vibrations, so I have been informed on numerous occasions. I know it to be true, but I also know that if one cannot escape the reality of one's situation, positive vibrations do nothing for you. I was not in the right space to attract anything good, nor was I when my business went bankrupt. I was of the notion that nothing would ever go right in my life, and certainly not while Dion du Toit was in it.

Having a few extra pennies from the children gave me the opportunity to buy a few necessary items. I also learnt lots of dollars could determine the amount of time you stayed in jail too! I couldn't help wondering who the deluded person was that came up with the phrase "money doesn't buy happiness".

It bought lots of happiness in jail and an abundance of it could buy a ticket to freedom. A lack of it, as was my predicament, meant I felt every bit of the harsh side of what life dished out behind bars in Japan, and money, or the lack of it, was why I was in this hell.

I witnessed what wealth could manipulate by being associated with a sweet young German lass. Her name was Heidi, and she had always had too much for free. Her family, particularly her father, dished out money when she wanted it. As a result, she grew up without values, leaving her exposed to the wrong type of people when she reached her mid-teens. Without the wisdom and guidance from parents, whose time was spent in pursuit of making more and more money, she didn't quite know how to stop wanting more herself. There's nothing wrong with wanting more, but it was how she was getting it that was the concern.

She was one of the sweetest young teenage girls I'd met in many years, and I was sure she had not fully comprehended the impact of her actions. She'd been caught carrying cocaine for the third time. This time, she expressed her fears that she would be spending a long time in jail and her fears brought on long fits of sobbing. Much like mine had been. Heidi told me how she'd pray at night that her rich daddy's lawyer could work his magic again. Despite this, Heidi was kind, considerate and amusing; a beautiful young girl spoilt by mega ego-driven parents. She was surprisingly unpretentious, which was unusual. It was all quite contradictory; she didn't consume drugs herself but moving them, she said, "had worked for her". I was shocked by the vast amount of pocket money she got from her father and how little her parents seemed to care about what she did.

"When money finished, I needed more. Smuggling cocaine paid better than Daddy," she shared with me.

However, her youthful vulnerability was showing now; she was a very frightened young girl. One night, with her hearing looming closer, she cried like that frightened little girl. She reached out to me for comfort and maternal reassurance. Though prisoners were not permitted to touch each other, I held Heidi in my arms and let her cry until there were no tears left.

"They tell me I'm in for eight years for smuggling marijuana. Cocaine is far worse."

Heidi raised her eyebrows and shook her head.

"Not eight years, nein, nein. Maybe three," Heidi reassured me. "I think I will do eight years this time. I'm scared, so very scared." And it showed.

Thankfully, we were not caught comforting each other. Heidi was younger than my daughters, and that night, while we hugged and cried together, satisfying each other's needs for physical comfort, we both agreed we felt calmer for it. There is nothing like a hug to make a person feel valued.

I hoped this scare would stop her from doing it again, but I never mentioned my thoughts to her. After her hearing, she came back with a smile that stretched from ear to ear. Heidi's father had hired the best criminal lawyer in Germany; her case was acquitted for the third time. It didn't go without warning though. If she was caught again, she would face serious consequences. And so, the many clichés like "with money you can get away with murder" and "money doesn't buy you happiness" had just played out in real-time, in front of me. Heidi wasn't directly responsible for murder, but the drug runs she was doing would have had catastrophic effects on young lives that could lead to death. Innocent children were always the victims, often dying from overdoses or the consequences of overdose, but Heidi didn't see that side of what she was encouraging. If we'd had more time to talk, I would have said something to her.

I sat in deep thought after the outcome of her trial. I knew what I had brought in was not right, but the physical consequences of consuming cocaine versus marijuana were worlds apart.

I was happy for Heidi that she was going free. I was going to miss her. Heidi's leaving brought on the ghosts of my life, the unfairness of it, the regrets, the shame and self-loathing, which wrapped itself around me like a serpent squeezing the life force from me. I had to stop feeding this anger and hatred, but it was a good companion sometimes. Real anger often prompted crystal clear thoughts for me, and the night Heidi left, I prayed for the first time in a very long time. I prayed for my little German companion, asking God to stop her doing what she was doing. If He never listened to my problems, perhaps He'd at least listen to hers.

I asked Him to help me remove the blame game I was playing. If Dion hadn't robbed me blind to feed his addiction to alcohol, I wouldn't be here. How was I going to forgive? If I'd listened to my instincts and not my middle child I wouldn't be here. I had to stop thinking these thoughts; it only made it all harder to bear. The bitter truth was, I was here because of… me! I had to take responsibility for *all* of my choices. It was me who'd made a choice to give Dion endless chances, it was me who'd given in to Vivienne's pleas to help her father. I'd said I would do the delivery of said unknown package to Japan, which took Andre out of the equation. I understood about choices and responsibility, or did I? The question was how was I going to convert my bitter thoughts into forgiving ones? What I'd done was not right – I'd accepted that – but I wasn't a criminal, and that was why it hurt so badly.

I couldn't deny the envy I felt when I hugged Heidi once more before she left. She was like a daughter. I missed her cheerful demeanour in the days that followed. She was a little ray of sunshine in the gloom. We'd understood each other, not just in spoken language. I spoke Afrikaans, she spoke German, and we managed to understand more of what each other said than we thought. It was good to talk in my mother tongue, even if it wasn't for long. Heidi and I exchanged a few letters after her release, but in her last one, she told me she'd been caught again, this time in Australia. After that, I never heard from her again.

Before she left detention, she generously gave me some of her clothing: a nightie, an expensive warm jacket I cherished, a T-shirt and two pairs of socks, all of which I graciously accepted. Winter was approaching, and the nights were cooling down rapidly. Those extra clothes helped keep me warm. I felt the warmth of her kindness keeping my toes snug. Because her clothing, having been privately owned, was never marked like the toothbrush saga, I could keep them without retribution. The socks were the most favoured, for my feet suffered the most.

Chilblains were the bane of my life. They often kept me awake as they throbbed painfully, but Heidi's expensive thermal socks kept the bitter cold out better than any other socks. Two weeks after Heidi left, six of us had our cases heard, and for the first time since arriving in Japan, I got a taste of being handcuffed – Japanese style. If it wasn't so humiliating, it would have been interesting. It was an intricate system of knotted ropes that tied us together in a long line, leaving a complicated and equally intricate sense of worthlessness. We were bound together like slaves, reminiscent of those cruel days back in the distant past and consumed by emotions of terror and mortification and an agonising vulnerability all entwined in rope. A ruthless pain, a cadaverous system that ensured there was no possibility of escape. We shuffled our way down to the courts, tied together in grisly bondage. I'd never felt more like an animal than I did in that moment.

Today would reveal what lay ahead for me. I had no fancy lawyer.

Visions of the courtroom were intimidating. My legs mirrored the terror I felt as they dragged along beneath me. My whole body was giving way to the terror I felt as we were unbound and taken into the courtroom.

I'd envisioned the courts to be a massive, menacing room with dark wooden benches and high louvred windows, unapproachable policeman marching around the perimeter, clerks of the court and translators all waiting for me. I wasn't that important. Though it was a small room, it didn't make it any less intimidating. Standing in the wooden pulpit, I began to shake while I faced the judge, feeling insignificant and feeble in this foreign land, convicted of drug trafficking. Me? A fifty-two-year-old grandmother who'd rarely done anything unlawful. My hearing didn't last long for I was the last on the list that day.

Japanese court etiquette and protocols were respected. The judge and officials did not recess for tea twice a day, lasting up to an hour each time, nor did they close court at 4 p.m. like they do in South Africa. Lunch was a quick fifteen-minute recess, and no one moved to pack up when the typical working day ended.

The proceedings continued until the list was complete and every case had been fairly heard, no matter how long it took.

The discipline, ordinance and general respect in Japan had a lasting impression on me. I swore I was going to try to adopt a similar way of life when I got out, not that my life had been that much different in the manners department before.

I was asked to confirm my real name and my South African identity number – I could hardly speak.

"Are you aware of your conviction?" the judge asked.

"Yes, sir."

After a lengthy exchange of papers and discussion in Japanese, the state lawyer, who'd been appointed to represent me, said my hearing was postponed until December. No reason was given.

I was devastated. Tell a lie once, it lives with you forever. I had always reinforced the importance of not fibbing with my children. They didn't need reminding though; they'd heard enough of them spill from Dion's mouth. But now they were living the real-time pain of mine, and the consequence of Dion's lies and devious actions.

I was told I would be notified of the date and then I was dismissed. This decision meant another three months in detention. The longer I waited, the longer my stay in Japan.

Even though I spoke the truth and tried to remain a model prisoner, I had to remind myself a prisoner's word had no value. The authorities didn't care what I thought. I was a criminal.

Chapter Thirty-Six

Winter was settling in fast. The cells were freezing during the day and even colder at night; pneumonia was probably going to get me before the hearing. It was already the first day in December, and I'd heard nothing of my pending court case.

I'd been in for eight months with no idea on what sort of sentence I was going to serve. I had no clue what prison they'd transfer me to either. The wait was cruel, but finally, notification came through. My case was to be heard on 5 December.

Standing before the judge once more, he asked the routine questions, and I answered without feeling the same level of nerves I had on the first appearance. The South African authorities had confirmed I was Elizabeth Johanna du Toit and the identity number I'd given them was correct. The judge turned to the state lawyer and engaged in quiet discussion. I kept my eyes focussed on them. My neck began to spasm as I prepared myself for the verdict. I didn't move an inch as he turned back to face me and began to speak.

"Elizabeth Johanna du Toit, I find you guilty on all counts. You are sentenced to four years' imprisonment, with an 800,000 Yen fine," the judge announced.

The sound of the gavel crashing down on the table in front of him reverberated through me. Numbed and immobilised by his words, the reduced number of years hadn't registered. It was the sting of the fine that was hard to bear. *How am I going to pay an 800,000 Yen fine?*

The rest of what the judge had said filtered in and settled somewhere in the dark recesses of my mind. During this hearing came the realisation of what a mistake it had been requesting a translator. He'd screwed up my case by suggesting that four kilograms of marijuana was a severe crime and could kill many Japanese citizens. I instantly thought of Heidi and thought I should remind the judge of her case.

The injustices caught in my throat as they had done before and burnt as I shifted irritably in the enclosed podium.

"Sir, you heard the case of—" I was quickly shut down.

What kind of justice was this?

I wanted a re-trial and appealed immediately; miraculously, he granted it.

It was late into the evening when I was taken back to the cells. The only people around at the end of the day were the driver, a lady warder I'd got to know, and me. Being the only prisoner, they didn't feel the need to cuff me, thankfully. As the van doors closed, my world came crashing down around me. I sobbed as deeply as I had done on the first day of my arrest. It was pitch black outside, mirroring exactly how I was feeling. My heart-wrenching sobs must have tugged at the warder. Being protected by the darkened interior, she took the liberty of comforting me and folded her arms around me, whispering in reasonable English.

"No worry, ma'am, prison not so bad, you see. Be smart, like you are here in detention and very good in holding cell, you have no problem."

They were the kindest words I'd heard in months. The warmth of the warder's arms around me stilled my quaking body. A few minutes later, I began to wonder how she knew that I'd conducted myself in an exemplary fashion in the holding cells. Was she telepathic or could she see I was not a regular type of criminal? She'd just read my mind. I'd been thinking about the man who had spoilt me in the exercise area.

The kind man was her brother, she told me.

"He say, you velly good woman."

How I wished Dion could have heard this woman's sentiment.

It was late when we finally got back to Chiba. I wearily climbed out of the bus and looked up at the night sky. There were glittering stars that danced across the black velvet sky like they did at home and tears came pouring down my cheeks again. Not only did the vast expanse of starlit skies tug at memories of home, I knew it would be a long time before I would gaze upon skies so beautiful again.

A solitary, lonely realisation of what lay ahead, a process of illusion and disillusionment, would go on endlessly, this I knew. Without anyone to share it with or talk through the difficulties, it was going to be tough. A desolate emptiness and a ghastly hollowing in the pit of my stomach filled me as I entered my cell. I sat on my futon rocking on my haunches again. As I rocked, my thoughts began to drift towards preparations for my appeal hearing. I nodded off occasionally, but I never slept. Four years was an eternity – a lifetime in those moments. The sentence added to the time I'd already done. But how was I to raise 800,000 Yen in jail? I couldn't ask my children to pay it.

Somewhere in between the tears and sleepless nights, I had to find the strength to go on as a model prisoner and get early parole.

Thankfully, Storm managed to scrape some money together for me to buy more stamps, another notebook and writing paper. In my next letter to her, I asked her to send me as many facts and statistics on cannabis as she could obtain officially. In my next hearing I had to prove that heroin and cocaine were considerably more dangerous to "Japanese people" than what I'd been carrying. Next time, I would represent myself.

During the agonising long days waiting for a reply from Storm, I learnt from kind lady warders that I would earn money once I got to jail. The relief was immeasurable, and I began to sleep less fretfully. A deduction off of my wages would go towards reducing the fine over the four years of imprisonment.

"You velly good. You will get fine job," one of the warders had said to me, which made me laugh.

I was sure there was no place on earth closer to hell than this, and there was certainly nothing funny about it, but her sweet words placated the living torment.

I couldn't begin to utter that I was "looking forward" to going to "proper prison", but with the first court case behind me, moving to the main prison meant I could commence my sentence and start working. I'd ached to do something constructive after all this time of torturous waiting.

Soon it would be Christmas. I was told we would get a few extra treats and the exercise area was more fun, but it only made it worse for me.

The Japanese do not celebrate Christmas, but out of respect to us "aliens" who do, a few little sweeties and a slice of fruit cake at dinner only served to trigger emotions so intense I found it hard to swallow. Chewing and crying couldn't be synchronised – all I wanted was my children. The birth of Christ showed me how tormenting the celebration was without family. He'd not listened to me. I was not one of His lambs. I was an outcast even though I'd faithfully prayed so hard, for so long. Through all the years of abuse from Dion, I'd prayed for his issues to be solved. I'd asked for God's help to guide me and protect my children – my prayers were never considered.

"Ask, and thou shalt receive." *Really?* I thought with acid cynicism.

The New Year filled the void – a time the Japanese people celebrate – but the only excitement I could muster was the knowledge I was one day closer to presenting my case and, hopefully, shortening the length of time I'd be in Japan. New Year celebrations were cheerier than Christmas and lasted three days. The food improved, which made us all more cheerful; we even got more sweets. It astounded me what pleasure and comfort I derived from a handful of sweets in those bleak times. That first Christmas and New Year passed quickly; a week I shall always want to forget, then life went back to the normal drudgery.

If any changes to a prisoner's situation happened or there was to be a transfer, we were only advised the morning it was going to happen. There was seldom anything to look forward to, and the celebrations were behind us until Easter. I had wished upon those magical stars floating around in the universe, that I'd gazed upon earlier, that my name would soon be called, but the days dragged on into weeks and I heard nothing.

Early one morning, with my nose dribbling from the cold and my fingertips numbed by the fierce, crisp air, I learnt that parole was not considered for the first two years. My next hearing would be for me to try to reduce the term and the fine. I resigned myself to two years, but, come what may, I had to adopt a more positive attitude, which I did. The reward for my new attitude was granted a few days later – I got a cigarette and a cup of coffee while in the exercise area. The first in weeks. I was so happy. After a cup of hot coffee and a ciggy, even the icy cold wind didn't chill me, and while I was busy with my two favourite things, I decided to take up lessons in Japanese and learn more about their culture – actions spoke louder than words in prison and they respected those that strived to be better.

I'd already noticed the warders and guards recognised I was not a "true" criminal, and they clandestinely looked after me from time to time.

Through my past years living with an addict – a selfish, alcoholic, sociopath, narcissistic psychopath – it forcefully taught me a great deal about tolerance! If nothing else had served me throughout the relationship, that lesson was serving me now. The little "niceties", like a cigarette and a cup of coffee provided for me occasionally by the friendly exercise warder, made the days in detention a little less wretched.

Chapter Thirty-Seven

Tochigi Prison

"Eee... lez... bet..." The warder's voice boomed out across the cells. My name was called at last, followed by the name of the prison. "Tochigi Prison."

A small smile of relief stretched my lips.

Tochigi is a prison mainly for lady "aliens". They called us aliens for the Japanese find it impossible to pronounce "foreigner". Having a phonetic alphabet, the word "alien" was easier for them to pronounce. This description for us foreigners was very apt, I thought, for everything around me, and my circumstances, was alien. Perhaps it wasn't quite as alien for some of the others and there were a lot of hard, nasty women in detention.

I was transferred to a single cell again, and just as before, everything I owned was re-counted and checked then packed and stowed for the day I would finally be released. The preciseness of the Japanese people left an indelible impression on me. Being a neat and orderly person myself, I respected the discipline, but the re-counting of the seventeen clean tissues I had arrived with was stretching it a bit! I had to smile as they went into the suitcase in perfect folds, like flawlessly ironed pillowcases.

The following day, 6 February 2003, after 278 grim days in holding cells and detention, I was about to begin my sentence. Another day closer to going home.

To suggest I was "excited" would be absurd, but the thought of being put to work and earning an income did make me feel more worthy. The income was a meagre amount to begin with, but it was a start.

Seven of us were being transferred to Tochigi that day. We were lined up, cuffed in the ghastly ropes and squashed into the transfer van. The windows were closed and the curtains drawn. I'd never experienced claustrophobic panic before, but I did on that journey.

It was snowing that day, and though I only got a glimpse of the exquisite beauty that surrounded us, I kept that picture in my mind and remained totally focussed on it. The heavy snowfall made the surroundings quite surreal; it was so quiet, and the first time I'd ever seen snow. A child-like urge to touch it and play in it was a healthy desire, I thought. As the waves of claustrophobia came, I breathed in the different visions of the sea of snow I'd caught a glimpse of, but as the journey progressed, it got stuffier and I fought to hold on to those visions as I inhaled the toxic breath of six other prisoners.

The transfer journey took four hours. We were cooped up like chickens; a journey that again hammered home the grim reality of being a criminal. Thankfully, the heavy snowfalls forced us to stop every so often, and a lovely icy wind blew into the bus, freshening the air within while snow chains were attached to the wheels, then the journey continued. As soon as we were out of the deep snow, the driver would stop and remove the chains. These "breather" stops were a lifesaver.

A letter from Storm had arrived the day I was transferred to Tochigi Prison, and they handed it to me once the booking-in process was complete. With the letter was an unexpected parcel containing some of their clothing and more money. How blessed I was to have such a loyal, loving daughter. I was so excited to have in my hands all the endless research she'd done on cannabis to present at my appeal hearing. Then I read her heart-wrenching explanation of why she'd sent me the selection of clothing she had. She'd asked each family member to contribute a piece of clothing that had an emotional attachment, a memory of me. This simple gesture was intended for me to *feel* the person close to me when I wore the item.

Two lady warders sorted through the clothing, piece by piece, and as I watched, little bits of my heart broke. I was only permitted to keep certain items, but I held them all close to me and breathed in the familiar smells as I cried, visualising the face of the person who'd parted with their piece of clothing. Then the items I was not allowed to keep were taken away and packed. The ones I could keep became the emotional food I craved.

Prison-issue was a dreary blue-grey dress. It was good quality, roomy, comfortable and practical; in line with the Japanese culture. As I signed for the issue of my prison garb, an absurd thought flashed through my mind and I could hear the sweet, innocent voice of Lena Zavaroni singing, "If my friends could see me now." I smiled.

Three pairs of panties, three bras, three thermal vests with matching long johns, two jackets (one was a warm lumber jacket, the other a lighter one), cotton socks, extra slacks, and an extra blouse were issued. My wardrobe for the next four years. Once we'd got our issue, we had to sew our name tags onto each article of clothing and each label was thoroughly checked to ensure the sewing was perfect and sewn central to the manufacturer's label, as instructed. If it was incorrectly sewn on, or untidy, the warders pulled it off, and the process was repeated. Some of the ladies had never used a needle and thread in their lives and it took them days to complete.

Once that tedious task was completed, they issued an item referred to as "the pot". The pot, similar to a thermos flask, was useful at night when I wanted extra water. We were also given the most disgusting toothpaste powder, a toothbrush, a face cloth, a futon, a woven head cushion and a bar of soap. At last, I didn't have to buy these necessities and I could brush my teeth every day. I hoped I would get used to the toothpaste. In addition, we were given a bottom sheet, a pillowcase and two woollen blankets. This was heaven.

The furnishings in the cell were sparse, but adequate. There was a small wooden table and chair, a chest in which to place my clothing, even a small television sat on the lid of the chest. Mounted on the wall next to the washbasin was a wooden shelf, and a tiny wall cabinet. Below was a western style toilet without the seat – at least I didn't have to share the loo now. A wooden partition separated the toilet from my "open plan" living quarters. Though I was still visible while seated, I got over that. One and a half metres by three and a half metres was my new cell size. I was put in the new block. These cells were considered "luxury" in size and the building was situated right on the edge of the prison grounds. I had a beautiful window in my cell. It obviously couldn't open, but it was over a metre in height and about sixty centimetres wide; my window to the world. A world where I intended to put my broken vision, shattered hope and lost sanity back together, piece by piece.

Being considerably taller than most ladies in the prison I was not able to stretch out entirely on my futon; my feet got squashed up against the wooden partition. Having always had circulation problems, this exacerbated the problem in my toes. After a few weeks, they began to change colour, and it wasn't long before I had minimal sensation in any of them. At night, I'd sit rubbing them for hours to get the circulation going, giving up precious sleep. Two toes on each foot had darkened to a deep blue, and I insisted on seeing a doctor. What started as painful chilblains changed into a condition bordering frostbite, though not quite as severe. I asked to have the warm woolly socks Storm had sent, but they wouldn't relinquish them. I couldn't see how they could be dangerous, but apparently some had ended their lives using socks, so I resorted to wearing three pairs of my other socks at night. I snuggled up in the fleece tracksuit top and the snug warm jacket Storm had sent me. Only then did I get a decent night's sleep. I was given medication and gradually the colour returned.

There were rules to walking, talking, eating, sitting and even sleeping correctly. These rules were pummelled into our brains during the first two weeks. Scattered within the vast prison grounds were an assortment of essential buildings; learning their whereabouts was of paramount importance. The square block closest to my living quarters was where most of the general activities took place, and I could see it from my window. My luck was changing. My cell was in an excellent position, and I wondered if this cell was selected for me because of my behaviour over the past eight months. I had endured the holding cells and detention far longer than anyone else ever had.

Whatever had caused this stroke of good fortune, my window was my saviour. Looking out every day, I became familiar with the prison grounds and had a perfect view of the mountains beyond.

I passed the humiliating physical examination on arrival; the X-rays revealed nothing hidden. The dental check was completed without a hitch and the medication I required to keep cholesterol at manageable levels was all in place. I learnt much later that I was one of very few who'd passed all this without the need to be questioned. I also had a brand-new futon, but my toes took weeks to heal.

I still had 104 weeks to endure without parole being considered.

My official prison number – "Ni sen ju itchi" – number 2011 was stored to memory.

Chapter Thirty-Eight

Nothing here was how I'd imagined it would be.

I kept asking when I would be put to work. I was sure we were left wondering on purpose.

I'd filled in the questionnaire on what I could do and in what fields my strengths lay. The waiting game continued for a few more days until I got the good news. I was to work in the paper bag factory! Me, working in a paper bag factory. This was not what I was expecting, nor was it on the questionnaire.

To begin with, I felt humiliated. But any form of work was better than the endless boredom and I could stop the useless practice of counting the days, weeks, months and years I still had to endure.

"The chains of the body are often wings to the spirit," I had heard someone say long ago and I'd never forgotten it.

My first working day began on day ten in Tochigi Prison. There were some grim-looking ladies in prison, ones I knew that keeping my distance from was a matter of survival. Some of them were in for life, some for murder, some manslaughter, child abuse and numerous cases of theft and rape. There was an assortment of horrendous crimes and plenty of short-term prisoners in for shoplifting and carrying drugs. Most were medium-term – up to five years. And like me, they were in for drug and other forms of smuggling. There were approximately 900 lady prisoners at Tochigi.

The morning I started work, the group of us who'd been selected to work with the paper bags were shepherded down to a large open room where boxes of paper bags were piled everywhere.

The instruction on how to fold them correctly began. It was a most unstimulating task. It puzzled me that I was given this task, so I did some investigating and was told that everyone starts with a menial task. It played the boredom tune to perfection. The senseis watched. They assessed your attitude towards mindless tasks.

The sensei's first impression was important. The book cover of who you are. It determined the type of working life you'd have in prison from then on.

Every week, boxes of paper bags got delivered to the prison. We unfolded each bag, secured thin tape along the bottom, folded it flat to seal it and stacked them. From there, they were sent on to another group who packed them back into boxes. It passed the time, and I got paid.

After a few weeks, I knew I'd go mad, but I kept telling myself things would get better. To break the boredom and motivate us, the sensei held weekly competitions. The individual who packed the most bags in a day won and earned incentives. These were not designed for fun, but to test our work ethic and to help motivate us. The more paper bags one folded, the better one's ranking became, and gradually, I began to understand their carefully planned system of individual assessment. Each prisoner had to prove they were worthy of their questionnaire. It was a carefully designed test to judge our ability, commitment and strength of character. I won the competition for sealing the bottom of the highest number of bags more frequently than anyone else in the group. I got promoted fast.

My first reward was a more extended stay in the exercise area. But the longer I stayed out, the more I craved a cigarette! However, my working life in prison progressed well, winning all the competitions for a few weeks in a row and I did get a few cigarettes. Then I was promoted to "checker".

Catapulted into a position of responsibility, it was now up to me to motivate my team. I worked along with the group, ensuring the bags were folded with precision, stacked accurately and we got ahead of the other teams.

Ten folded bags lay in the box one way, then ten across those in the opposite direction. They all had to lie perfectly flat before the box was sealed. Monkey see, monkey do. Despite this, I managed to inspire my team to follow my example. We won every competition: first for the neatest, first for the most substantial quantity packed in a day and so on. Our sensei told me other prisoners were asking to join my team. That was a huge compliment and noted by the senior sensei. The next competition we won was an extra shower a week – a significant treat for me for we only had two showers per week.

It was backbreaking work, all done on the floor. I was even called "old alien" for I was at least fifteen years older than the rest of my group. The rewards kept coming and, as a team leader, my pay went up. My first pay was the princely sum of 32 Yen for three weeks, but it was Yen in the right direction and soon I got promoted to "packer". A packer was considered a responsible position and an honour to achieve so quickly. It was only awarded if the sensei found the person trustworthy because, at the end of the working day, the packer took the boxes from the packing room and put them in the store and went there unaccompanied by a guard and the packer was to return without trying to escape.

Both senseis were impressed with my work ethic. I quickly earned their respect and trust. I was one step closer to my goal.

During the sixth week, I got another promotion. I was to leave the paper bag factory and join the factory that manufactured dainty pink ballet shoes – one step closer to what I'd put on the questionnaire.

The sensei also rewarded my efforts by telling me I was one of the few prisoners who'd ever got promoted so quickly. I was delighted. I hoped it would be reported to the right people and work in my favour at my appeal hearing and early parole would be noted for future.

I worked on my appeal every evening before the lights were switched off at 9.30 p.m. Storm had sent a copy of the South African police papers on cannabis and I trusted this would stand me in good stead.

During this time, I'd cautiously befriended another Filipino girl who was in for murder. There was something gentle about her that suggested to me she wasn't a murderer, let alone a criminal, much like me. She had a sad warmth about her. I could sense there was something wrong. My assumption proved to be correct.

We became close, as close as one can get to another prisoner, and she spoke English. Her story was a tragic tale of being cruelly framed. An intruder had fatally stabbed her husband in their home. She found him on the floor in their sitting room. Lying on the floor, bleeding from the stab wounds, her natural reaction had been to rush to him and hold him close to her while she grieved her loss, then she called for help. She had his blood all over her and was accused of murdering him. A team of lawyers was still fighting Darna's case. She was a gentle woman with a beautiful porcelain face which was now etched with lines of pain and grief. Her large antelope-like eyes spoke of the hurt and suffering she'd endured. Their youthful sparkle was lost with her husband and now she'd lost her freedom too.

She was appealing her case for the second time and offered me some useful tips. She suggested my written defence should be checked by one of her lawyers before my hearing. They seemed to think it was well presented and should impress the judge, so I felt confident to hand it in. It was given to my lawyer to submit to the judge, requesting an appeal date.

Cannabis, a "mayaka" (Japanese for drug), ingested or smoked was not dangerous. I also compared it to alcohol and cigarettes, both available on the open market, but more hazardous than cannabis.

The mortality statistics were given by The National Institute on Drug Abuse in America. (Which I thought were extremely important and included them.) They proved, I thought, that "many Japanese people would not die". The statistics went like this:

American Deaths Caused by Addictive Substances – 2001 Survey

Tobacco: 400,000
Alcohol: 100,000
All legal drugs: 20,000
All illegal drugs: 15,000
Caffeine: 2,000

Aspirin: 500
Cannabis: 0

I felt this said it all. Shortly after submitting my case, I received a small notelet in the post from Storm with this little poem written in her hand.

"Diamond droplets in the tree, twinkle there for you and me. Little stars in the darkest night, they are there to show us the light."

I needed the light more than ever. I couldn't stop reading it and each time I did, tears welled up in my eyes.

Oh, how I longed to stand beneath the African skies again, clear and unpolluted, and see those twinkling stars.

Based on the evidence, the judge would then decide if my case was worthy of appeal. A week later, the lawyer informed me the judge had not accepted my case, saying I must have been an active part of an organised drug syndicate, considering the depth of my knowledge on cannabis. Appeal denied.

Aghast, I said to the translator, "Tell the judge I obtained the information from my daughter who is a police woman in the South African police force. Tell him I am not a hardened drug criminal. Before now I knew nothing of drugs. I am a mother who was trying to protect her children from a dangerous sociopath, and I did not know there were drugs in the suitcase. I was told they were uncut diamonds."

I was shouting, and my lawyer scowled with disapproval. I wasn't letting go of this opportunity, and he finally agreed to explain to the judge the misinterpretation of my first trial. I waited, holding my breath, dripping with sweat and consumed by frustration. I was granted another appeal hearing the following day. I sat in a dreary little office beside the court while the lawyer and the judge decided on my fate. An hour passed, the most extended hour of my life, but the news was not good.

"The judge says your sentence is suitable. There will be no changes and no further appeals permitted. Eight years is the regular sentence. You are only serving four. After two years, you may request an appeal for parole."

I gasped. Speechless. I wanted to know if they counted the two years from my capture date. I never got an answer.

The lawyer did his best to calm me, but nothing anyone said helped.

Case closed. That was it. No little diamonds were glittering in the sky for me.

I went back to my cell and sobbed for hours. Then I was sure I heard a voice saying, "You will get through this. Just open the doors to faith again."

I looked around me to see where the voice had come from. There was no one near my cell. Who'd just spoken? The message sounded so clear I shook my head and stood up. There was no one in sight.

Yes, I'd make it. Parole was 104 weeks away. I had to make it.

I'd turned one corner successfully and gained the sensei's trust. There were ten factories within the prison grounds, and each factory had several divisions which contributed to a considerable part of the income derived for running the prison. The sensei clearly understood the value of placing prisoners in a factory that produced happy workers, even encouraging us to speak up if we needed to be in a different section, providing we had proved ourselves first, of course. It was essential to them that each prisoner had the opportunity to reach their full potential. There was such wisdom in their methods.

Administration and office work were the best paid positions. Though I had exceptional administration and accounting skills, I avoided this work for I needed to be creative. More importantly, I'd highlighted my sewing and upholstery skills on my questionnaire, and now I could prove it, being in the ballet slipper factory.

Prisoner sentence identification was indicated by wearing coloured badges above the breast pocket on the left-hand side of our shirts. Short-term prisoners and new prisoners wore a red badge. Prisoners in for more than six years wore a green badge and prisoners in for life wore a white badge. The white badge bearers filled me with an uneasy fear. I steered clear of them whenever possible. Not one of them expressed a glimmer of emotion in their dark lifeless eyes. Most of them were bullies and caused terrible misery amongst the short-term prisoners. Fortunately, most of the time, they left me alone. Some jeered at me or deliberately bumped into me and tried to fleece me, but I always managed to knock them away before they got a grip of me.

The day arrived when I was to start my new assignment. Sixty-four of us left the paper bag factory.

Only the most skilled got to the ballet shoe factory. I learnt later the only reason they were giving me a chance in the ballet shoe manufacturing process was that I'd proven to be trustworthy. The fact I had many years of experience working on sewing machines was only a minor consideration at this point. I also learnt this was an impressive assignment, but the best part for me was the significant monthly pay rise.

I must have made a good impression in my new role. Only a few days into starting, I got a brand-new pillow as a reward. This reward was for proving I could sew, and I hadn't lied in my questionnaire. I was delighted. Little rewards like the pillow made some days more tolerable than others.

Any reward was considered a prestigious recognition in jail. Recognition was celebrated for all prisoners to witness, but getting them as often as I did was a double-edged victory. I gained very little favour with fellow prisoners and there was a backlash of nasty jealousy. I wasn't there to gain respect from fellow prisoners. I wanted to earn the trust and respect from the sensei.

Stupid things become significant in jail – things one takes for granted in ordinary life. Food had never been a priority for me. I thought of it only as a necessity, but in jail, it became an important part of my day.

There was a vile dish called "azuki" – a maroon-coloured bean which was served often and prepared as a sweetish paste and always accompanied with either a potato salad or a slice of tomato and two or three leafy salad greens. I never got used to the taste of it.

What I missed was my coffee serving with each of my meals. Coffee or "black tea" was always served black and only on the "alien meal" days, those being Tuesday and Saturday. On those days, we could have milk in our tea or coffee. Tamanegi (onion), egg or nori (a thin compacted seaweed) accompanied by fermented beans, served in a Styrofoam bowl with a sachet of soya sauce (known as "shoyu") was another meal I loathed.

A few others were also positively repulsive. But after a year in prison, the acid reflux I'd suffered with never plagued me again. I put that down to the green tea that neutralised and detoxed my system. However, the post-meal mouth inspection did plague me. An utterly humiliating routine. After every meal the sensei gaped into our mouths, one by one, checking we'd not hidden anything in the smelly depths. Then we were checked to make sure we had not concealed anything in our clothing.

"Goodie packs", a preposterously exciting privilege, generally consisted of a packet of crisps, a handful of biscuits and sweets with either a sugar-loaded fruit juice or a sugar-loaded flavoured milk. These were a treat we all looked forward to. They became the mainstay of my dreary, awful existence. But these goodie packs became a terrible dilemma for me too; I could never finish one at a sitting, and if I took one, it was marked on the purchase sheet and deducted off my salary. I could not afford that, but in the end, denying myself became pointless and only made me crave them more.

Retail therapy was a thing of the past, ruined by rules and the scarcity of funds, so every purchase had a carefully monitored life expectancy. For example, a bar of bath soap and a tube of toothpaste had a life span of two months. If it didn't last, they required a reasonable explanation as to why it hadn't lasted. But no matter what reason, it was never considered reasonable. This happened to me once – my soap and toothpaste always lasted two months to the day after that. Shampoo, face cream and washing powder had the same rule tag, and empty containers had to be handed in and accounted for. No empty container, no replacement. True to Japanese culture, there was always a pay-off to motivate prisoners to follow the rules.

A good work ethic earned respect. Mine was exemplary and had earned me two extra showers a week, so I had to recalculate how much soap to use.

Sometime during the first month, new prisoners were shown to the library. When they took us, I was astounded at the massive selection of books that were housed there. There were thousands upon thousands of book titles in seventeen different languages, and each language had hundreds of different titles in assorted genres. Amongst so many books, I never found one written in Afrikaans. I wondered whether that was a good sign, or not, for me.

We were permitted to select five books and one magazine, which we exchanged every two weeks. Each visit, I went quickly to the English section, affording me an additional ten minutes to get a better selection of my favourite love stories. The "happily ever after" fluffy ones became my favourite, helping me overcome anxiety and depression.

The maze of five-foot-high book-cased passages was a sanctuary I loved. I felt safe in those quiet moments being nourished by such a variety of intellectual nectar, stimulating my imagination.

In one of Pieter's letters, he'd suggested I look for an author called Stephen King.

"Mom, they're brilliantly written!"

So, on our next visit to the library, I took out the novel *It*. Though the contents of the book didn't prompt even the remotest smile, the choice of author my precious son had selected for me did. In an obscure way, it made me happy that Pieter had no concept of what I was experiencing. The dark, sinister and scary Stephen King novel did nothing to lighten my already sombre mood, so I stuck to soppy love stories with a happy ending. Hard-wired horror and suspense I lived with daily. I didn't need it in book form too.

The days got busier; the nights remained an emotional hell. No matter how often I fought against negative thoughts, the yearning for my children was so powerful, my heart felt like it would explode and shatter. I craved to feel the warmth and touch of my children.

Chapter Thirty-Nine

Working in the ballet slipper factory gave me renewed hope for early release. Every morning, I'd get up and say to myself, "Elizabeth, you will get parole. Keep being positive." Then I'd send gratitude and love to the universe in meditation and that little ritual would begin my day.

The promotions and rewards kept coming. With every exciting move up the ladder came more significant pay rises and some great bonuses. The morning ritual I'd put together was my lighthouse during the tough, stormy times. I got knocked about when jealousy turned calm waters into raging torrents, which happened every time I got a reward.

Once I was caught down one of the passages in the library after my new undies reward. A green badge prisoner grabbed me and sank her teeth into my arm, but I didn't dare yell out. Bruising easily anyway, her teeth marks stayed on my arm for weeks. I was furious. Jealousy comes out in all ugly forms in jail, and after I'd received my new uniform, naked and vulnerable while in the shower, a white badge woman tried to rape me. Stunned, I nearly broke her arm trying to get rid of her for it got caught between my thighs. Suppressing an agonising scream, she fled quickly before being caught. She stayed away from me after that. I had thought of reporting it, but that would have attracted a worse situation.

The third reward in quick succession, all of them earned within five months, was a brand-new Parka type jacket. That was deemed to be one of the grandest honours and a silent warning for me to stay on high alert after receiving it, even for as long as a few weeks. Hatred, jealousy and envy... emotions like these were dominant in prison. They filled the air, they filled the cells, they filled the workplace and permeated through the exercise areas; there was no escaping them.

As far as fellow prisoners were concerned, I'd progressed from a paper bag packer to manufacturing ballet slippers too fast. The next post I was awarded meant few spoke to me. The sensei trusted me enough to recommend the post of chief machinist. I was thrilled for it meant a considerable hike in my pay. With each passing month, my fine was reducing.

In the trimming section, I checked every stitch. Yes, every stitch, then I'd trim off excess thread, so when I progressed to machinist, I knew what I was in for. No trimmer was going to throw a slipper back for me to re-do.

I had a perfect source of natural light from the window I sat next to. I could also look out into the distance when I became cross-eyed from intense concentration. I was lucky enough to catch these moments to rest my tired eyes and had the good fortune of being able to utilise the natural light, though I still needed the sharp light of the machine's bulb shining down on the slipper fabric. I knew every stitch I sewed was perfect.

The ladies seated deeper into the factory area struggled with the lighting and strained their eyes. None of this work was kind on any of our eyes and shoulders. The process of making ballet shoes, worthy of the dancer that wore them, was an intricate process of manufacture I'd never appreciated before.

Prior to becoming head machinist, I was put through the rigors of stitching on a square of material with pre-marked lines drawn on it. When I first sat down at the machine and was given this marked square of fabric, I considered it quite an insult to my machining ability. I laughed at my reaction when I understood the system and the level of difficulty. To get into the swing of making these delicate slippers, I was made to sew two or three stitches along the pre-marked line then stop, lift my foot off of the controls, then sew a few more stitches and so it went on until my ankle screamed and my calf muscles resigned. I could hardly walk after that first day.

Once I'd perfected that phase, I moved on with a whole new appreciation of the importance of this training, for the seams on a ballet slipper are very short, with endless curves. It is impossible to sew fast when such precision is required. If the quality controller returned more than four slippers, a black mark was issued. I ensured black marks against me rarely happened. As good as I had been on a sewing machine, I learnt foot control with considerably more skill.

The sensei's eagle eye was as skilled as the keenest bird of prey. She recognised a good catch when she saw one and swooped on me as a prize catch. She'd spotted I had the right attention to detail. I was accurate and committed to excellence. She respected that, and it was that commitment that shot me up the income highway.

Within our factory, there were clearly defined divisions. Each division head was a long-term white badge prisoner who'd proved herself. She loomed over her podium, carefully watching over her assigned brood of machinists. She was also the only person a prisoner was permitted to communicate with, and the only person authorised to move around freely.

After several weeks of excruciating immobility, legs tingling or burning, I progressed from those tiresome steps, got my rewards and left that painful work behind me, becoming the leading seamstress, but it was insufferable monotony.

I continued manufacturing pink satin ballet slippers for months and began to wonder if it was what I would be doing until I left prison. I'd been in the slipper factory for roughly a year when I started making the more specialised leather ones. I had the top post. Another substantial income boost and elevation to my status, and now, at last, I was left alone, and the bullying and threats ceased.

Once the top part of the slipper was complete, binding was sewn around the top edge of the shoe. This was where the cord slides through and must run freely inside the binding to allow the dancer to tighten the slipper to fit the foot perfectly. My machine had a specialised binding attachment and the concentration required was more intense – it was good for me, keeping my mind focussed. I wasn't sure how many more promotions were open to me in this factory, but the one position I wanted was to head one of the divisions. Once I got there, I could move around and talk to some of the lady machinists.

Sitting at my cell window one evening, revelling in my last promotion and staring longingly at the mountains, I was interrupted by the delivery of a letter from Storm. Inside was a photograph of my second grandson. For long minutes, I stared at the picture, sadness eating away at my insides while another deep sense of guilt persecuted me. Delighted though I was to receive the photograph and knowing it was sent with all the best intentions, it left me weakened by a renewed self-loathing. I should be with my children, not Japan.

Unfolding my legs, straightening my back and closing my eyes, I heard that voice again. A powerful light flashed bright and beautiful, then it was gone.

At the end of a busy day, the sensei signalled to switch off all machines, then I saw that light again beam across the skies. These messages I understood to be the signatures of reassurance that I was not alone. That night, I crawled onto my futon and thanked God for coming to my rescue; even the stigma of being a criminal became more comfortable to bear.

A brand-new futon with brand-new bedding came with an abundance of brand-new problems I'd thought were over. But this time, I handled the nasty bullying with God's guidance. Even sleep was more peaceful; terrifying nightmares didn't plague my nights quite as often. At last, I began to feel I was on the fringes of accepting this journey and the lessons. Standing alone, watched by those with folded arms and lots to say, I'd been torn and whipped about by the storms of life, my body maimed, and my clothing torn, but with honour, I'd leave.

I'd just finished my umpteenth pair of slippers when I was called to the head sensei's office. Being summoned to the head sensei's office generally meant trouble.

He was one of the few male staff in the jail. Stress levels peaked; I couldn't think of anything I'd done wrong. It was the primary response in jail, and sure enough, his opening question wasn't encouraging.

"Why are you not putting more of your earnings towards paying off the fine?" he asked, like this alone was a crime.

I stood there, not knowing how to answer. I had no control over the deductions.

"Elizbet, you must pay 1,000 Yen per week now," he insisted.

I would be left with very little to buy the few things that made my life bearable, and I expressed my concerns. Stamps, pens and notepads were my number one priority; I could go without the rest, if I had to.

He nodded and dismissed me.

Hope, my powerful weapon against depression, had been dashed. To my surprise, at the end of the month, my income, even after the new deduction, brought hope racing back. He'd doubled my earnings; my fine was reducing significantly.

I realised then, as I had previously in my life, even when things were dark and grim, when I'd tried and tried and hadn't allowed others to discourage or insult me (even those who enjoyed humiliating me after Dion's disgusting escapades), I could hold my head high. Even now, I could be proud of me. I was brave for an innocent farm girl who'd grown up in the humblest of environments. The sensei recognised these traits and dished out the honour I deserved.

While taking a moment to look out of the factory window before switching on my machine, I noticed a spider hard at work in the most distinct web I'd ever seen. The spider's hard labours captured my attention to such an extent that I didn't want to look away. I had been so absorbed by the miniature battles going on within the web, I never realised the sensei was watching me as carefully as I was watching the spider. She interrupted my spider moment by saying in broken English that she was impressed with my work and would ask the senior sensei if she could teach me to be the overall supervisor of all the divisions. My mouth dropped open. I could have hugged her. This was huge. Perhaps it had been worth spider watching with such intensity.

This was an astounding promotion. I became the highest paid, short-term prisoner they'd ever had at Tochigi. I was proud of my achievements under such trying circumstances.

God was answering my prayers at last.

The boredom and immobility I'd endured for months were over. At last, I could move around and put my spoken Japanese skills to good use.

Issuing new machine needles was one of my new tasks, though it didn't happen often. Breaking a needle was seriously frowned upon because a broken machine needle could do severe damage or even kill someone if thrust deep into an unsuspecting jugular. And one thing I knew for sure, I didn't want to meet my end as a jealous inmate plunged a broken needle into my neck. So, when a needle did get broken, every single piece of it had to be handed in before I would issue a new one.

I introduced a reward scheme to stop needle breakage, for there were some who broke them on purpose. Isn't it true that there are always those who ruin everything for others who are good? This system soon stopped those engaged in the practice of needle breaking. Apart from issuing them, I changed them, altered tensions, taught newcomers and operated a machine if one became empty.

The days were more varied, and sometimes I was even asked to fix a machine if the sensei couldn't or was having difficulties fixing it. (The only benefits of owning a sewing shop years ago.)

Despite the job variety, emotional emptiness remained a close companion and as hard as I tried not to become cynical, a disposition I always disliked, I found I couldn't help it.

So, there I was, in the top post. I couldn't help wondering if I got parole, would the balance of the fine be written off? Was that possible? Did that sort of thing happen?

My new position meant I had to go back to Japanese lessons and brush up on what I had learnt previously. I found Japanese difficult to learn to speak; it is an agglutinative, mora-timed language I'd found impossible to get my tongue around. Its history dated back to the eighth century. Simple phonotactics with a pure vowel system, spoken in subject-object-verb. These extra lessons helped me communicate as the head of the ballet slipper division.

"Keimusho kara no shakuhoo." Released from prison. *This is what I will sing when I get parole*, I thought.

"Irasshaimase, doozo ohairi kudasai." Welcome, please come in. That was a tongue twister, and it took lots of practice to get that right.

Once I was confident enough to ask, I approached the head sensei, asking if it would be permitted to begin our days in the factory with singing the Japanese national anthem, "Kimigayo". He was delighted and soon the other factories followed suit. It was a motivational, patriotic way to start the day. There is a verse in the song that reflects the culture and expresses respect. The basic meaning of the anthem is, "May the reign of the emperor continue for 1,000, nay, 8,000 generations and for the eternity that it takes for small pebbles to grow into great rocks and become covered with moss."

The words resonated with me.

Many days during my imprisonment, I'd have what I called my "mind wanderings". These wanderings took me back into the veld (bush), into the wild wide open spaces where I grew up.

How one appreciates those unspoilt spaces when they are gone. I thought of my rooms in Paris. I had the same thoughts there, pitying those who knew nothing of that amazing African space. Inhaling deeply, I pretended I could smell the dust or the freshly fallen raindrops on thirsty dry earth. The deeper my thoughts became, the freer I felt, and my mind tricked me into believing I could smell those wondrous smells of my African childhood.

It was when immersed in these blissful thoughts that I received the first letter from "Gogga": Dion. To begin with, I didn't want to read it. His timing was impeccable, as it always was. It took me days to open the envelope and call on the courage to read it. He was writing to tell me he hadn't had a drink for weeks and was very proud of himself.

"I feel clean, clear and calm. I wish you were here with me."

I didn't have the same sentiment, but the contents, when he wasn't talking about himself, had some surprising tender touches; he even admitted to having sensations of guilt, something I didn't think he was capable of.

He seldom asked how I was coping. The worst part about all the letters I received was that I knew all these deeply personal things had been read by a third person – the censor – and I cringed.

"You know, I've always thought that you viewed me as a nothing, a failure, someone who never learns from mistakes. But now, I finally see how you tried your best. It was me who saw the wrong side of you. I promise to 'make a plan' to pay for your ticket home. Love you always, Dion."

I read that letter repeatedly and cried endless tears each time. I hated the bastard, or did I? I couldn't fathom my reaction.

Chapter Forty

Once a year, the Sakura Festival is held, creating a wave of excitement within prison that spreads like an infection. The sakura is the national flower. Translated, it means cherry blossom. The festival is internationally renowned and enjoyed by many visitors to Japan, even those of us visiting behind bars.

On the morning of the opening day, we were marched to the sports grounds to participate in what I know as boere (farm) sports. It was a refreshing change; a day of rope pulling, volleyball, skipping and rounders competitions, plus other games I'd not played before.

The factories were divided into groups, and I opted for the skipping competition. It brought back memories of boarding school days and we won it.

After the festival, and on an occasional Saturday, they introduced inter-factory games and pop music festivals. It seemed absurd that the first song I heard at a "pop" festival was a Japanese rendition of "New York, New York", and it left me desperately homesick.

Since my encounter with God while sitting at my cell window, the pull to attend church became quite intense. I felt the need to be a part of His flock again. The options were Catholicism or Buddhism. I knew nothing of Buddhism and was somewhat hesitant about Catholicism. I took the Catholic option and joined their prayer meetings and services; they were of the Christian faith, which I understood, and the meetings were conducted in English.

The opening blessing had a powerful effect on me. We stood in front of our chairs, ready to welcome the priest, when suddenly a voice echoed through the building, sending shivers down my spine. It was the priest singing the sensational hymn "Amazing Grace" as he walked into the congregation. Moved by the timbre and magnificence of his voice, tears rolled down my cheeks on their own, lifting some of the darkness I'd stored for twenty long months.

That evening, I sat cross-legged on my pillow at my window, which in my mind mimicked an altar, and in a jerky whisper, I sang my favourite hymn, "Jerusalem", and closed my eyes. Later that night, while I lay meditating, I found a new connection to my inner soul. I'd worked on a multitude of thoughts, but deeper stuff seemed to be happening now, feelings I'd seldom allowed myself to acknowledge. Picking up one of the books I'd sourced in the library, a little poem fell out of the book, and I read it.

The poem taught me a little more about me and added immense warmth to my chilled soul, blending beautifully with the thawing the minister had begun.

"Life's threads all form a pattern,
Some silver, some gold.
And there are new and finer threads
To mingle with the old.
Some tiny threads are broken
A stitch or two is skipped,

But when the work is finished
The pattern isn't ripped,
It forms a perfect blending
Of all of life's great dreams
With love we form the border
With sorrow, sew the seams
So, fold the pattern to your heart
Sweet memories are the dearest part."

From then on, the moment a negative thought came to mind, I'd think of the poem. It didn't take long, and I could recite it word for word. Those words were the thread of gold that helped keep me motivated. I pasted the little piece into my journal and considered it another lesson that would serve me for the rest of my life.

All the hurt, pain, shame, regret, resentment, bitterness and hate had been like open festering wounds. In tiny increments of self-love, others' love, kindness and remarkable thoughtfulness from sources I'd never anticipated, the uncomfortable sensations within were being put back together. But no matter how my thoughts had changed, the first Christmas in Tochigi Prison was the greatest torture in this adversity. It was different to the Christmas I had spent in the detention cells. A tsunami of the most difficult emotions smothered me, magnified by desperate loneliness and, once again, a mournful need to be with my children arose. An agony so indescribably devastating it set me back the months of hard work I'd done on myself.

It began on 19 December 2003, at the Christmas Mass.

On that morning, the mountains were quite different. They were sprinkled with a splattering of light snow, a vision like a picture postcard. The air was crisp, though the sun was shining, and the wind whipped at my cheeks as we marched from the dining hall to the hall where Christmas Mass was being held. On the way across, I noticed a pigeon sitting in the snow, its feathers all puffed up, and for a fleeting moment, I wondered if its feet were as cold as mine. This was my first experience of a Catholic Christmas Mass.

When Father entered the hall, he was carrying with him a porcelain baby doll dressed in swaddling clothes, and today, it represented baby Jesus. At the end of the service, Father passed "baby Jesus" around, asking each of us to hold him in our arms, to look deeply into his eyes and give thanks for our lives.

I had the most poignant connection to the Holy Spirit I'd ever experienced. I cradled the child in my arms, who, for a moment, felt so real and I tearfully whispered my gratitude for sparing my life, a life I had so often wanted to end. Baby Jesus' face, hands and feet were porcelain, but the body was soft; as real as the emotion that was pouring out of me. I saw life in those glass eyes as the lids flickered open and closed while the doll-child moved in my arms. I knew, in that instant, God was beside me. He understood the depth of my pain and guilt. It was time to forgive myself. During the divine celebration of an extraordinary life, and before I passed baby Jesus on to my neighbour, I rejoiced at the birth of the new me.

It was one of the most meaningful Christmas services I'd ever experienced.

On 23 December, we celebrated the emperor of Japan's birthday, quite different celebrations from the 19th. The variation in food during the festivities had more meaning to us "alien" inmates than the emperor's birthday, as there were all sorts of delicacies like icing sugar coated doughnuts and other cakes we rarely saw.

On Christmas morning, the church distributed a printed Christmas prayer and a heart-warming thought-provoking letter to carry us faithfully into the New Year; there was no service.

Joy is to be shared. Let us pray to Jesus our Lord that the Good News of his coming may warm the hearts of all, and let us pray:

> *That today may be a feast of joy for all our families and for all to whom we bring a bit of happiness today.*
>
> *That today may be a feast of joy for all children far or near, to those who are happy and those who hunger and suffer.*
>
> *That today is perhaps a feast of faith for those who know the Lord and for those who do not yet know him.*
>
> *That today may become again a feast of peace for those divided by quarrels, for countries divided by war.*
>
> *That today may be a feast of joy for all our Christian communities and that we may share that joy as we go together in the Lord's way of peace.*
>
> *Let us pray to the Lord.*
>
> *Lord Jesus, you are one of us. Help us to become more like you, that we may become your joy, as you are ours, now and forever. Amen.*

The prayer held a more profound meaning now. As I read, I cried softly and often that day. I cried for my children, I cried for the "old" Dion, and I prayed for them all. My sobs were no longer gut-wrenching blasts of intolerable physical pain and unimaginable suffering, but gentle sobs of personal forgiveness and messages of unconditional love.

I asked the Lord to show Dion the road to recovery. The children's letters told me he was still drinking heavily, though he'd have weeks where he wouldn't drink, but those were short-lived. He'd been job hopping as usual, either resigning or getting himself fired. My fantastic once-prosperous business that had collapsed because of him still stung. In one of Storm's letters, she mentioned having banned Dion from entering her home. Now, under normal circumstances, it would have infuriated me that his behaviour was so unacceptable that even his own daughter wouldn't allow him into her house. Instead of feeling this intense anger and disappointment, I found comfort in offering up a little prayer for them both.

That night, after consuming a rather unusual but special Christmas dinner, I went to bed holding baby Jesus in my mind; it was a treasured peaceful night.

The following day was the last working day of the year in Japan. We gave the factory a spring clean, closed at three o'clock, and as I locked the factory door, I was handed another letter from Storm. The timing could not have been more perfect. Though this first Christmas in Tochigi had been an emotional mix of emptiness and enlightenment, reading her letter was still extremely hard.

Throughout the Christmas week and into New Year, we received a variety of interesting goodie packs we could take into our cells, but they had to be finished by the 31st. On the eve of 27 December, looking out my window was like looking at a real life fairy tale. Everywhere was white with snow. The trees sparkled in their white coats; the roofs of the prison were blanketed in snow. It was magnificent. A white Christmas was not something Africans experience. I knew this New Year would be a better year for me.

Weirdly, on the morning of the fourth day into 2004, my waking thoughts were of "Gogga". I opened my eyes and found myself praying for him. And later that day, I received a letter from him, and like Pieter's letters, he too asked if I remembered various songs we had loved so much. The one he mentioned in this letter was "You Can Make Me Whole Again". Dion couldn't make me whole again, though I heard in my mind his exquisite voice singing it to me. I wished with all my heart that the man I had married all those years ago hadn't changed into the ogre he was. Perhaps my prayers of forgiveness were being transmitted, for this letter contained unusual emotional dialogue. I wondered if he finally meant what he was expressing. *Would I ever be ready for him to serenade me again?*

Even with God's help, I doubted it. Even with God's help, I wasn't sure I could forgive him for all he'd put me through. I'd endured twenty-five years listening to empty apologies and endless lies, being physically abused and emotionally dragged through thorns. Now it was time for me, even if it was in this godforsaken place. Because I'd never forget all that he had inflicted on me and our children, I knew it would take more than just one deeply moving Christmas Mass in Japan to forgive him. His letter ended by saying, "Be strong, my love, your ever-loving husband. I love you." That didn't feel good.

If I'd read that, even days before the Christmas Mass, I would have angrily torn the letter into tiny bits. Though I still had a long way to go on this journey of forgiveness, I was considerably calmer in my response to his empty words.

That afternoon, we watched a movie called *Pay It Forward* with Haley Joel Osment. It was excellent. The theme song was "Call on Angels". I wondered if that was another message. The following week, while in the library, I went in search of spiritual and religious books to add to my uplifting love stories, even if they were only fantasy.

Chapter Forty-One

The Christmas celebrations had done me good. I realised how hard I had always been on myself. My mother, bless her, had done an excellent job of entrenching a powerful belief system in me. I had to remain strong and in control of absolutely everything I did. I had lived with the illusion that I *had* been strong and in control. It was only now, after all I had endured and still had to endure, that I could see how detrimental that belief was. The only thing I was in control of now were my thoughts, and with them, I was going to carve out a better future for me here. I accepted, with warm gratitude, that there was nothing wrong with the framework of Mother's teachings. Her intentions were pure. Her admirable inner strength had served her when Papa passed away and when she was raped, but they'd left an ingrained fear of failure within me. This was the fear I was struggling to crawl my way out of now, even with God's assistance. Though I felt more confident, my journey to redemption would be more manageable with Him in it.

I smiled as I thought back on my initial horrified thought of being forced to attend a "Catholic Mass" on Christmas Day, not being of the Catholic faith. It completely went against all my beliefs, and I realised then how inflexible we could become.

During Bible study or in a service, when Father read from the Bible, he explained "his" perspective, then he asked us all to give the wise words some thought from "our" perspective. It was a perfect unobtrusive way of allowing the interpretation to become our own. He never forced us to pray or beg the Lord for atonement of our terrible deeds and sins. Instead, he filled us with hope and an intricate understanding of being human.

Slowly, like the passage of a tortoise, I began to see life through the angelic eyes of the hare. I was able to reach out to Vivienne, now that I understood her struggles from a different perspective. Her letters, and mine to her, took on new meaning.

"Love the unlovable" I was taught in Bible study. It was a concept I struggled with to begin with. Jail was indeed a lonely, solitary life. The little choices we must make:

Will chart the course of life we take

We either choose the path of light

Or we wonder in the darkest night

The author of this poem was unknown, but I found it in the library and copied it into letters to my children with the hopes that they'd make better choices than I had.

Storm's letters and poems kept me motivated and often I would speak with Father Bradly.

"Elizabeth, my dear, you need to remember a famous quote... I'm sorry, it escapes me who said it, but it goes something like this... 'People are not disturbed by the things that happen, but by their opinion of the things that happen.'"

I thought long and hard on the wisdom of those words, for they had deeply resonated with me. I have never forgotten them.

Chapter Forty-Two

I watched, from my window, the dazzling sunsets. Their colours changed the fluffy white clouds that brought snow to puffs of orange, gold and yellow, each with a perfect silver lining until the last rays of light were gone. Songs I'd forgotten would fill my mind as I watched the sun slowly fade and I'd sing them quietly until it was dark. Once the last rays were gone, I'd turn my attention to the photographs Storm and the family sent. The most recent was of Storm standing with her father, still so handsome. I was surprised by the desires the image of him provoked, desires I didn't want to deal with in prison, sensations I never thought I'd feel again. There was never a moment's doubt; I still loved the Dion I'd first married.

In the morning, I'd see another glorious day bloom, showing a completely different palette of colours that washed across the skies and helped brighten my day.

April 2004: the second-year anniversary of my arrest. Sublime, but it was a great celebration for me. I was halfway there if I had to complete the full sentence.

I walked into the factory with sensei and switched on the radio. "Have You Ever Seen the Rain" was playing. I loved that song. It was a perfect song to listen to as I secretly hoped the possibilities of a parole hearing were approaching.

I'd given up daily exercises for the past two weeks. My entire body hurt from the machining. I'd asked to go to the dispensary to get painkillers, but they said I wasn't sick. Because I wasn't considered sick, I requested to see the doctor to have my cholesterol checked instead. It was dangerously high. He cautioned I could have had a heart attack. After those results, he advised it was essential for me to have checks done every three months. I still never got the painkillers.

During this horrid low, burdened by awful joint and back pain, my assistant, a vicious, long-term prisoner whom I disliked immensely, chose this time to come on to me. Like a lioness watching and stalking a sick animal, she cornered me. She was strong and rubbed herself hard against my body, telling me I was very pretty, which thoroughly repulsed me. I managed to push her away with more force than I'd anticipated and knocked her to the floor. I was terrified there were going to be terrible repercussions, delaying my parole application or, worse still, losing my responsible position. Thankfully, not a word was spoken of the incident, though she told me later she wanted to get me into trouble. Bitch!

She left me alone and a few days after my medication was changed and I was feeling stronger, I got notification that I would only be permitted to apply for a parole hearing in July 2005 – fourteen months away. I sank back into a dark emotional pit, rawer and more devastating than before.

Seven weeks later, Japan was shaken by two earthquakes. I was sitting in my usual position, looking out my window at the mountains, trying to re-establish some positivity, when a deep rumbling filled the air, followed by a frightening shaking of the earth. The whole building shuddered, and I thought it was about to crash to the ground. For a fleeting moment, I wished it would. A few minutes later, it was over, but the following day, during the morning, we got hit by a stronger tremor. The senior sensei sent an urgent instruction that echoed through the factories: "Switch off machines and sit on the floor."

We all slid off of our chairs and put our heads between our knees as the building shook.

Sitting cross-legged next to senior sensei, I got the chance to question why my parole hearing had been shifted. He informed me there was nothing he could do to bring it closer, but assured me he'd submitted many "good behaviour" notices.

The earth tremors settled, but the internal ones stayed with me all day. I found it impossible to concentrate and cried off and on throughout the day. I had tried so hard; this news was so demoralising.

That day, during afternoon exercise routine, sensei brought me a cigarette. I hadn't had a cigarette for months. Even that didn't help.

I stopped looking out of my window with sparkling eyes. I stopped praying. I even stopped going to Bible study and performed all the daily routines robotically. I felt no emotions. They had rumbled into the earth with the quake, where they were to be stored until my release. I sank back into nothingness, my soul needing to hibernate for the winter of my life. I was dead, but my body worked and worked and worked on autopilot. This was cruel, this was merciless, and for the next three long months, I lived in this pit of ever-increasing depression until an accident in my section stirred me from the dangerous spiral I found myself in.

Under my watch, in front of my eyes, I witnessed, with traumatising horror, an inmate emotionally snap. I was shattered, but what struck me was I wasn't far away from mentally snapping too. The once balanced and powerful internal self-control my mother installed was gone. I was teetering on madness. I could feel its talons gripping harder. The shock of witnessing the most gruesome dance of self-destruction any human could witness stopped me in my tracks and woke me from the madness slumber: a numbed state where I didn't care anymore.

The girl was Polynesian, petite and shy, and seldom spoke to anyone. She was in for drug offences. I had observed her carefully. Well, I thought I had. I remember wondering why she was so reserved. She was a good seamstress and very meticulous. Externally, she appeared to be focussed, but her demons got the better of her after she made a trivial mistake on a pair of ballet shoes. It began with her rocking on her seat. I had noticed that, but thought she just needed to get the circulation back in her butt. Then as human tolerance became more and more stretched by her internalised emotional trauma, weird sounds hissed out of her mouth, followed by strands of saliva, then she erupted with agonising screams as if she was being torn apart by some invisible force. She threw herself on the floor, writhing and jerking in spasmodic asthmatic-like gyrations, banging her head against the floor as if she was beating a ragdoll to death. Blood burst in spurts from her head while she repeated the thrashings, then she grabbed the ballet shoes she'd tossed on the floor and hurled them across the room.

My immediate reaction was to rush to her and stop her from doing herself more damage, but I knew I could not do it alone. Her mind had gone; her body was performing a grotesque suicide for all of us to witness. By the time senior sensei entered the factory, it was too late. She completed her macabre dance of death so quickly and with such power. She stood up, smashing her head into the top of my sewing machine. The metal thread holders became embedded into her skull and the needle arm ripped through the flesh of her face, tearing it away from its moorings. Then she sank my cutting scissors deep into her chest with a departing deathly groan as she fell forwards over my machine, her body twitching and spasming before it hit the floor with a horrifying thud. Her body shuddered violently and she heaved out her last breath, then she lay still. We all stood watching, in rigid horror, as the emergency siren rang out, chilling even the most hardened inmates.

I could have been next, I thought grimly as we silently watched her limp, torn body being lifted onto a stretcher, covered with a sheet and removed from the factory.

The mood was grim, but as I was the one in charge I chose two others I could trust to help clean up the morbid mess. Sensei's voice exploded in my head and brought me back into the room. He'd shouted at me twice before I acknowledged his instruction, so intensely disturbed was I. Sensei helped organise cloths, bowls of water and disinfectant. It took immense effort to stop myself from vomiting as we removed pieces of facial flesh, tangled up with hair and congealed blood off of the cotton holder and needle tensioner of my machine. One of the helpers could take no more of it and fainted. It was a gory reminder of what could happen when the human mind could take no more isolation and punishment.

Once we'd got the area cleaned and my machine was free of human flesh, blood and hair, we were marched out of the factory and down to the exercise area where we could mingle, rest, communicate and reboot. Two off-duty senseis came to talk to us, and then Father visited us, offering words of wisdom to soothe our battered thoughts from the horror we had all witnessed. Her suicide made me doubly vigilant from that day forward, and I always kept my cutting scissors in my uniform pocket from then on.

On 16 July 2005, I was informed my first application for parole had been submitted, which gave me hope. I was so excited I wrote a letter to Storm letting her know I would be home soon, then I had to let them in on the devastating news I wasn't coming home. Parole had been denied without explanation.

I applied again, but again it was denied. This time, I insisted on a full explanation as to why I was being denied parole. I had done everything in my power to prove I wasn't a criminal, in the real sense of the word, and would never consider doing anything illegal again in my life, no matter the circumstances, for this was a mistake too enormous ever to contemplate making again.

The only answer I got was: "It is still too early." I was furious.

"Too early for what? Too early for whom?" I screamed at the senior sensei.

So practised were they at not answering prisoners' demands and cries for help, he stared past me in uncomfortable silence.

On Sunday 18 December, three prisoners were released on parole – that was more punishing news for me. A fellow prisoner understood my anger, and while in the exercise area she came to me, pointing with her index finger to her head.

She said, "Stupido, you."

"What you mean?" I asked, gesturing with my arms.

"You! You too good to go, make too many slippers, too honest. Sensei needs you."

The penny dropped, but I was still spitting mad. The three released were green badges.

What to do? I wouldn't drop my work standards. I felt sure there was more to it. I'd learnt many years back that no one was indispensable, but now I found I'd worked myself into a position of being indispensable. There was precious little I could do to change it. The factory closed early that day – a movie was being shown for the afternoon, turning my burning anger into deep sorrow.

The movie was of the life of John Lennon, 1940–1980, and the theme song was "Stand by Me".

I wept through the whole movie struggling with crushing conflicting thoughts. Gogga used to sing that to me, on the infrequent occasions he ever felt guilty.

"When the night has come, and the land is dark, and the moon is the only light we'll see…" I remembered his smile. "Darling, darling, stand by me…"

Oh, how I had. I'd stood by him through thick and thin. I'd tried so hard for him and look what it got me: four years in jail versus taking his life. Now it appeared I'd tried too hard for parole, sealing my fate. I wondered if I'd ever get out early. The ongoing battle between negative and positive emotions fought each other for lead position in my head and my heart, while fear and the encroaching cold weather kept me alert.

Winter was back with a vengeance, chilling my mind, my body and my soul, all of which hovered around freezing point, battered by cold winds from Siberia.

Christmas Day 2005 came and went, and "Oujaar" celebrations were about to begin. This one was just like the last, except for a letter from Pieter who'd enclosed a little poster for an indoor cricket match he'd organised as a fundraiser towards my flight home. God had given me amazing children. It was time to start working on those positive affirmations again and go back to communicating with God.

"Goodbye, 2005." Time was passing. The winds had dropped, and it was almost peaceful, but for my thoughts. Sometime during 2006, I would be home with my family. I did not stay awake for midnight that year. Instead, I drifted off to sleep, my night filled with fitful dreams and visions of me being reunited with my family once more.

At 9.30 a.m. on 3 January 2006, I was holding in my hands, with disbelief, another request for an interview for parole. I'd just about completed my sentence; their timing was ruthless and inexplicable.

"Third time lucky," I prayed.

The difference in the questionnaires gave me hope. There were three strange questions this time, ones I'd not had before.

What things have you thought about during these past four months? Describe what you feel and think about your crime.

In order not to commit a crime again, what kind of life are you going to have in the future?

I was worried my answers in English may be detrimental to the outcome. "Lost in translation" had happened to me before. Now I had to depend upon my newfound faith and belief that God would guide my answers.

Thoughts over the last four months? The previous four years, I could honestly say they had been plagued by shame and guilt. I was desperate to get home to redeem myself with my family. I was returning home a criminal – an international criminal. It was an impossible thought. A colossal mistake of trust and misjudgement that any sane, functioning, loving mother could have made was my justification. God knew I'd never had any intention of doing anyone harm. I'd allowed my ex-husband to destroy my success and force me into a disgusting muddle of lies, deceit and despicable behaviour, which had finally led me to a four-and-a-half-year jail sentence in Japan. This was his final gift to me, instead of murdering him.

The last four months? I'd lived with regret, grief, heartache and despair. I'd wallowed in self-pity – what more did they want me to say? How many times did they want me to agree I'd made the biggest mistake of my life?

How do I feel about my crime?

Demeaned, humiliated, shamed… They knew I loathed what I'd done, but I had accepted the responsibility of my actions. I believed I had proved that my morals and ethics were sound and unquestionable. Why did I have to regurgitate the disgrace again? The wound in my heart would always fester.

I had a few days before I had to hand in my answer sheet and decided to allow the process to happen on its own. A new set of suitable answers would slip out from somewhere. The answers came to me while watching the movie *Titanic*, hidden in the hauntingly beautiful musical lyrics.

Thursday, 12 January 2006. The day they were to call me for the interview where I would be asked to read the answers I'd carefully scribed and await the decision of one man. I always hated this "waiting to be called"; it made my hands damp and clammy, and a cold sweat of apprehension covered my body. This time, the Titanic wasn't going to sink. This time, love and divine guidance would steer me around the icy cold hard places I'd been kept in for four years, and I'd come out in the sunshine, victorious.

That day also marked the day I had completed three-quarters of my sentence; the worst was already over.

Finally, I was called. I stood up and I read out my answers, my voice filled with honest sincerity, then I sat down again. I kept my eyes cast towards the floor, and my hands clasped together, gripped between my thighs. The tension was spreading across my shoulders, and a dull ache had snuck into my temples as I waited.

"Elizabeth, did you hear…?" the parole officer asked again.

"Hear what?" I asked, amazed I'd even been spoken to.

"Internal parole is approved."

I heaved in sadness at his familiar words.

"Internal parole was approved last time, sensei, and I'm still here."

I curtsied and left the room with a heavy heart. Nothing I did or said worked with these people, but I noticed the parole officer shake his head and he said something in Japanese I didn't understand. A month passed, and I still had no idea of when I would be called and notified of the decision taken by the external parole officer. It was Pieter's birthday soon, and I desperately wanted to be home for that.

Monday, 20 February – still no news. I was missing Pieter's birthday; another year celebrated without me. I was not just counting the days, the weeks and months, but the hours, the minutes and the seconds now, even though I knew it was a pointless exercise. It just made it all go slower, but I couldn't help myself.

The only real positive thought was I would never have another Christmas or New Year in jail.

Chapter Forty-Three

Parole

I woke in a better mood than I had in months. Perhaps this was the day, 22 February 2006. Dare I hope? I greeted my section as always, suppressing a smile I wanted to wear for no apparent reason.

"Ohayoo gozaimasu (good morning)," I said, using a monotone voice and they responded the same way. None of them were waiting on parole advice. It was only me this time.

The drone of the machine motors whined as they started up, marking the beginning of another day of precision work after we'd sung the national anthem. The monotonous humming continued throughout the day and became so lodged in my brain that it took hours for the sound to leave my consciousness at the end of the day. But more beautiful ballet shoes would be completed today and shipped around the world, and despite the daily repetition, I was proud of what my girls produced. The phone had rung in the factory a few times and each time I jumped at the sound. A few ladies noticed and smiled at me. They knew I was waiting for that parole call.

Checks complete, I settled back on my machine and started it up. My gut twisted with anticipation; I found it hard to concentrate, let alone sew. I switched off the machine and walked up and down the rows of machinists, checking each one and asking if anyone needed help, but it was more to quell my anxiety. Just before the lunch bell rang out, so did the phone. This time it was for me.

Tears of relief streamed down my face, and my hands automatically closed in thanks as I raised my eyes to the imaginary skies above and thanked God for His loving guidance. My group of seamstresses all rejoiced and clapped for me. I bowed in grateful thanks and quietly asked for Him to bless those I was leaving behind. Then they all stood and bowed, silently returning the respect, sat down and went on with their work. It was an incredibly touching response. I knew then I'd done an excellent job and that mattered to me more than anything.

Sensei gave permission for me to thank each one individually for their dedicated work and for taking care of me. I really wanted to give each one a hug, but that was not permitted.

I stood at my podium and waved to them all for the last time.

"Sayonara, goodbye, we will never meet again, but I will never forget you either. God bless you all," I said in Japanese.

The external parole board had only deducted six months off of my sentence. It was hardly parole, considering I'd spent a total of nine months in detention and the holding cells, but it was better than nothing.

I was going home. I had to say it aloud for it to penetrate.

"I'm going home!" I shrieked happily as I was escorted back to my cell: cell number 248. A number I would never forget. Like a coil unravelling, I could barely contain myself.

To utilise the burst of energy that had filled me, I got to work spring cleaning every inch of my cell. This amount of happiness coursing through my veins was a brand-new sensation; I had to do something useful with it.

I scribbled a short note to Storm and handed it in for posting. This time I was definitely coming home, no false alarm. Busying myself with getting my cell clean and tidy, I thought about our meeting at the airport. It was going to be hard on us both, poignant but complex. I let her know I wanted no one else to meet me but her and I wanted no one else to know I was coming home. A date I couldn't give her yet.

Everything moved fast after that. The following day, I was moved from my spotless cell to a single waiting cell. To all intents and purposes, I was free, but when you are a criminal, you're never free, and I was still within the prison walls.

I couldn't help but feel free. How else was I supposed to feel? I had a private shower cubicle, and I could shower every day. That was exhilarating, that was freedom, the ultimate heaven and worth celebrating, and I had my hair cut and styled for the first time in five years. I felt alive.

Then the warders and I carefully checked the inventory against every single item I'd ever possessed from the moment I'd arrived in Japan. There, amongst the clothing and other articles, were the seventeen tissues I'd had when I was captured. I looked on in awe, then I couldn't help myself and burst out laughing. The gentle lady warder looked at me. I suddenly realised how disrespectful that was and apologised to her. Freedom had gone to my head, and I'd forgotten my manners in that moment of elation.

Seventeen tissues – all still there, neatly folded and accounted for in precise Japanese style. Absurd, but anyway. My old tooth-brushes, toothpaste, even the half bottle of shampoo were there! The warder's petite round face lit up, satisfied it was all still there, then finally she laughed, two little dark eyes became slits in a round creamy-coloured face, and I laughed with her. The suitcase filled very quickly, so she kindly arranged another bag for me, and we filled that too. I'd be overweight. I left some of the unnecessary things behind and shoved the tissues into my handbag. I'd be needing those.

I waited in my new cell for a week and imagined myself walking out of the prison gates, head held high, breathing freedom deep into my lungs. I pictured myself climbing into the cab. There'd be no need for curtains this time, no need for rope handcuffing. I wasn't a criminal anymore; I'd paid my dues. I was looking forward to seeing a small part of the countryside for the first time, other than the view from my cell window.

The vision I'd had and reality were starkly different. It really wasn't how it was shown in the movies, and I had to keep reminding myself of that.

I went out the same way I came in: cuffed and bound with horrid rough sisal ropes and transported in a curtained vehicle. I never did get to see any of the country. What I did learn on my way to the vehicle was they could not have released me any earlier, for it was only a week ago that my fine was fully paid. My dreams of parole after two years had been in vain, and I wasn't indispensable.

It was clammy and humid inside the vehicle; a fleeting moment of excitement was quickly overtaken by nausea. When we stopped a few hours later, I was off-loaded and marched to the basement of a tall building that was marked "Immigration Cells". The cuffs were removed, and I was locked in my cell, the last cell in the line of cold concrete boxes. I could only assume this mysterious building was part of the airport, but it was very different from the holding cells coming in. These cells were like a dingy catacomb. They were icy cold from air conditioning blasting freezing air that whipped around the bare concrete walls. Freedom doesn't come without enormous cost, just as my fellow countryman Nelson Mandela once told. And "freedom" is an all-embracing word that has many meanings, as I discovered. Just a few short weeks away and I'd be free from the burden of imprisonment, but what lay ahead emotionally was making me feel rather anxious. I prayed the work I'd done on myself was strong enough to withstand the coming emotional onslaught. It was going to be huge. I knew that. My darling brother was still my rock. Though I'd not mentioned him while I was in prison, I heard from him and I had replied and he was always in my thoughts and prayers, but my children were the mainstay of my sanity, the powerful voice within my head and in my journal ramblings. He knew I had limited funds for stamps.

I sat entombed in the basement of an unknown building. A chilly reminder I was still regarded as a criminal. I learnt from the others that this was where all foreign criminals were brought when they'd reached the end of their term and were either waiting for travel documents, airline tickets, or family to collect them. I had no idea how long I'd be in this cell block, how quickly travel documents could be attained by Storm, when I'd be given my airline ticket or what would happen next. All I knew was I was almost "free".

A line of stark white washing machines stood in a row against the wall opposite to the cells. Their doors lay open like gaping mouths, ready for dirty clothes to be fed in, cleansing away the stench of captivity for the last time. The showers were good; civilised cubicles where my breasts were no longer exposed to forty prying eyes, thankfully. For these cells were multi-sex. Another thing that unnerved me somewhat.

Scattered around were a few gaming machines, dispensing machines and a couple of table tennis tables. There was the normal assortment of candy, crisps, sodas, fruit juices, chocolates and chewing gum in the dispensers.

At 9 p.m., the guards came around and locked our cells. They opened them again at 6 a.m.

Two public telephone booths stood, bold and blue, near the washing machines, beckoning us to connect once more with the outside world. It was the most sought-after spot in this cold, characterless basement, and we stood in queues to make that one important call.

My gut churned as I stood in the line, wondering how I'd deal with hearing Storm's voice again. I had to hold myself together. The call I'd dreamt of making, the announcement of my freedom at last. A call I'd so dearly hoped to have made much sooner. Standing in the queue suddenly made "freedom" a more significant reality and quelled the horrors of my nightmares, but initiated a whole lot of others I'd have to face.

A call to South Africa was expensive; money was tight and there was a seven-hour time difference. When I finally reached the head of the queue, I mentally calculated it was about 2 a.m. in South Africa and Storm would be fast asleep, but this news required me to wake her. I stood nervously, fiddling with my fingers and hair and shifting my weight from one foot to the other, wondering if it was fair to wake her. Should I call her now or wait? But I'd waited too many long years for this moment, so the decision was made. It was worth taking the chance.

Storm had just completed a twenty-four-hour police shift. The national elections in South Africa were in full swing. She'd just come off duty and was about to fall into an exhausted sleep when she answered my call unenthusiastically.

The telephone reception was dreadful, so I kept shouting down the line, saying, "Hello, hello, hello."

In a final attempt to make her aware it was me, I shouted her nickname as loudly as I could and heard muttering in the queue behind me.

"Meid, meid, it's me. I'm free. I need to get home."

"Ma... Ma," I heard her say, her voice breaking up, husky with emotion.

The crackling made conversation difficult, so we arranged a time to call the following day, and I placed the earpiece back on its holder. Turning away, not quite knowing what to do with myself, I walked slowly away from the queue of others waiting to do the same thing I'd just done and sat in my cell sobbing tears of relief. Everything I was dealing with at that moment and everything I had dealt with over the years came crashing down on me – a mingling of outrageous happiness and bitter regret all churning in the cauldron of the love I was feeling for my daughter. Nothing I'd thought of or primed myself for had prepared me adequately for this.

Tomorrow, we would talk again and arrange my exit from Japan.

Freedom, yes, the one from jail, was indeed just around the corner. Emotional freedom I hoped would follow later.

Chapter Forty-Four

Our Reunion

So, my life's journey had been one filled with difficulty and insurmountable tests of courage, tenacity and wit. What other nasty surprises lay ahead?

This final test of endurance was colossal enough, then I learnt I had to endure another month of hell in these freezing cells, waiting for my airline ticket to arrive.

My telephone call had led to a few hectic weeks for Storm dealing with inefficient bureaucracy while I impatiently waited and, of course, time went really slowly.

Before I could fly home, a temporary South African identity document had to be issued. Inevitably delayed by the jumble of autocratic red tape and the application of things being done in African time within the Internal Affairs department, it took an unusually quick three weeks. Only once Storm had my official ID document could she book my ticket home. Then as timely as the other setbacks, planes only departed from Tokyo to Johannesburg on Tuesdays and Sundays. Storm had booked my flight for a Tuesday departure, but unbeknown to her, that Tuesday was a public holiday in Japan. Only a skeleton staff was on duty, which meant another excruciatingly long week's wait. Apart from being the longest month imprisoned, the last week was one of the longest weeks of my life.

Once the flight was confirmed, I learnt I was not where I thought I was. I was not living in the guts of the airport buildings at all; I had another four-hour journey to get to Narita Airport in a curtained minibus. I was still considered bad enough for them to handcuff me, only this time in conventional handcuffs. As we were permitted to talk to the warders, I wanted to know why I needed to be handcuffed and why we couldn't look out of the windows and view the passing countryside for I was no longer a prisoner.

"You do not have a visa to be in Japan as a South African resident," she answered. "You are an illegal visitor."

I finally made that longed-for exit from Japan on 28 March 2006.

The stigma of being a prisoner stayed firmly glued. I still had more disgrace to live through.

At the airport, foreign ex-prisoners were dealt with in the basement of the building and shoved into vile-smelling cells, nothing like the clean holding cells when I came in. I'd learnt to deal with just about every form of humiliation, but this final blow was the hardest. I'd psyched myself up for the fact that the passage to freedom was going to be an easy, happy occasion.

I was collected a few hours later, handcuffed again, and led to the plane via airport passages not used by regular commuters and formally handed over to a hostess who led me down the aisle to a seat at the very end of the plane. I was the first onto the aircraft.

Normal travellers can't have their space violated by a criminal like me, I thought with bitter cynicism.

I was seated in a special seat hidden behind the galley that housed the last block of passenger ablutions. I was not permitted to carry hand luggage of any sort – just in case I blew up the aircraft! Anyone would have thought I was a mass murderer. I could understand this type of treatment for serious criminals, but I wasn't one of those. I had spent nearly four years proving it. I was a normal South African grandmother who'd made an error of judgement and was dying to get home. I'd paid dearly for my mistake and wanted this whole ordeal to be over without adding more degradation. My hand luggage was taken and stowed elsewhere; it would all be handed back to me upon landing in Singapore where we would be changing planes.

Upon landing, I was escorted directly to the other plane ahead of all the other passengers and taken straight to the back of the plane again and ordered to fasten my seat belt. Stripped of all dignity and being so close to "home", I cried more tears of shame, tears of happiness at knowing I was on the last leg, tears of processing the meaning of freedom, tears of haunting hardships. I cried tears for every human emotion with intensity. The air hostesses were very kind to me though.

After take-off, and once the plane had levelled off, I was served the meal first. Probably because I was in the galley where the food was stowed. After four years of prison food, aeroplane food tasted tantalisingly good. The only plus of being stuck at the very back of the plane was that I had two seats to sleep across, and after my long sobbing session and a good meal, I fell into a deep, emotionally exhausted sleep and was woken by the stewardess asking me politely to fasten my seat belt for landing.

"Am I home?" I asked her, rubbing my eyes, amazed.

"Yes, ma'am, we will be landing in twenty minutes."

I quickly went to the toilet, splashed cold water on my face, and ran my fingers through my hair. I could feel the excitement rising as the plane was dropping in altitude, rapidly descending towards the earth I loved so dearly, and moments after taking my seat, we touched down on African soil. Choked with emotion, I had to keep swallowing as the lump in my throat threatened to rise.

The plane taxied into its allocated parking spot, and I heard everyone unclip their safety belts in unison. I was instructed to remain seated – I would be collected by airport security personnel.

When I eventually exited the plane via the door furthest from the front of the aircraft, I could smell the ground, the earthy smell of Africa and it took all my strength to remain poised as I stepped onto the luggage carrier platform, which criminals share with the cargo. Nothing was normal, and every process took ten times longer. I began to panic, for I knew Storm would be waiting for me at the standard international arrivals area – as one does.

I didn't know what to do. Then I was taken into a hall and told to sit; someone would come for me.

Eight o'clock came and went. I was frantic, agonising over the thought that Storm may assume I'd missed my flight and possibly leave the airport, but that was an absurd thought. Amazing how bizarre one's thoughts can be when panicked and common sense flies out the door. I illegally left my seat and went to find someone who would get a message to Storm to tell her to wait. There were more formalities I had to complete. I found no one who could be bothered to help and was met with a barrage of "no" answers. Then I found someone who enlightened me.

"Excuse me, sir, but why is this taking so long? I need to let my daughter know she must wait for me," I urged.

"They are checking your luggage," the official answered.

I felt like saying, "Looking for bombs, are they?" I refrained from being sarcastic.

"What, again?" I asked with an irritable shake of my head.
"Yes, ma'am, again."

Two hours later, on 29 March 2006, after flying for nineteen hours and waiting for many others, I was technically a free woman. A kind porter loaded my luggage onto an airport trolley, and for the first time in over four years, I was free of handcuffs or rope bonds, dressed in civilian clothing and pushing my luggage trolley, free to go where I pleased without a security escort. It was liberating, but oddly frightening too.

I walked through a different set of immigration and customs gates and there, standing forlorn and alone under the glaring artificial airport lights, stood my precious daughter. I was horrified by how thin and gaunt she looked. Her once beautiful glowing skin was now sallow and grey with the etchings of sadness, worry and fear that had woven a delicate web around her friendly warm brown eyes, that even at a distance, I could see were sunken back in her head. Guilt, oh, the guilt, along with a collage of other emotions at war with each other dampened the happiness at seeing her and being on home soil.

Then she saw me. We ran into each other's arms, sobbing, holding each other tightly, savouring the smell and feel of each other, storing it to memory, never to be forgotten. I pulled back from her first to release the grief-filled space between us, giving space for happiness to pour in.

"Why are you so thin, meid? All I saw was a big nose." I giggled through my tears, holding her close again and breathing in the smell of her soft brown hair that was lightly fragranced.

For a moment, she couldn't answer and cried harder. Finally, unlocking ourselves from each other, looking questioningly into my eyes like she used to as a small girl when something had gone wrong, she said, "Mama, you are so thin and fragile too. Look at you."

The years without me and the stigma attached had been a far greater strain on her than I had understood. My last vision of her when I'd left, she was carefree and happy, now she was ravaged by shame, loss and heartbreak and I had caused it.

For the next half an hour, we couldn't stop touching, hugging, giggling, crying – drunk on a surreal relief. Emotionally disorientated, Storm struggled to find where she'd put my passport, lost somewhere in her handbag while we stood in the queue at Bureau de Change, but it came to light, and we giggled again. After doing the exchange, still giddy with the joy of being reunited, we couldn't find where she'd parked – somewhere in the covered parking. This time we looked at each other and erupted in laughter. It was a joyous disorientation and, eventually, we were on the road home.

There was so much to say, but where did one begin when there were raw truths to deal with? The drive home was a concoction of awkward moments that swung from tears to laughter and back to sadness.

"How is my darling boy?"

"He's coped, Mama, we all have. You taught us how to cope, but our grief and yearning for you has been hard on us," Storm answered truthfully.

Tears rolled down my cheeks again.

"Mama, we all forgave you long ago. It was not your fault," Storm said quietly with depth and tenderness, provoking continued sobbing. "Papa should have been jailed, not you," she added bitterly. Forgiveness didn't resonate in her voice.

The mention of Dion brought about other questions I needed answering.

"He doesn't know I'm home, does he? I don't want to see him." It would take me a few weeks to settle back into "normal" life, and Dion was not going to disrupt that if I could help it.

"No, Mama, he doesn't, and for now, you don't have to see him, but you will at some stage."

I nodded.

Our journey home passed with only glances at the passing countryside. I'd missed so much of it, but our constant chatter was more essential and soon we were pulling into the driveway of Storm's new house where my precious grandchildren waited.

Little Rick, born while I was in jail, was now seventeen months old. Rika, who'd been seven months old when I was jailed, was now five. All those years of her childhood I'd missed. She came tearing out of the house to greet us. I jumped out of the car wrapping this precious child in my arms, her little body close to mine and I knew in that moment no other hug compared to the unquestioned purity of one from a child.

As I walked into their new home, arm in arm with Storm and holding Rika's hand, a familiar tune was playing, I assumed it was on the radio, one I'd not heard for years. I didn't associate it with my homecoming, then it hit me – it wasn't the radio.

"Tie a Yellow Ribbon Round the Old Oak Tree" was playing, welcoming home the prisoner who'd returned to her family. Standing on the coffee table in the lounge was a love palm, bound with yellow ribbons and a big chocolate cake sat next to it. The sights and sounds were so touching, their meaning so real. With little Rika looking up at me with expectant eyes, I knew in an instant I was forgiven and loved unconditionally.

Could a mother dream of anything more?

I stood and unashamedly sobbed while Rika looked down at the floor, not sure what to do with a sobbing grandmother she didn't know. She squeezed my hand, just as her mother had done when she was a child, then she looked up at me again, and I smiled awkwardly through my tears. Little Rick was sleeping soundly in his cot, as if the music had extended his peaceful slumber. We'd meet later. Time was no longer a pressing issue that had dominated every second of the last four years.

Chapter Forty-Five

The delicate and delicious smells that wafted from Storm's kitchen made my mouth fill with saliva. I felt like a labrador desperate to get hold of food, any food. Storm had insisted I was not allowed in the kitchen; she wanted to spoil me with the kind of meal I missed and had often expressed in my letters.

Eating with a knife and fork was an absurdly alien experience. I hesitated a moment, letting my hands rest on the cutlery, thinking back to the holding cells and how I'd sobbed with frustration at the difficulty of eating with chopsticks, how I'd longed to hold a knife and fork then. Slicing through a juicy piece of South African beef, I felt the family's eyes on me. I looked up. Storm and Robert were watching me, amused as I sliced through the roast beef and put it my mouth. Nothing had tasted this good for such a long time. I swallowed quickly to appease the callings in my stomach, savouring long-forgotten flavours and cherishing the moments of being home with family once more.

From one taste sensation to another, Storm had provided it all. The second course of "koeksisters" was nectar to my numbed taste buds, creating a delightful chaos of rejection in my tummy.

Storm had taken a week off of work to celebrate my homecoming. After dinner, exhausted but refusing to part from each other, we curled up on the sofa together and kept up the constant chatter like two hungry hyenas at a kill.

Robert discreetly disappeared, leaving us the intimate space we needed as mother and daughter to tear away at the pain we'd endured for so long.

"I prayed so hard for you, Ma. While you were in the holding cells, I prayed for your release, prayed that they'd discover there had been a mistake, the same when they moved you to detention, but you never came back. I remember you telling me you had lost your faith in God, and I did too, for a time, when anger couldn't find the answers to my questions. Work was a continuous night-mare. Everyone knew you'd been caught smuggling drugs. So, working in the drug squad, I was under constant surveillance.

"For a few months, I even hated you, Ma, then all I could think of was you rotting in a jail thousands of miles from home because of Papa, and I was helpless to protect you. So, I redi-rected my focus and cultivated a more positive approach, but it took longer for me to forgive Vivienne, and I hated Andre. I banned Papa from coming to my house. I hated the world then too. Only boetie and Robert could enter my shattered world. Boetie was so strong. Sometimes it was just a veneer to hide his pain, but I was so proud of the way he sorted out his own life without Papa's help."

I sat listening to Storm. There was so much she couldn't say in her letters, and I knew that during the next week she would have the time to clear away the nasties and we could begin our healing journey together.

"Oh, my angel, remember if God had answered my prayers and sent me back when you asked Him to, I would have come home and committed murder, and that would have been worse.

I hated Papa. I hated him with such venom. It poisoned my mind and there was no clarity in my thinking then. If I'd been chucked in jail here, we wouldn't be sitting together talking as we are."

I hesitated while I tried to find the appropriate words to what I wanted to say next.

"There are no gentle ways of putting this, but I would have strung myself up or slit my wrists had I been jailed here. I'd even considered it a few times in Japan."

Storm nodded. She knew what life in a South African jail looked like, being in the police.

I yawned, too much emotion and a belly full of forgotten taste sensations. It was time to sleep.

"Just one more question, Ma." Storm smiled with a pleading look in her eyes.

"Okay, then we must get to bed." I yawned again feeling more relaxed than I had in years, despite the emotional exhaustion.

"Why didn't you answer my phone call the day after you left?"

It was the one question I'd been waiting all these years for her to ask.

"I couldn't, meid, I just couldn't. Not only was I sickened by guilt, I would have lied to you again. Plus, I was scared to death, alone in Paris. Why do you ask?" I leant forwards and pinched her cheek affectionately and then she dropped the bombshell.

"The day after you left, I received a call during my lunch break. And if you had only answered my call when you were in Paris, I would've told you that I'd just won 246,000 Rand in a competition I'd forgotten I'd even entered, and you need never have gone to jail. I could never bring myself to tell you until now."

Epilogue

Despite learning the devastating news of the reason for Storm's phone call shortly after I arrived in Paris – the one I could not bring myself to answer – I slept well.

I'd grown in jail. I'd shamed myself, blamed myself, loathed myself and had reached the very depths of depression where suicide had become a comforting thought. Now the rarity of living happily fragile, and accepting that human fragility, allowed me to sleep well without yearning for what could have been.

The following morning, I called Pieter. I was longing to see him. Longing to hold him in my arms. He was thrilled to hear my voice and excited I was finally home. Another emotional conversation happened, of course. Rather than shying away from hard truths, I looked forward to understanding his deepest feelings and how, together, we could all heal the wounds of the trauma and the emotional pain and learn from it.

Twenty-four hours after arriving back in Bethlehem, the editor of the local newspaper called Storm asking if I would permit an interview, which I reluctantly agreed to, even though I felt mildly annoyed by the intrusion. I wondered how the news of my homecoming had already leaked out. Someone must have seen Storm and me in her car on the way home. What the heck, I had to stand tall. I didn't need to make

413

apologies to anyone except my family; the public just wanted some juicy news. I had learnt how humans thrive on others' heartache and hardships.

It took another twenty-four hours before I called Viv and Andre. This was a more difficult conversation to cope with. No matter what one tells oneself, it had taken time to process their part in what happened to me and it still stung. Forgiveness and love are always forefront in my mind, and it was finding the right vocabulary to articulate my feelings over the phone in that moment. I had to face the injustice of their actions appropriately and that was hard. There had been many letters back and forth from Viv over the years in jail, but speaking to her seemed to conjure up what I'd not dealt with correctly. I'd learnt in prison that whatever happened in my life I had choices and I had to take responsibility for them, which I had. The vision of Vivienne's angry face, begging me to employ her father, remained. I could not get that vision cleared from my mind, nor the tone of her voice that rung in my ears when I thought back. Choices or no choices, I still felt the resentment. That meant there was still work I had to do on myself. It saddened me that she had never said a word to her father when my business failed, which he was directly responsible for. And then there was Andre. I could not blame him; I had made the choice to go. I could lay no blame. It was the relationship between Vivienne and I that needed mending.

The following week, Dion rang. He'd seen the newspaper article and wanted to know why none of the children had told him I was home. After all these years, it was still all about him, and though I felt annoyed, I also felt sorry for him. His entire life was a plea for attention; it was so entrenched.

My inner peace was almost complete. I was reunited with my family, and to my amazement, I also received an incredible number of unexpected "welcome home" calls from people in the community. Their thoughts touched me deeply. With so many of them, there was no finger pointing and gossip, but admiration and awe of what I'd endured.

I spent hours discussing with myself, and Storm, what I was going to do, where I was going to live, how I would earn an income. Who in this town would employ me, knowing I was a convict? Should I remain in Bethlehem? The only thing I was sure of was I didn't want to be far from Storm.

A month later, I found an insignificant little job that helped raise my self-confidence when dealing with and facing the public. I sold milk, cream, butter and eggs for a farmer who had a dairy shop in town.

Facing the challenge of reintegrating into "normal" life was very difficult. I knew it would be, I'd accepted that, but with the overwhelming love and support from my family and more friends than I realised I had, they eased the transition from being a cocooned pupa to a beautiful butterfly. I began to spread my wings and fly.

Of all the many lessons I'd learnt from my experience in Japan, how and why I got there, the most rewarding was the feeling of what unconditional love and forgiveness meant. From that followed a deep understanding and need for setting personal boundaries without feeling guilty. It was this that enabled me to allow Dion back into my life. After much persuasion, we shared a house, living as friends and we enjoyed our family together.

After many odd jobs and then permanent employment that lasted three years, I finally went back to work for the lady who had taken over my upholstery business all those years ago!

One Monday morning, Adelle, the business owner, swept across the reception floor towards me. Her vibrant energy was lost on me that morning. I woke with a burdening feeling of apprehension. Not the normal Monday blues. Dion had been away all weekend. It had been a blissfully peaceful one too. I should have been feeling on top of the world.

As Adelle swept passed me on her way out to quote on a complete interior revamp, she left a trail of expensive perfume in the air. I sat mesmerised by the scent. Soon the memory of the sounds of the rain that had fallen heavily on our tin roof on Sunday, comforted me. The rain had come pelting down in sheets, but my reverie was soon shattered by Mariah as she burst into the reception looking stressed. Mariah was the head seamstress. She seldom got so rattled. I asked her what was causing her that level of stress. She explained she had made a terrible calculation error. The curtains she was working on had to be hung the following day, and the client was a particularly difficult one. She was short of three metres of curtain tape to complete the last curtain. Mariah stammered apologetically. She loathed making mistakes. I reassured her that I had three metres of the same tape at home. I would not say a word to anyone about the mistake. Doing it this way meant that no money would be drawn from petty cash for the purchase of the shortfall. No explanation needed. She shot me a beaming, toothy grin which spread across her wonderful round face. She stood for a moment, holding the edges of her threadbare apron and her shoulders visibly drooped with relief.

Mariah stammered apologetically. She loathed making mistakes. I reassured her that I had three metres at home. I would not say a word to anyone about the mistake. Doing it this way, no money would be drawn from petty cash for the purchase of the shortfall. No explanation needed. She shot me a beaming, toothy grin which spread across her wonderful round face. She stood for a moment, holding the edges of her threadbare apron, she visibly drooped with relief.

I finished a few small errands in the office, downed my tea, gathered up my bag, front door keys, car keys and cell phone and left Veronica in charge of the reception.

"I'll be back in twenty minutes. I forgot something at home," I said as I left.

"No problem," Veronica replied without interest.

I pulled up to the automatic gates in front of the housing estate where we lived and pressed the button. While waiting for the gates to open, I glimpsed the back of Dion's car parked in the driveway and wondered what had brought him home early. I'd been expecting him back the following day. I suddenly felt annoyed, which added to my frazzled mood. It had been so peaceful without him. I'd enjoyed my own space more than I cared to admit and had primed myself for another quiet evening alone. I allowed the instant testiness to wane as the gate slid open. Our friendship was reasonably comfortable now, I supposed. I knew he'd never change. I had finally accepted that. He paid his way; I paid mine. If I was truly honest with myself, sometimes I felt closer to him now than I had in years; he'd mellowed with age. It was just when he went on his booze binges that I kicked myself for letting him back into my life. I had a feeling this was one of those weekends that had ended in excessive indulgence, and he was suffering with an enormous hangover.

I parked beneath the shade of the massive rubber tree that grew near the entrance to our house and noticed our front door was ajar and instantly felt uneasy. Neither of us ever left the front door open, even though we were in a secure housing estate. It was one of our mutual rules. My first thought was perhaps we'd been broken into, and the cops had called Dion, hence his early return. There hadn't been any break-ins in the past two years, but living in South Africa, it was always a possibility.

Pulling the keys out of the ignition, I quickly headed towards our front door and stepped into the house. Dion's keys and cell phone were lying on the kitchen counter. I expected to see him in the kitchen, but the house was silent. I called out, but there was no reply. It was then that an eerie sensation trickled down my spine, raising the hair on its way. I shivered involuntarily. Something felt wrong.

I put my bag and car keys on the counter next to Dion's and went through to my room. He wasn't there, nor was he using my bathroom. I checked his room. He wasn't there either. My mind was racing though it didn't appear that anything was missing or that there'd been a break-in. Maybe he was outside with the police, though I hadn't noticed any police vans around. I checked in the other bathroom quickly, then checked the spare room, calling out his name as I went. Where on earth could he be? And why had he left the front door open?

As I entered the spare room, a spine-chilling, throaty rasping sound was coming from outside, instinctively warning me of something ominous. Rushing forwards to see what was making that awful noise, I peered out of the window. That was when I saw Dion.

I knew in an instant why I'd been battling with the blues. Instinct. I ran outside, looked at him and moaned, a deep painful sound, so chilling I was sure it didn't belong to me. A sense of heart-wrenching loss filled me, followed closely by other feelings I couldn't interpret in that moment, but they took a stranglehold on my chest and breathing became very difficult.

The nurse in me desperately wanted to go to him, but I couldn't. I didn't dare touch him. He was still alive, but only just. I had felt this ghastly familiar feeling of utter helplessness before.

I ran back inside, grabbed my phone, dialled 911 and waited outside. I couldn't go back and look at what Dion had done to himself. He sat slumped in one of our deck chairs, fresh blood was still dripping from his temple, and the .22 calibre rifle had fallen across his knees in a sinister reminder of a life weighed down by a fearsome, deeply embedded guilt.

"Why, Dion? Why end it this way?" I whispered, and though I wanted to cry, not a tear left my eyes while I waited for the ambulance and the police to arrive. He'd put me through too much to shed a tear now.

The urge to go to him grew stronger as I waited, but I knew there was nothing that would save him now. I stood in silence, willing him to hold on to his life for a few minutes longer. I wanted to say goodbye before he took his last breath, even though I feared he might have already taken that last gasp. My body began to shake involuntarily as the shock of what he'd done penetrated. I reached out for the sturdy trunk of the rubber tree to support me. I leant against it, trying to absorb some of its life force until help arrived.

If I'd been here fifteen minutes earlier, I could have stopped him, I thought miserably. While I waited, only the cherished moments of our life together flashed through my mind. I had been told when one was close to death one only feels love, and prayed he was feeling that now. I never imagined Dion possessed the courage to end his life and certainly not in this way. Was this an indication that he did have a conscience after all? What he had done to me, his family and many others must have finally got the better of him.

I felt instantly sickened by that thought. I always knew guilt may have been buried somewhere in the deep recesses of his twisted mind. Everyone who knew him, even his own children, swore he never had a conscience. Now, the years of suppressed regrets, vile uncontrolled actions and dishonesty must have finally struck at his subconscious, wounding it, while excessive alcohol consumption had sunk him into a dark depression and burst the abscess of a lifetime of accumulated shame. Thinking back, maybe not! I'd not noticed a change in his mood on Friday. I felt sure he must have made the decision not to go on living before he left, and it brewed for two long days.

He was a master of disguise, right to the end.

His mood had been cheery when he left. He'd not said where he was going, and I never asked.

"What a macabre end to a life," I whispered, looking up to the heavens through the large green leaves of the canopy above me, searching for some mystical comfort and divine reassurance as I stood trying to understand. I prayed then that when he took his last breath, whether I was beside him or not, he'd go to a beautiful peaceful place surrounded by love and light as I'd been informed happened. However, a part of me felt he didn't deserve it, but now was no time for thoughts like that.

Somewhere in the distance, I heard the ambulance siren bellowing out its torturous reminder that Dion would soon be taken away in it.

I clicked the gate opener. The gate ground its way along the tracks, scattering sand as it went. The sound reminded me of the rasping sounds coming from deep within Dion when I had found him. I covered my ears as the ambulance raced in and parked. Two medics jumped from the vehicle. I ran with them to where Dion's slumped body waited for an escape from his suffering.

So many unanswered questions would be buried with him.

I watched as the medics carefully laid him down on the floor. Minutes later, the police walked in. I glanced up at them briefly. They all knew Dion, and they knew my history too. I looked back to the medics and our eyes connected; they seemed to understand my silent question.

It was now safe for me to say goodbye in their presence. I would not be accused of murder.

I knelt beside Dion's lifeless body and finally surrendered to my grief. Would there ever be a day when I'd think of Dion and feel nothing? His breathing was very shallow as I leant in close to him and whispered in his ear.

"Gogga, I will always love you."

The faintest quiver moved across his lips, acknowledging my words, then his chest shuddered, and he let out his final breath. I gently closed his haunted brown eyes for the last time.

It was then that it struck me. Life really did revolve the same way as our wondrous planet: round and round in big, astounding circles, and so often there is simply no explanation for the way it turns out. The only difficulty I faced then, was telling the children.

Printed in Great Britain
by Amazon